The
HIKERS GUIDE to the
HAWAIIAN ISLANDS

The
HIKERS GUIDE to the
HAWAIIAN ISLANDS

Stuart M. Ball, Jr.

 A Latitude 20 Book

University of Hawai'i Press
HONOLULU

05 04 03 02 01 00   5 4 3 2 1

Library of Congress Cataloging-in-Publication Data

Ball, Stuart M., 1948–
    The hikers guide to the Hawaiian islands / by Stuart M.
Ball, Jr.
        p.   cm.
    Includes bibliographical references (p.   ) and index.
    ISBN 0-8248-2223-4 (alk. paper)
    1. Hiking—Hawaii Guidebooks.   2. Trails—Hawaii
Guidebooks.   3. Hawaii Guidebooks.   I. Title.
GV199.42.H3B35   2000
919.6904'41—dc21   99–36621
                                                          CIP

    Maps by Manoa Mapworks

Designed by Santos Barbasa Jr.
Printed by Edwards Brothers, Inc.

CONTENTS

Color photos follow pages 116 and 212

ACKNOWLEDGMENTS

Lynne Masuyama, my wife, joined me on all 44 of the hikes in this book. She is an ideal hiking partner, providing support, guidance, and good company.

Accompanying us on some of the hikes were John Hoover and Marcia Stone, Spencer Nitta and Michele Middleton, and Jason, Cera, and Kimberly Sunada. They are all good friends and hiking companions.

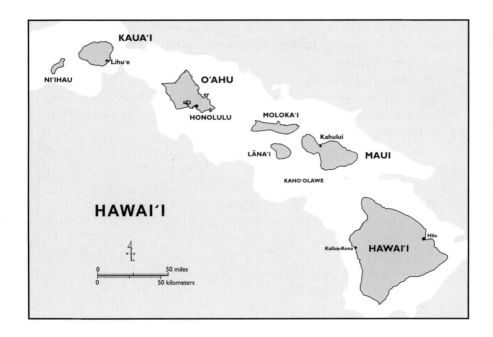

KAUA'I

Lihu'e

NI'IHAU

O'AHU

HONOLULU

MOLOKA'I

Kahului

LĀNA'I

MAUI

KAHO'OLAWE

HAWAI'I

Kailua-Kona

HAWAI'I

Hilo

0   50 miles
0   50 kilometers

INTRODUCTION

Hawai'i is truly a paradise for hikers. While tourists and locals alike flock to the beaches, the mountains and remote shorelines remain surprisingly deserted. This book aims to change that just a little. It will take you where few people go, to active volcanoes, lush valleys, cascading waterfalls, secluded beaches, and windswept ridges and sea cliffs.

This guidebook includes 44 of the best day hikes on the islands of Hawai'i (the Big Island), Kaua'i, Maui, and O'ahu. Each island is equally represented with 11 hikes. All of the hikes are open to the public; none requires a permit or liability waiver.

Each hike has a section on highlights, directions to the trailhead, and a detailed description of the route. A narrative section covers points of interest and major hazards along the trail. As applicable, there are short notes about the plants, birds, geology, history, and legends of the area. Each hike also has its own topographic map keyed to the route description.

As you will see, this guidebook is very detailed. The information in it, however, is neither perfect nor up-to-date because of changing conditions. New housing construction may alter the approach to a trailhead. Recent lava may force a trail to be rerouted. A winter storm may cause a landslide that blocks the route. Do not rely entirely on this book; use your own judgment and common sense as well.

Good luck and good hiking!

HIKING TIPS

Climate

Hawai'i has two seasons, summer (May to October) and winter (November to April). Summer is the warmer and drier season. Daytime temperatures at sea level are in the 80s, and nighttime temperatures are in the 70s. Trade winds from the northeast blow steadily to cool the Islands. The trades, however, do produce cloud buildup over the mountains and some rain there.

Winter is the cooler and wetter season. Daytime temperatures at sea level are in the 70s and low 80s, and nighttime temperatures are in the 60s and low 70s. The winds are more variable in strength and direction, sometimes coming from the south or west. Southerly Kona winds produce mainland-type weather—clear skies or heavy cloud cover and rain.

Clothing

For short, easy hikes, wear:
    hiking boots, running or walking shoes (with tread)
    socks
    lightweight pants or shorts, cotton, cotton blend, or nylon (no jeans)
    lightweight shirt, short or long sleeve, cotton or cotton blend
    rain jacket, breathable fabric
    hat, broad brimmed

For long, difficult hikes, add:
    light sweater or jacket, wool or synthetic fabric

Equipment

For short, easy hikes, bring:
    daypack
    1 liter water

food
sunscreen

For long, difficult hikes, add:
    extra water
    extra food
    first-aid kit
    space blanket
    flashlight and extra bulb and batteries
    whistle
    compass
    topographic map

Pack It Out

Most of the hikes in this book are trash free. Let's keep them that way. Pack out all your trash, including cigarette butts, gum wrappers, orange peels, and apple cores.

Heiau

Heiau are early Hawaiian places of worship with stone or earth platforms. Do not disturb *heiau*, other ancient sites, or artifacts you may come upon while hiking. In addition, do not build new *ahu* (rock cairns) because they may confuse other hikers and local archaeologists.

Pest Plants

Unfortunately, the Islands have a number of introduced pest plants, including *Clidemia hirta*, *Melastoma candidum*, and banana poka. All three overrun native forests and overgrow hiking trails. The pests are spread by birds, feral pigs, and, yes, hikers. Clean the soles and sides of your boots carefully after hiking in the wet areas of all the Islands.

All three are easy to recognize. *Clidemia* is an agressive shrub with heavily creased, elliptical leaves. Mature plants have hairy, blue berries containing lots of tiny seeds. *Clidemia* is widespread on O'ahu and also occurs on the Big Island, Kaua'i, Maui, and Moloka'i.

Melastoma is a shrub or small tree found on Kaua'i and the Big Island. It has velvety, elliptical leaves with a slightly curved tip and large pink flowers.

Banana poka is a woody, climbing vine and a member of the passion flower family. It has deeply three-lobed leaves and a yellow fruit resembling a small banana. The vine is a serious pest on Kaua'i and the Big Island, where it climbs native trees and shades them out.

Emergencies

Don't have any! Seriously, come prepared with the right clothing and equipment. Bring along this book and follow the hike description closely. Memorize key junctions. Constantly be aware of the route you are traveling. You can never be lost if you know where you came from. Above all, use your common sense and good judgment.

Always tell someone where you are hiking and when you will be out. Make sure they know to call the emergency number (911) and ask for Fire Rescue if you don't call or show up on time.

The mountains are a dangerous place for exhausted, disoriented, and/or injured hikers. If you do get into serious trouble, settle down for the night and wait for rescue. You did let someone know where you were hiking, right? You did bring your sweater and space blanket, right?

Hazards

There are hazards in hiking, as in any sport. Described below are the main hazards you should be aware of while hiking in Hawai'i. With the right clothing and equipment, and good judgment on your part, you should be able to avoid or minimize these hazards and have an enjoyable outing.

Too Hot

Hiking in Hawai'i is usually a hot, sweaty experience. Drink plenty of water throughout the hike because it is very easy to become dehydrated. Prolonged lack of water can lead to heat exhaustion and heat stroke.

The need for water on a hike varies from person to person. As a general rule, take 1 liter of water on the short, easy hikes. Take two or more liters on the long, difficult hikes. If you have to ration or borrow water, you didn't bring enough.

The sun in Hawai'i is very strong, even in winter. During midday wear a broad-brimmed hat and use lots of sunscreen. Be particularly careful of the sun on the shoreline and at high altitudes.

Too Cold

Hiking in Hawai'i can sometimes be a wet, cold experience. A winter Kona storm with high winds and heavy rainfall can make you very cold very quickly. Insufficient or inappropriate clothing leads to chilling, which leads to hypothermia.

Always bring a rain jacket to protect you from wind and rain. Most of the time you won't even take it out of your pack but bring it anyway! On the high-altitude and long ridge hikes take a light wool or synthetic-fabric sweater or jacket that will keep you warm even when wet.

Altitude Sickness

Altitude sickness occurs when you climb to high elevation too quickly for your body to adjust to the thin air. Symptoms can show up as low as 8,000 feet, depending on the individual. Symptoms include shortness of breath, headache, dizziness, loss of appetite, nausea, and general fatigue. The cure is to stop climbing, rest, drink plenty of liquids, and eat sparingly. If the symptoms persist or get worse, descend to lower elevation immediately.

Leptospirosis

Leptospirosis is a bacterial disease found in freshwater ponds and streams contaminated with the urine of rats, mice, or mongooses. The bacteria can enter the body through the nose, mouth, eyes, or open cuts.

Symptoms resemble those of the flu—fever, chills, sweating, head and muscle aches, weakness, diarrhea, and vomiting. They may persist for a few days to several weeks. In rare cases the symptoms may become more severe and even lead to death.

What to do? First, never drink any stream water unless you have adequately boiled, filtered, or chemically treated it. That's easy. None of the hikes in this book is so long that you cannot bring all the water you need with you. Second, wear long pants to avoid getting cut and don't go swimming in freshwater. That's harder to do. After all, people come to Hawai'i to wear shorts and go swimming. Only you can decide how much risk you are willing to take.

High Streams

Island streams can rise suddenly during heavy rainstorms. Do not cross a fast-flowing stream if the water is much above your knees. Wait for the stream to go down. It is far better to be stranded for half a day than swept away.

Narrow Trail

Hawai'i is known for its knife-edge ridges and sheer cliffs. Trails in those areas tend to be very narrow with steep drop-offs on one or both sides. Oftentimes, the footing is over loose, rotten rock or slick mud.

If narrow sections make you feel overly uneasy, don't try them. There is no shame in turning back if you don't like what you see.

Rough Lava

Lava is tough on your boots and feet. Wear sturdy hiking boots with plenty of ankle support and cushioning. Don't take new boots on lava unless you want to age them prematurely!

As you will soon find out, there are two types of lava, 'a'ā and pāhoehoe. 'A'ā flows are jumbled-up heaps of rough, clinkery lava. They are virtually impassable without a trail. Even a well-worn path through 'a'ā is difficult to walk on because of all the loose, uneven rock.

Pāhoehoe is lava with a smooth or, sometimes, ropy surface. The terrain of a pāhoehoe flow ranges from relatively flat to very humpy. A well-used trail on older pāhoehoe makes for easy hiking. Be careful, though, on new flows without an established treadway. Their crust may be thin and brittle in spots and can collapse when walked on.

Goat/Pig/Bird Hunters

On the trips in the state forest reserves you may meet goat, pig, or bird hunters. They are friendly people, and their dogs generally are, too. They use hiking routes to access hunting areas; however, the hunt usually takes place off trail. Stay away from areas where you hear shots fired or dogs barking.

Marijuana (paka lōlō) Growers

The danger from marijuana growers and their booby traps is much exaggerated. The growers do not plant their plots near recognized trails. All of the hikes in this book travel on established routes. Stay on the trail, and you should have no *paka lōlō* problems.

The Ocean

All of the shoreline hikes visit beaches with no lifeguards. If you decide to swim, you're on your own. Ocean swimming is usually less hazardous in summer and along leeward coasts. The waters off windward coasts are often treacherous because of large swells and strong currents.

While exploring along the shore, remember the saying—never turn your back on the ocean.

Tsunamis

Tsunamis are huge on-shore waves that can rapidly inundate coastal areas. The waves are generated by earthquakes, either locally or along the Pacific Rim. If you feel an earthquake or the ocean recedes suddenly, move to high ground immediately.

Hurricanes

Hurricane season in Hawai'i is usually from June to December. Before starting a hike during that period, check the weather report to make sure no hurricanes are approaching the Islands.

A Final Caution

The hazards just described are the main ones you may encounter, but the list is by no means all inclusive. Like life in general, hiking in Hawai'i carries certain risks, and no hike is ever completely safe. YOU HAVE TO DECIDE HOW MUCH RISK YOU ARE WILLING TO TAKE.

HIKE CATEGORIES

Length

Length is the distance covered on the entire hike. If the hike is point to point, the length is one way. If the hike is out and back, the length is round trip. If the hike is a loop, the length is the complete loop.

Distance is given to the nearest tenth of a mile. The mileage is taken from park signs or trail maps, when available. Otherwise, distance is measured on the U.S. Geological Survey topographic maps. The plotted value is then increased by 10 to 20 percent to account for trail meandering too small to be shown on the map.

To convert the length to kilometers, multiply the miles by 1.609.

Elevation Gain

Elevation gain includes only substantial changes in altitude. No attempt is made to account for all the small ups and downs along the route. Measurements are taken from the U.S. Geological Survey topographic maps and then rounded to the nearest 100 feet.

To convert the elevation gain to meters, multiply the feet by 0.305.

Suitable for

Use this index to determine which hikes best match your ability. The categories are novice, intermediate, and expert. Novices are beginning hikers. Experts are experienced hikers. Intermediates are those in between.

Novice hikes generally follow a short, well-graded, and marked trail with gradual elevation changes and few hazards. Expert hikes have a long, rough, sometimes obscure route with substantial elevation changes and multiple hazards. Most hikes fall between those two extremes. Some are even suitable for everyone because they start out easy and then get progressively harder the farther you go.

How difficult a hike seems to you depends on your hiking experience and physical fitness. An experienced, conditioned hiker will find the novice hikes easy and the expert hikes difficult. An out-of-shape beginner may well find some of the novice hikes challenging.

Use the index only as a rough guide. Read the route description and notes to get a better feel for the hike.

Location
Location tells the general area of the hike. Given is the island and the nearest town or subdivision, if applicable. Also mentioned is the national park, state park, state forest reserve, and/or the mountain range where the hike is found.

Topo Map
Topo map refers to the U.S. Geological Survey quadrangle that shows the area of the hike. All maps referenced are in the 7.5-minute topographic series with a scale of 1:24,000 and a contour interval of 20 or 40 feet depending on the terrain.

You can purchase topographic maps directly from the Geological Survey. The address is USGS Information Services, P.O. Box 25286, Denver, CO 80225.

In Honolulu, topo maps for all the islands are available from Pacific Map Center at 560 N. Nimitz Highway, Suite 206A; phone 808-545-3600.

Highlights
Highlights briefly describes the hike and its major attractions.

Trailhead Directions
Trailhead directions are detailed driving instructions to the start of the hike. On the Neighbor Islands the directions begin at the town with a major airport nearest the trailhead. On O‘ahu the directions start from downtown Honolulu.

If you are at all familiar with the Islands, these directions should be sufficient to get you to the trailhead. If this is your first visit, bring along James A. Bier's reference maps to supplement the directions. You can purchase his maps for each island at local bookstores and tourist shops.

For some hikes the directions stop short of the actual trailhead. There is a reason for suggesting that you do some extra road walking. In certain areas it is generally safer to park your car on a main road, rather than at the trailhead. Wherever you park, never leave valuables in your vehicle.

On Oʻahu the directions also mention the bus route number and the stop nearest the trailhead. For route and schedule information, phone The Bus at 808-848-5555. Both Kauaʻi and the Big Island have bus systems with limited routes. For their current schedule, call Hele-on Bus on the Big Island at 808-961-8744 or Kauaʻi Bus at 808-241-6410. Maui has no public transportation.

Route Description

This section provides a detailed description of the route that the hike follows. Noted are junctions, landmarks, and points of interest. Also mentioned are specific hazards, such as a rough, narrow trail section. Out and back hikes are described on the way in. Loop hikes and point-to-point hikes are described in the preferred direction.

Each hike has its own map. The solid line shows the route. The letters indicate important junctions or landmarks and are keyed to the route description. For example, map point A is always the point where you start the hike.

The maps are reproductions of the U.S. Geological Survey quadrangles for the immediate area of the hike. As in the originals, the scale is 1:24,000, and the contour interval is 20 or 40 feet depending on the terrain.

This section sometimes uses Hawaiian words to describe the route. They are listed below with their English definition.

ʻaʻā	rough, clinkery lava
ahu	a pile of rocks indicating the route through treeless areas; known as cairns on the mainland

kīpuka	an island of vegetated older lava surrounded by newer flows
makai	seaward; toward the ocean
mauka	inland; toward the mountains
pāhoehoe	smooth, sometimes ropy lava
pali	cliff
puʻu	hill or peak

The word *contour* is sometimes used in the route description as a verb (that is, to contour). It means to hike roughly at the same elevation across a slope. Contouring generally occurs on trails that are cut into the flank of a ridge and work into and out of each side gulch.

Notes

The notes section provides additional information about the hike to make it safer and more enjoyable. Included are comments about trail conditions, major hazards, and the best time of day or year to take the hike. Also mentioned are scenic views, deep swimming holes, ripe fruit, and hungry mosquitoes. In addition, there are short notes about the plants, birds, geology, history, and legends of the area. At the end is a brief description of any alternatives to the basic route.

HIKE SUMMARY

Hike	Location	Length (miles)	Elev. Gain (feet)	Suitable for Nov.	Int.	Exp.	Views	Swimming	Native Plants/Birds	Historical Sites	Volcanic Features
Hawai'i (the Big Island)											
1. Kīlauea Iki	Hawai'i Volcanoes National Park	4.0	400	X			X		X		X
2. Halema'uma'u	Hawai'i Volcanoes National Park	6.9	600		X		X		X	X	X
3. Kīlauea Crater Rim	Hawai'i Volcanoes National Park	11.6	500		X	X	X		X	X	X
4. Makaopuhi Crater	Hawai'i Volcanoes National Park	8.3	600	X	X		X		X		X
5. Ka'aha	Hawai'i Volcanoes National Park	8.2	2,300		X	X	X	X			X
6. Kealakekua Bay	Kona	4.2	1,300		X		X	X		X	
7. Waipi'o Valley	Hāmākua	5.7	2,100		X		X	X		X	
8. Kalōpā Gulch	Hāmākua	2.8	600	X			X		X		
9. Pu'u 'Ō'ō Trail	Saddle Road	10.0	200		X		X		X	X	X
10. Mauna Loa	Saddle Road	12.6	2,700			X	X			X	X
11. Mauna Kea	Saddle Road	12.0	4,600			X	X			X	X
Kaua'i											
12. Awa'awapuhi	Kōke'e	6.5	1,600		X		X		X		
13. Nu'alolo Cliff	Kōke'e	11.4	2,200			X	X		X		
14. Alaka'i Swamp	Kōke'e	8.0	1,400	X	X		X		X		
15. Kawaikōī Stream	Kōke'e	9.1	1,200		X		X	X	X		
16. Waimea Canyon Vista	Kōke'e	6.0	700		X		X	X			
17. Kukui	Kōke'e	5.0	2,200		X		X	X			
18. Nounou Mountain –East	Kapa'a	3.8	1,100	X			X				
19. Kuilau Ridge	Kapa'a	4.3	700	X			X	X			

#	Trail	Area	Distance (mi)	Elevation (ft)									
20.	Powerline Trail	Kapaʻa/Hanalei	11.3	1,700		X			X				X
21.	Hanakāpīʻai Falls	Hanalei	7.9	2,000	X	X	X		X		X		X
22.	ʻŌkolehao	Hanalei	3.6	1,300	X	X	X			X	X		X

Maui

#	Trail	Area	Distance (mi)	Elevation (ft)									
23.	Kaluʻuokaʻōʻō	Haleakalā National Park	5.0	1,600		X					X		X
24.	Sliding Sands–Halemauʻu	Haleakalā National Park	12.1	1,500		X	X			X	X	X	X
25.	Hōlua	Haleakalā National Park	7.8	1,700		X			X		X	X	X
26.	Waiakoa Loop	Kula	4.5	700	X	X			X		X		
27.	Polipoli Loop	Kula	4.9	1,200	X	X	X		X		X		X
28.	Skyline Trail	Kula	15.0	3,500		X	X		X		X		
29.	ʻOheʻo Gulch	Hāna	4.0	900	X	X		X	X		X	X	
30.	Hāna-Waiʻānapanapa Coastal Trail	Hāna	4.6	100	X	X		X	X		X	X	
31.	Hoapili Trail	Kīhei	4.2	200	X	X		X	X			X	X
32.	Lahaina Pali	West Maui	5.0	1,600		X	X		X		X	X	
33.	Waiheʻe Ridge	West Maui	5.0	1,500		X	X		X		X	X	

Oʻahu

#	Trail	Area	Distance (mi)	Elevation (ft)									
34.	Kuliʻouʻou Ridge	East Honolulu	5.0	1,800	X	X			X		X	X	
35.	Lanipō	East Honolulu	6.7	2,000	X	X			X		X	X	X
36.	ʻAihualama	East Honolulu	6.0	1,400	X	X		X	X				
37.	ʻAiea Loop	Central Oʻahu	4.8	900	X	X			X				
38.	Waimano Ridge	Central Oʻahu	14.6	1,700	X	X	X		X		X	X	X
39.	Mānana	Central Oʻahu	11.6	1,700	X	X	X		X		X	X	
40.	Maunawili Falls	Windward Side	2.6	400	X	X		X	X			X	X
41.	Kahana Valley	Windward Side	6.4	400	X	X		X	X			X	X
42.	Hauʻula-Papali	Windward Side	7.4	1,500	X	X		X	X				
43.	Maʻakua Gulch	Windward Side	6.0	900		X		X	X		X		X
44.	Keālia	North Shore	6.6	2,000	X	X			X				

HAWAI'I
(the Big Island)

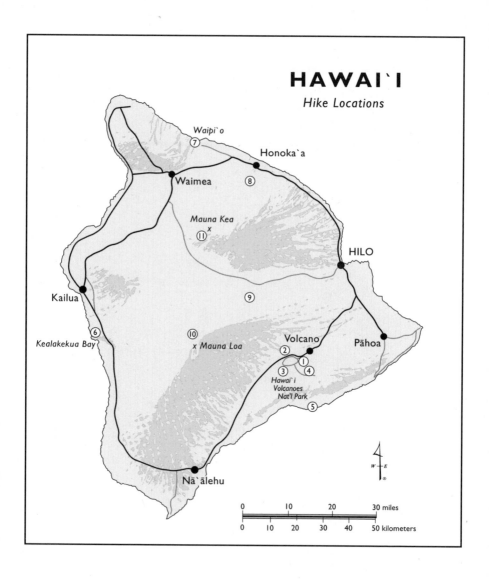

HAWAI`I

Hike Locations

Waipi`o
⑦

Honoka`a

Waimea
⑧

Mauna Kea
x
⑪

HILO

Kailua

⑨

⑥

Kealakekua Bay

⑩
x Mauna Loa

Volcano
②

Pāhoa

③
①
④

Hawai`i
Volcanoes
Nat'l Park

⑤

Nā`ālehu

| 0 | | 10 | | 20 | | 30 miles |
| 0 | 10 | 20 | 30 | 40 | | 50 kilometers |

HAWAI'I VOLCANOES NATIONAL PARK

1 Kīlauea Iki

Length:	4.0-mile loop
Elevation Gain:	400 feet
Suitable for:	Intermediate
Location:	Hawai'i (the Big Island): Hawai'i Volcanoes National Park
Topo Map:	Volcano, Kīlauea Crater

Highlights:
Kīlauea Iki Crater was the scene of a spectacular eruption in 1959. This short loop hike crosses the crater floor past steaming vents and lava ramparts. Along the rim are scenic overlooks and lush native rain forest.

Trailhead Directions:

Distance: *(Hilo to Kīlauea Iki overlook) 30 miles*
Driving Time: 3/4 hour

From Hilo take Kanoelehua Ave. (Rte 11) toward Volcano. Kanoelehua Ave. becomes Hawai'i Belt Rd. (still Rte 11).
Just past Kea'au, the road narrows to two lanes.
Ascend gradually, passing the villages of Kurtistown and Mountain View.
Pass turnoffs to the village of Volcano on the right.
Enter Hawai'i Volcanoes National park.
Shortly afterward turn left at the sign for the park entrance.
Pay the fee at the entrance station.
Almost immediately reach an intersection. Turn left on Crater

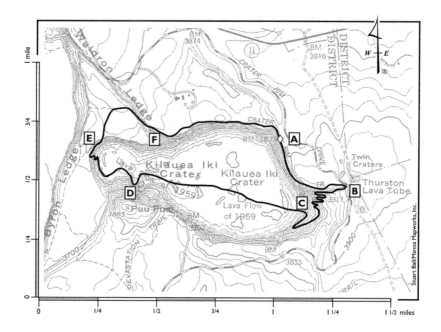

Rim Dr. (Straight ahead on the right is Kīlauea Visitor Center with restrooms, drinking water, and trail information.)

At the stop sign turn left again, still on Crater Rim Dr.

Reach Kīlauea Iki overlook. Turn right into the lot and park there (elevation 3,874 feet) (map point A).

If you are starting from Kailua (Kona), you have a considerably longer drive. Take Hawai'i Belt Rd. (Rte 11) and follow it around the southern tip of the island to the National Park. Turn right at the park entrance sign and pick up the directions above. The distance to the trailhead is 98 miles, and the driving time is about 2 1/2 hours.

Route Description:
At the overlook take the Crater Rim Trail to the left past the display case.

The gravel path hugs the rim of Kīlauea Iki Crater through native 'ōhi'a-hāpu'u forest. To the right are several overlooks.

Reach the parking lot for Thurston (Nāhuku) lava tube (map point B). Keep to the edge of the lot on the sidewalk.

At the crosswalk turn sharp right and down on the Kīlauea Iki Trail.

Descend, gradually at first, and then more steeply on five switchbacks. Initially, the trail is lined with hāpu'u tree ferns. There is a shady bench, presumably for those hiking up.

After another switchback, break out of the rain forest onto open lava. On the far side of the crater is the main vent, backed by its cinder hill, Pu'u Pua'i.

Descend briefly to the crater floor (elevation 3,520 feet) (map point C). Here small 'ōhi'a trees, 'ōhelo shrubs, and kupukupu (swordfern) are already gaining a foothold in the cracks and crevices of the barren lava.

Cross the crater on smooth *pāhoehoe* from the 1959 eruption. The route is marked by piles of rock, called *ahu* in Hawai'i and cairns on the mainland.

Pass several small steam vents.

Near the main vent the trail winds through huge, desolate lava ramparts.

Bear left and ascend briefly to reach an overlook of the vent (map point D). A short side trail leads down to its lip.

Climb gradually across a rough *'a'ā* lava flow. Watch your step on the loose, sometimes jagged rock.

Near the edge of the floor the trail ascends steeply on broken-up *pāhoehoe*.

Climb steadily out of the crater on seven switchbacks. There are rock steps in the steeper sections. Look for pūkiawe shrubs and bamboo orchids on the way up.

Reach a junction and another bench (map point E). Continue straight on the Kīlauea Iki Trail. (To the left a connector trail leads to the Byron Ledge Trail and views of Kīlauea Caldera.)

Stroll through the 'ōhi'a-hāpu'u forest. Introduced ginger forms much of the understory here.

Reach a second junction. Keep right on the Kīlauea Iki Trail. (To the left another connector trail leads to the Byron Ledge Trail.)

Climb steadily. Cross a rockfall and pass a bench.

Reach a third junction at an overlook (map point F). Turn right on the Crater Rim Trail. (To the left the rim trail leads to Volcano House and the park visitor center.)

Cross an indistinct trail. (To the right it leads to an overlook by a concrete platform.)

Walk along the rim of Kīlauea Iki Crater. Along the way are several overlooks.

Climb several stone stairways.

Reach Kīlauea Iki overlook (map point A).

Notes:

The descent into Kīlauea Iki (little spewing) Crater is a breathtaking half-day introduction to hiking in Hawai'i Volcanoes National Park. This short loop provides a close-up look at a major eruption site and at the plants that make up the native rain forest. You can also visit Thurston (Nāhuku) lava tube as a side trip. The route is described clockwise so as to approach the main vent after crossing the crater floor. You can, of course, walk the loop in either direction.

Before starting the hike, spend a few minutes at Kīlauea Iki overlook to get oriented. Directly below is the desolate crater, mostly covered with smooth lava. You can easily trace the hike route across the floor. On the far (south) wall is the main vent of the 1959 eruption. Behind is Pu'u Pua'i (gushing hill), built by that eruption. In the distance to the right (west) is Halema'uma'u (fern house) fire pit inside Kīlauea (spewing) Caldera. In back looms massive Mauna Loa (long mountain).

The Kīlauea area was the legendary home of 'Ailā'au, the ancient Hawaiian god of fire. His name means one who devours trees. Time and again he sent lava from his fire pits to devastate the surrounding forest and the fields of the Hawaiian people. One day, the goddess Pele arrived on the Big Island looking for a new home to build her fires. 'Ailā'au immediately recognized her superior power and simply vanished. Pele now reigns supreme as the goddess of fire in nearby Kīlauea Caldera.

Along the rim of Kīlauea Iki Crater is the native 'ōhi'a-hāpu'u forest. With their sweeping fronds hāpu'u tree ferns form much of the understory. Their trunks consist of roots tightly woven around a small central stem. 'Ōhi'a trees have oval leaves and clusters of delicate red flowers. Native birds, such as the 'apapane, feed on the nectar and help in pollination.

If you're lucky, you may catch a glimpse of an 'apapane in the forest canopy. It has a red breast and head, black wings and tail, and a slightly curved black bill. In flight the 'apapane makes a whirring sound as it darts from tree to tree searching for insects and nectar.

As you emerge onto the crater floor, notice the small 'ōhi'a trees and 'ōhelo shrubs beginning to colonize the bare lava. 'Ōhelo has rounded leaves and delicious red yellow berries, about the size of blueberries. According to legend, 'ōhelo is sacred to Pele. She changed her dead sister, Ka'ōhelo, into the shrub and named it after her.

As you approach the main vent, imagine the evening of 14 November 1959. At 8:08 p.m. a fissure opened along the southwest wall of the crater. Lava cascaded down to the split level floor from a line of fountains over a half mile long. A few days later activity concentrated at the main vent. A single majestic fountain spewed red orange lava to the delight of thousands of viewers at the overlooks behind you. The fountain eventually reached a height of 1,900 feet, a world record. Cinder and ash from the fountain accumulated downwind to form the hill Pu'u Pua'i. Underneath your feet, the lava from the eruption is 414 feet thick. The crust solidified quickly, but the core remained molten for over 20 years.

2 Halema'uma'u

Length:	6.9-mile loop
Elevation Gain:	600 feet
Suitable for:	Intermediate
Location:	Hawai'i (the Big Island): Hawai'i Volcanoes National Park
Topo Map:	Kīlauea Crater

Highlights:

This magnificent loop hike traverses the caldera of Kīlauea, the world's most active volcano. Our destination is Halema'uma'u, the summit crater and home of Pele, the Hawaiian goddess of fire. Along with way, barren lava and steaming vents contrast with the green native rain forest.

Trailhead Directions:

Distance: *(Hilo to Kīlauea Visitor Center) 29 miles*

Driving Time: *3/4 hour*

From Hilo take Kanoelehua Ave. (Rte 11) toward Volcano.
Kanoelehua Ave. becomes Hawai'i Belt Rd. (still Rte 11).
Just past Kea'au, the road narrows to two lanes.
Ascend gradually, passing the villages of Kurtistown and Mountain View.
Pass turnoffs to the village of Volcano on the right.
Enter Hawai'i Volcanoes National Park.
Shortly afterward turn left at the sign for the park entrance.
Pay the fee at the entrance station.
Reach Kīlauea Visitor Center. Turn right into the lot and park there (elevation 3,974 feet) (map point A). The visitor center has restrooms, drinking water, and trail information.

If you are starting from Kailua (Kona), you have a considerably longer drive. Take Hawai'i Belt Rd. (Rte 11) and follow it around

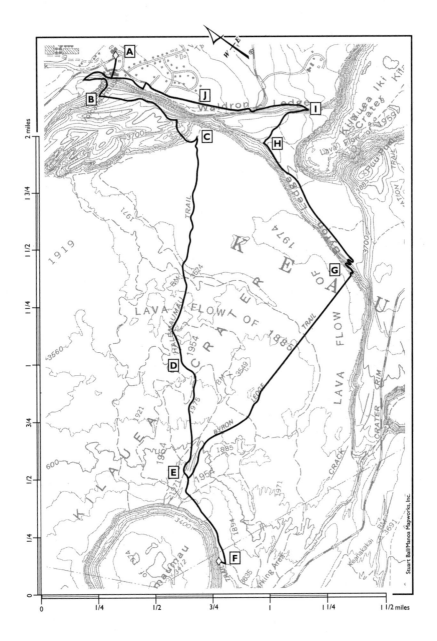

the southern tip of the island to the National Park. Turn right at the park entrance sign and pick up the directions above. The distance to the trailhead is 97 miles, and the driving time is about 2 1/2 hours.

Route Description:

From the visitor center take the paved path crossing Crater Rim Drive to Volcano House.

Enter the hotel and then exit through the back door, marked Crater View.

Reach a signed junction and an awesome view of Kīlauea Caldera. The goal of this hike, Halema'uma'u fire pit, lies on the far side of the caldera.

Turn right on the paved Crater Rim Trail along the stone wall.

Pass the site of the original Hawaiian Volcano Observatory on the right.

A paved trail from the visitor center comes in on the right.

After descending some steps, the path becomes a dirt trail. Along the way are wooden posts, identifying some of the native plants.

Reach a signed junction. Turn left on the Halema'uma'u Trail. (To the right the Crater Rim Trail continues to Uwēkahuna Bluff and the volcano observatory.)

Descend gradually through native 'ōhi'a-hāpu'u forest. The understory includes uluhe ferns and introduced ginger.

By a bench reach another signed junction (map point B). Turn left, still on the Halema'uma'u Trail. (To the right the Sandalwood Trail leads to Steaming Bluff.)

Descend gradually toward the floor of Kīlauea Caldera.

Pass a small picnic shelter on the right.

Climb briefly over the tip of a rock fall from the cliff above.

Enter a dark, dense grove of introduced firetree, a serious pest in the park.

Large boulders loosed from the crater wall line the trail. Look for bamboo orchids in this area.

Break out into the open, bear right, and descend to the crater floor.

Reach a signed junction (map point C). Keep right on the

Halema'uma'u Trail. (The Byron Ledge Trail on the left leads to Kīlauea Iki Crater.)

Begin crossing the crater on smooth *pāhoehoe* lava from the 1974 flow. Piles of rock, called *ahu*, mark the way. They are known as cairns on the mainland. Native kupukupu (swordfern), 'ōhelo shrubs, and small 'ōhi'a trees are already gaining a foothold in the barren lava. There are 'ama'u ferns near the steam vents.

Traverse the light gray, humpy *pāhoehoe* of the 1885 flow.

Cross the 1954 flow on relatively smooth *pāhoehoe* (map point D).

Pass through an area with steam vents. White sulphur lines the cracks in the lava crust.

Walk across the jumbled-up 1975 flow. Steam vents near the trail produce a warm, sulphuric breeze.

Climb gradually toward a line of spatter ramparts on the broken-up *pāhoehoe* from the 1982 eruption.

Parallel the ramparts on a smoother trail.

Bear left and cut through the rampart line. Reddish brown cinders from the eruption are underfoot.

Reach a signed junction (map point E). For now, keep right on the Halema'uma'u Trail. (The Byron Ledge Trail to the left leads to Kīlauea Iki Crater and is the return portion of the loop.)

Cross the 1844 flow of weathered gray lava covered with grass.

Begin circling the rim of Halema'uma'u Crater.

Reach a viewing platform surrounded by a fence (map point F). The fire pit lies directly below.

After viewing the fire pit, backtrack to the junction with the Byron Ledge Trail (map point E). Turn right on it.

The trail initially parallels the spatter ramparts and then works away from them to the right.

Descend gradually over rough *pāhoehoe* from the 1982 eruption. The trail is indistinct in spots; watch for the *ahu*. Look to the right where the 1982 flow has poured over the rim into the crater.

Recross the 1885 flow on flat *pāhoehoe*. Pūkiawe, 'ōhelo, and 'ōhi'a are becoming established there.

Traverse the 1974 flow again on billowy and then very smooth *pāhoehoe*.

Reach the foot of the crater wall and begin the ascent to Byron Ledge (map point G).

Climb steadily out of the crater on three switchbacks.

Walk along the ledge through an open 'ōhi'a forest. The pumice underfoot is from the 1959 eruption of nearby Kīlauea Iki.

Pass a crater overlook with a railing.

Reach a signed junction. Continue straight on the Byron Ledge Trail. (The trail to the right connects with the Devastation Trail.)

Go through a wire fence.

Reach a second signed junction. Continue straight. (The trail to the right leads to Kīlauea Iki Crater.)

Reach a third signed junction (map point H). This time, turn right on a connector trail. (Straight ahead the Byron Ledge Trail descends to the crater floor and rejoins the Halema'uma'u Trail.)

Reach a signed junction with the Kīlauea Iki Trail. Turn left on it. (To the right the trail heads down into Kīlauea Iki Crater.)

Reach a signed junction with the Crater Rim Trail (map point I). Turn left on it. (To the right the trail leads to the Kīlauea Iki overlook and the Thurston (Nāhuku) lava tube.) At the junction are superb views of the Kīlauea Iki vent and cone, Pu'u Pua'i, from the 1959 eruption.

Climb briefly, following the rim above Byron Ledge.

Cross an abandoned section of Crater Rim Drive and parallel it on the left.

Jog left and then right onto the paved road. Parts of the rim trail fell into the crater during earthquakes associated with the eruptions of 1975 and 1983.

Pass the turnout for Waldron Ledge on the left (map point J).

Another paved road comes in on the right.

Sections of the road are fenced off because of huge cracks and potholes.

Reach a junction. Turn left off the road onto the paved Crater Rim Trail. (The road continues to Volcano House.)

By a small picnic shelter turn right, along the rim.

Reach the back door of Volcano House by some picnic tables.

Retrace your steps through the hotel lobby and the paved path to Kīlauea Visitor Center (map point A).

Notes:
If you only take one hike in Hawai'i Volcanoes National Park, make it Halema'uma'u. This moderate loop traverses the scene of much of the activity of Kīlauea (spewing) Volcano. The hike also provides a close-up look at the native plants that make up a mature native rain forest and those that colonize new lava flows. The route is described counterclockwise so that you reach Halema'uma'u after hiking the full extent of the crater. You can, of course, walk the loop in either direction.

Before heading out on the rim trail, take in the awesome, eerie view from Volcano House overlook. Below lies desolate Kīlauea Caldera, carved out of the surrounding rain forest. Across the barren floor is the pit crater Halema'uma'u, the heart of Kīlauea Volcano. To the right plumes of steam drift into the caldera from vents along the bluff. In the distance looms massive Mauna Loa (long mountain), the other active volcano on the Big Island.

In front of the west wing of Volcano House is the original site of the Hawaiian Volcano Observatory, founded by Thomas Jaggar in 1912. All that remains is a concrete piling that served as a base for cameras and surveying instruments. A nearby mound covers the Whitney Seismographic Vault, used to measure the size of earthquakes. The observatory is now located 2 miles farther along the rim on Uwēkahuna (weeping priest) Bluff.

On the descent to the crater floor you pass through a lovely native 'ōhi'a-hāpu'u forest. With their sweeping fronds hāpu'u tree ferns form much of the understory. Their trunks consist of roots tightly woven around a small central stem. 'Ōhi'a trees have oval leaves and clusters of delicate red flowers. Native birds, such as the 'apapane, feed on the nectar and help in pollination.

If you're lucky, you may catch a glimpse of an 'apapane in the forest canopy. It has a red breast and head, black wings and tail, and a slightly curved black bill. In flight the 'apapane makes a whirring sound as it darts from tree to tree searching for insects and nectar.

As you emerge onto the crater floor, notice the small 'ōhi'a trees, 'ōhelo shrubs, and 'ama'u ferns beginning to colonize the bare lava. 'Ōhelo has rounded leaves and delicious red yellow berries, about the size of blueberries. 'Ama'u ferns have short trunks, usually 1 to

2 feet high. Their fronds are bright red when young, gradually turning green with age. Halema'uma'u means fern house; temporary shelters in the area were thatched with 'ama'u fronds.

Halema'uma'u is the main and most active pit crater of Kīlauea Volcano. Currently, the fire pit is about 1,000 yards across and 270 feet deep. Lava from the 1974 eruption covers the floor. Throughout its almost 200-year existence Halema'uma'u has changed shape with each new eruption. In the early 1800s and 1900s a sunken molten lava lake occupied the site. In 1924 the lake drained, and the pit collapsed to a depth of 1,200 feet. Since then, 17 eruptions have refilled Halema'uma'u to its current depth.

Kīlauea Caldera is the legendary home of Pele, the Hawaiian goddess of fire. Many years ago she journeyed to the Hawaiian Islands in a canoe provided by her brother, Kamohoali'i, the god of sharks. With her, Pele carried *pāoa*, a magic tool to dig fire pits. She stopped first at the island of Ni'ihau and began digging. Just as the fire kindled, Nāmakaokaha'i, Pele's older sister and goddess of the sea, flooded the pit with water. Pele then traveled down the Hawaiian chain, digging on Kaua'i, O'ahu, and Maui. On each island her elder sister prevailed, dousing the fires with seawater. Finally, Pele and Nāmakaokaha'i fought in the ocean between Maui and the Big Island. Pele lost and died, but her spirit form occupied Kīlauea Caldera. As you can see, she lives there to this day.

There are several attractive variations to the route as described. You can hike across the crater one way if you have two cars. Park the second one in the large lot next to Halema'uma'u along Crater Rim Drive. The resulting 3.2-mile walk makes a nice novice hike. For a longer outing, combine the Halema'uma'u and Kīlauea Iki hikes. After climbing Byron Ledge, turn right at the second junction and walk the Kīlauea Iki loop in reverse. Before closing the loop, keep right on the Crater Rim Trail to Volcano House. Total distance of the combination is 10.1 miles.

3 Kīlauea Crater Rim

Length:	11.6-mile loop
Elevation Gain:	500 feet
Suitable for:	Intermediate, Expert
Location:	Hawai'i (the Big Island): Hawai'i Volcanoes National Park
Topo Map:	Kīlauea Crater, Volcano

Highlights:

This loop hike circles the great caldera of Kīlauea Volcano. Lush native rain forest alternates with hot desert and barren lava. Along the rim are scenic overlooks, steam vents, pit craters, lava tubes, native birds, and even a museum.

Trailhead Directions:

Distance: *(Hilo to Kīlauea Visitor Center) 29 miles*

Driving Time: *3/4 hour*

From Hilo take Kanoelehua Ave. (Rte 11) toward Volcano.
Kanoelehua Ave. becomes Hawai'i Belt Rd. (still Rte 11).
Just past Kea'au, the road narrows to two lanes.
Ascend gradually, passing the villages of Kurtistown and Mountain View.
Pass turnoffs to the village of Volcano on the right.
Enter Hawai'i Volcanoes National Park.
Shortly afterward turn left at the sign for the park entrance.
Pay the fee at the entrance station.
Reach Kīlauea Visitor Center. Turn right into the lot and park there (elevation 3,974 feet) (map point A). The visitor center has restrooms, drinking water, and trail information.

If you are starting from Kailua (Kona), you have a considerably longer drive. Take Hawai'i Belt Rd. (Rte 11) and follow it around the southern tip of the island to the National Park. Turn right at

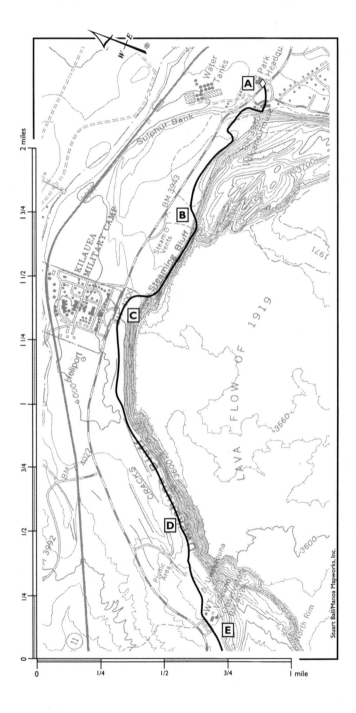

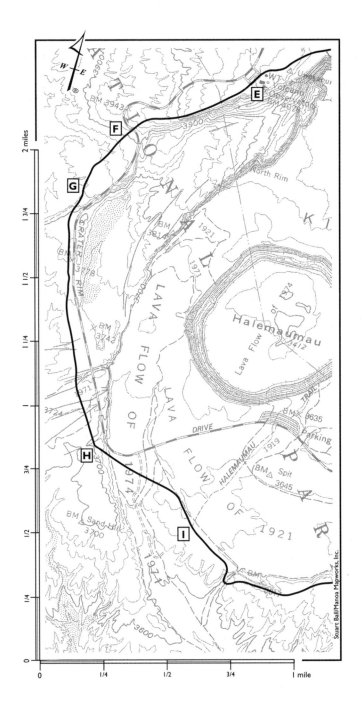

the park entrance sign and pick up the directions above. The distance to the trailhead is 97 miles, and the driving time is about 2 1/2 hours.

Route Description:
From the visitor center take the paved path crossing Crater Rim Drive to Volcano House.

Enter the hotel and then exit through the back door, marked Crater View.

Reach a signed junction and an awesome view of Kīlauea Caldera and much of the hike route.

Turn right on the paved Crater Rim Trail along the stone wall.

Pass the site of the original Hawaiian Volcano Observatory on the right.

A paved trail from the visitor center comes in on the right.

After descending some steps, the path becomes a dirt trail. Along the way are wooden posts, identifying some of the native plants.

Reach a signed junction. Keep right on the Crater Rim Trail. (To the left the Halemaʻumaʻu Trail heads down into Kīlauea Caldera.)

The trail jogs left and then right along the rim.

Stroll through native ʻōhiʻa forest with uluhe ferns underneath. There are some bamboo and Philippine ground orchids along the path.

Steam vents line the trail.

Reach a four-way junction (map point B). Continue straight, on the rim trail. (To the left is the Sandalwood Trail and to the right, the Sulfur Banks Trail.)

Walk through an eerie stretch of steam vents and open grass known as Steaming Bluff or Akanikōlea.

Pass a series of overlooks and a stand of koa trees. The shrubs along the trail are native ʻōhelo and pūkiawe.

An unmarked trail to the right goes to Kīlauea Military Camp (map point C).

As the vegetation thins, join a semipaved trail coming from the camp. Mauna Loa is the massive, rounded mountain to the right (northwest). In the distance is Mauna Kea, which is sometimes snow-capped in winter. On the left are superb views into Kīlauea Caldera.

Pass a parking lot on the right and an official overlook on the left (map point D).

Pass a triangulation station on the left.

Go around to the right of the buildings of the Hawaiian Volcano Observatory.

Reach the observatory parking lot and entrance (elevation 4,077 feet) (map point E). On the left are restrooms and drinking water. Beyond are the Jaggar Museum and a crater overlook. From it are views into Halemaʻumaʻu fire pit. Across the crater are Kīlauea Iki Crater and in the distance Mauna Ulu.

Pick up the Crater Rim Trail at the far end of the parking lot.

Descend gradually along the rim. The trail is indistinct in spots. The native shrub ʻaʻaliʻi lines the trail.

Work right, away from the rim and cross Crater Rim Drive (map point F). Look out for cars.

Walk on a wide, level path through scattered ʻōhiʻa, ʻōhelo, and pūkiawe.

Reach a signed junction (map point G). Keep left on the rim trail. (To the right the Kaʻū Desert Trail leads to the Footprints Exhibit.)

Descend gradually toward Crater Rim Drive as the vegetation gradually disappears. Underfoot are red cinders.

Parallel the road. The trail crosses several small washes on rock causeways. On the right is a huge fault crack.

Cross a larger causeway and then bear right away from the road following a series of trail signs and *ahu* (cairns).

Parallel a gully on the right and then cross it.

Turn left, back toward the road, following the signs.

Turn right and cross a wide crack, partially filled in.

Veer left toward the road on barren *pāhoehoe* lava from the 1971 flow.

Resume walking on brown cinders, following the trail signs.

A service road comes in on the left, and the route follows it briefly.

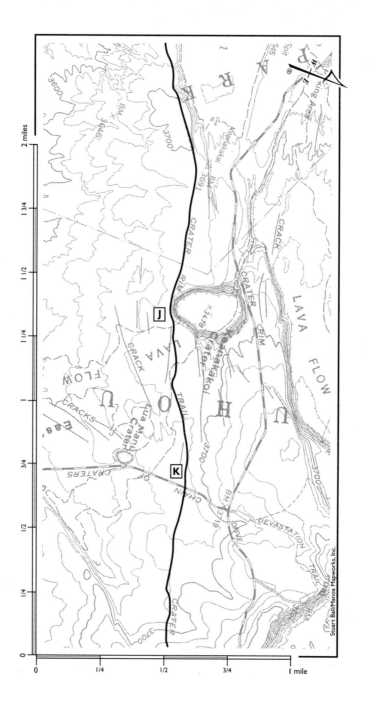

Stuart Ball/Mānoa Mapworks, Inc.

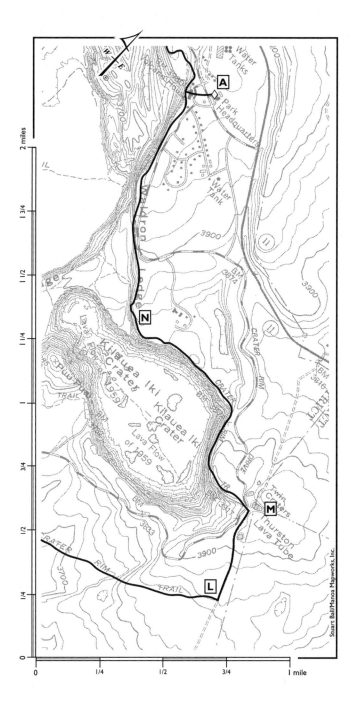

Turn left off the service road back on to the trail.

Descend briefly next to a gully (map point H).

Traverse the 1974 flow with its silvery, billowy *pāhoehoe*.

Switch back to red brown cinders and, almost immediately, cross another service road.

Follow the edge of a cliff.

Reach a signed junction (map point I). Continue straight, uphill on the rim trail. (To the left the Halemaʻumaʻu Trail leads to the Halemaʻumaʻu fire pit.)

On the right pass a blob of *pāhoehoe* all by itself. In the area are various scientific monitoring devices.

Cross a river of lava from the 1982 flow. It runs from the basin on the left, downslope to the right.

Cross a finger of lava from the 1982 flow.

Parallel a gully and then cross it to the left.

Work left, staying near the edge of the cliff. Vegetation, mostly ʻōhelo and pūkiawe, gradually reappears.

Pass another monitoring device on the left.

Join a service road.

Bear right, off the service road as it curves left to rejoin Crater Rim Drive.

Cross a tongue of *pāhoehoe* from the 1974 flow.

Pass to the right of Keanakākoʻi (map point J). Look for koaʻe kea, the white-tailed tropicbird, soaring inside the crater.

Go through a fence, closing the gate after you.

Traverse the brittle, mustard-colored 1974 flow that poured into Keanakākoʻi Crater.

Pass several lava trees on the right. Bleached ʻōhiʻa trunks lie on the ground.

Enter a dry forest of ʻōhiʻa trees, and ʻaʻaliʻi, ʻōhelo, and pūkiawe shrubs.

The trail skirts the edge of the 1974 flow. Underfoot are cinders from the 1959 eruption of Kīlauea Iki.

The path becomes wide and level.

Cross Chain of Craters Road (map point K). Be careful; traffic makes this the most dangerous part of the hike!

Pass through some dark groves of introduced firetree, a serious pest in the park.

Enter the native rain forest with large 'ōhi'a trees and hāpu'u tree ferns. Look for the native birds 'apapane and 'elepaio.

The trail climbs gradually.

Reach a junction with a dirt road, called Escape Road (map point L). Turn left on it.

Go through a gate.

Descend briefly to reach the start of the trail to Thurston (Nāhuku) lava tube.

Turn left by the information bulletin board. (Straight ahead are restrooms.)

Cross Crater Rim Drive in the crosswalk (map point M). Again, watch for traffic.

Reach a signed junction. Turn right along the edge of the lava tube parking lot. (To the left is the Kīlauea Iki Trail.)

Climb briefly; the path is initially paved and has guardrails.

Walk along the rim of Kīlauea Iki Crater.

Reach Kīlauea Iki overlook. The trail becomes paved around the parking lot.

Cross an indistinct trail.

Reach a signed junction (map point N). Keep right and up on the Crater Rim Trail. (To the left and down is the Kīlauea Iki Trail leading to the crater.) At the junction are superb views of the vent and cinder hill (Pu'u Pua'i) from the 1959 eruption.

Climb briefly, following the rim above Byron Ledge.

Cross an abandoned section of Crater Rim Drive and parallel it on the left.

Jog left and then right onto the paved road. Parts of the rim trail fell into the crater during earthquakes associated with the eruptions of 1975 and 1983.

Pass the turnout for Waldron Ledge on the left.

Another paved road comes in on the right.

Reach a junction. Turn left off the road onto the paved Crater Rim Trail. (The road continues to Volcano House.)

By a small picnic shelter turn right, along the rim.

Reach the back door of Volcano House by some picnic tables.

Retrace your steps through the hotel lobby and the paved path to Kīlauea Visitor Center (map point A).

Notes:

This circle hike is a grand tour of the Kīlauea (spewing) area of Hawai'i Volcanoes National Park. Although long in distance, the route never fails to fascinate with its varied terrain, vegetation, bird life, and volcanic features. The section of the trail from Volcano House to Thurston (Nāhuku) lava tube is very popular. The rest of the loop you may have to yourself.

Start early in the morning. You can then set a leisurely pace and have time to visit Jaggar Museum. Also, you avoid the Ka'ū Desert section in the hot afternoon.

Before heading out on the rim trail, take in the awesome, eerie view from Volcano House overlook. Below lies desolate Kīlauea Caldera, carved out of the surrounding rain forest. Across the barren floor is the pit crater Halema'uma'u, the heart of Kīlauea Volcano. Beyond the crater is the southwest rift zone extending into the Ka'ū Desert. To the right (west) is Hawaiian Volcano Observatory atop Uwēkahuna (weeping priest) Bluff. In the distance looms massive Mauna Loa (long mountain), the other active volcano on the Big Island.

Kīlauea Caldera is a basin about 2 to 3 miles across and several hundred feet deep. It was formed by successive episodes of collapse, the last one occurring in 1790. During the 1800s and early 1900s nearly continuous eruptions created molten lava lakes that overflowed, partially filling the caldera. The eruption of 1974 produced the band of new lava on the near side of the floor.

In front of the west wing of Volcano House is the original site of the Hawaiian Volcano Observatory, founded by Thomas Jaggar in 1912. All that remains is a concrete piling that served as a base for cameras and surveying instruments. A nearby mound covers the Whitney Seismographic Vault, used to measure the size of earthquakes.

After a pleasant walk through 'ōhi'a forest, you emerge suddenly into a meadow, known as Steaming Bluff or Akanikōlea (cry of the plover). Steam billows from vents along the rim and drifts into the crater. Hot volcanic rocks underground heat the ground water to produce the steam. The area is covered with shallow-rooted grasses because tree roots cannot survive the boiling temperatures. The dramatic legend of Akanikōlea is retold on a sign overlooking the crater.

Once past Steaming Bluff, look for the native shrubs ʻaʻaliʻi, pūkiawe, and ʻōhelo. ʻAʻaliʻi has narrow, dull green leaves and red seed capsules. Pūkiawe has tiny, rigid leaves and small white, pink, or red berries. ʻŌhelo has rounded leaves and delicious red yellow berries, about the size of blueberries. According to legend, ʻōhelo is sacred to Pele, the Hawaiian goddess of fire. She changed her dead sister, Kaʻōhelo, into the shrub and named it after her.

Take a short break at Hawaiian Volcano Observatory on Uwēkahuna Bluff. The museum there has some excellent exhibits on Hawaiʻi volcanoes and the instruments that track their activity. The bluff is the highest point along the rim and provides a commanding view of the crater.

After leaving the observatory, the trail crosses the southwest rift zone of Kīlauea Volcano in the Kaʻū Desert. A rift zone is an area of structural weakness that is laced with cracks providing passageway for rising molten rock, called magma. The vegetation here is sparse because of new lava, lower rainfall, and the volcanic fumes from Halemaʻumaʻu (fern house) Crater.

Halemaʻumaʻu is the legendary home of the fire goddess. One day Pele looked up from her fire pit and saw Kamapuaʻa, the pig god, coming to visit from Oʻahu. Pele made an unfortunate remark about his appearance. Kamapuaʻa then taunted Pele about her fire and the destruction it caused among the Hawaiian people. An angered Pele stirred up her fire pit again and again to destroy the pig god. Each time he emerged from the flames unscathed. Finally Kamapuaʻa appealed to the gods of the skies who sent rain to cool the inferno. The rain weakened the fires, but did not put them out. Pele and Kamapuaʻa then agreed to a truce. Because fire and water are equally powerful, the two gods decided to divide the Big Island in half. Pele kept the districts of Kaʻū, Puna, and Kona where her fires still rage. Kamapuaʻa received the rest of the island where rain falls and forests and gardens can grow, untouched by lava.

After crossing a series of recent lava flows, you come to Keanakāko'i (adze quarry cave) Crater. Early Hawaiians shaped the dense basalt of the crater wall into stone tools. Eruptions in 1877 and 1974 poured lava into the crater and buried the adze cave. Just beyond the crater are some deformed lava trees. They form when *pāhoehoe* lava surrounds the trunk of a tree and solidifies against it. The lava then drains downslope, leaving a shell of cooled lava around the tree. The tree burns, resulting in a hollow pillar.

After miles of barren lava and cinders the lush native 'ōhi'a-hāpu'u forest is a welcome sight. With their sweeping fronds hāpu'u tree ferns form much of the understory. Their trunks consist of roots tightly woven around a small central stem. 'Ōhi'a trees have oval leaves and clusters of delicate red flowers. Native birds, such as the 'apapane, feed on the nectar and help in pollination.

If you're lucky, you may catch a glimpse of an 'apapane in the forest canopy. It has a red breast and head, black wings and tail, and a slightly curved black bill. In flight the 'apapane makes a whirring sound as it darts from tree to tree searching for insects and nectar. Another fairly common native forest bird is the 'elepaio. It is brown on top with a chestnut-colored breast and a dark tail, usually cocked. 'Elepaio are very curious, which is why you can often see them.

After the solitude of desert and rain forest, the mob of tourists at Thurston (Nāhuku) lava tube comes as a shock. If you haven't already done so, take the short walk through the tube. Then stroll the final section of the rim trail past Kīlauea Iki (little spewing) Crater and Waldron Ledge to Volcano House.

There are several variations to the route as described. You can, of course, hike the loop in reverse; however you then traverse the hot, dry side of the crater in the afternoon. For a shorter loop, cross the crater on the Halema'uma'u Trail, following the route description of that hike. At the trail end turn left or right on the Crater Rim Trail and circle back to Volcano House. Total distance is 8.7 miles for the loop on the observatory side and 10.3 miles for the loop on the Thurston (Nāhuku) lava tube side.

4 Makaopuhi Crater

Length:	8.3-mile round trip
Elevation Gain:	600 feet
Suitable for:	Novice, Intermediate
Location:	Hawai'i (the Big Island): Hawai'i Volcanoes National Park
Topo Map:	Makaopuhi Crater, Volcano

Highlights:

This hike leads across barren lava flows to Makaopuhi Crater, a deep pit created by Kīlauea Volcano. Along the way you see volcanic shields, spatter cones, lava trees, and patches of native rain forest. The view from the top of Pu'u Huluhulu is one of the best in the park.

Trailhead Directions:

Distance: *(Hilo to Mauna Ulu parking area) 36 miles*

Driving Time: *I hour*

From Hilo take Kanoelehua Ave. (Rte 11) toward Volcano.
Kanoelehua Ave. becomes Hawai'i Belt Rd. (still Rte 11).
Just past Kea'au, the road narrows to two lanes.
Ascend gradually, passing the villages of Kurtistown and Mountain View.
Pass turnoffs to the village of Volcano on the right.
Enter Hawai'i Volcanoes National Park.
Shortly afterward turn left at the sign for the park entrance.
Pay the fee at the entrance station.
Almost immediately reach an intersection. Turn left on Crater Rim Dr. (Straight ahead on the right is Kīlauea Visitor Center with restrooms, drinking water, and trail information.)
At the stop sign turn left again, still on Crater Rim Dr.
Pass Kīlauea Iki overlook on the right and Thurston (Nāhuku) lava tube on the left.

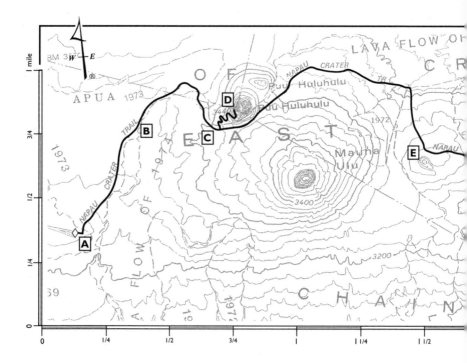

Wind through a tree fern and 'ōhi'a forest.

Pass the turnoff to Pu'u Pua'i on the right.

At the next intersection turn left on Chain of Craters Rd.

On the right pass the turnoff to Hilina Pali overlook.

Just past Pauahi Crater turn left to Mauna Ulu parking area. Leave your car in the lot there (elevation 3,220 feet) (map point A).

If you are starting from Kailua (Kona), you have a considerably longer drive. Take Hawai'i Belt Rd. (Rte 11) and follow it around the southern tip of the island to the National Park. Turn right at the park entrance sign and pick up the directions above. The distance to the trailhead is 112 miles, and the driving time is about 2 3/4 hours.

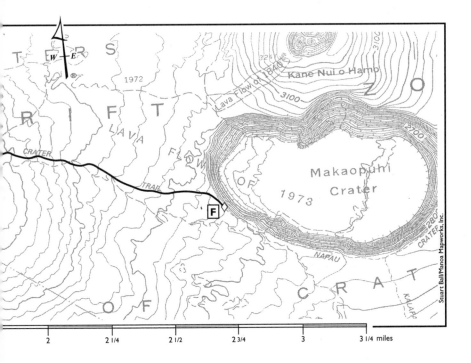

Route Description:

At the far end of the parking area walk past a barrier across the road.

Shortly afterward reach a junction. Turn left off the road onto the Nāpau Crater Trail. (The road continues straight for a short distance and then is blocked by a massive lava flow.)

On the right pass a wooden bulletin board displaying trail maps and information.

Cross the 1973 flow from Mauna Ulu on relatively smooth *pāhoehoe* lava. The trail is marked by piles of rocks, called *ahu* in Hawai'i and cairns on the mainland. Look for native pūkiawe and 'ōhelo shrubs, kupukupu (swordfern), and small 'ama'u ferns.

Enter a remnant native 'ōhi'a forest, untouched by the surrounding new lava. The huge flow on the right issued from Mauna Ulu in 1974.

Resume crossing the 1973 flow (map point B). To the right is another remnant 'ōhi'a forest.

Pass some short, deformed lava trees. A few have double or triple trunks.

Bear right through large 'ōhi'a trees.

Break out onto the barren 1974 lava flow.

Climb gradually along the edge of the flow toward a forested cone, Pu'u Huluhulu.

Reach a signed junction (map point C). For now turn left up Pu'u Huluhulu. (The main trail continues straight, to Makaopuhi Crater.)

Climb Pu'u Huluhulu on 12 short switchbacks through a remnant 'ōhi'a forest. Look for native 'ama'u ferns and 'uki, a sedge with sword-shaped leaves.

After passing a hitching post, reach the summit with its awesome view (elevation 3,440 feet) (map point D).

Backtrack down Pu'u Huluhulu and turn left on the main trail.

Initially the trail hugs the base of Pu'u Huluhulu.

Descend gradually and then swing right, around Mauna Ulu.

Climb to a small pit crater (map point E).

Bear left and pass some steam vents.

Descend gradually toward Makaopuhi Crater on the 1973 lava flow. The hill to the left of the crater is Kāne Nui o Hamo, an old volcanic shield similar to Mauna Ulu.

Reach the rim of Makaopuhi Crater (elevation 2,940 feet) (map point F). (The Nāpau Crater Trail continues around the rim through native 'ōhi'a-hāpu'u forest.)

Notes:

The route to Makaopuhi (eye of the eel) Crater follows the upper east rift zone of Kīlauea (spewing) Volcano. The zone is an area of structural weakness, marked by a line of spatter cones, volcanic shields, and pit craters. Lava from recent eruptions has engulfed huge patches of the rain forest growing on older flows.

Native plants are already colonizing the barren lava flows along the first section of the trail. Watch for pūkiawe and 'ōhelo shrubs, kupukupu (swordfern), and 'ama'u ferns. Pūkiawe has tiny, rigid leaves and small white, pink, or red berries. 'Ōhelo has rounded leaves and delicious red yellow berries, about the size of blueberries. 'Ama'u ferns have short trunks, usually 1 to 2 feet high. Their fronds are bright red when young, gradually turning green with age.

Just past the remnant 'ōhi'a forest is a desolate stand of lava trees. They form when *pāhoehoe* lava surrounds the trunk of a tree and solidifies against it. The lava then drains downslope, leaving a shell of cooled lava around the tree. The tree burns, resulting in a hollow pillar.

About a mile in, climb Pu'u Huluhulu (shaggy hill) for a bird's-eye view of the ravaged landscape. The hill is actually a spatter cone that formed 300 to 400 years ago. Next to it to the north is a small forested crater. Recent lava flows have almost completely surrounded both the cone and the crater.

At the top a weathered compass points out the sights. Close up to the south is Mauna Ulu (growing mountain), a volcanic shield with a lava lake. To the east lies the route of this hike to Makaopuhi Crater. Beyond the crater is Pu'u 'Ō'ō cone and vent, the scene of intermittent volcanic activity since 1983. Mauna Loa (long mountain) is the massive mountain in the distance to the west.

Leaving Pu'u Huluhulu, the trail skirts Mauna Ulu, the source of most of the lava you are walking on today. Mauna Ulu is a volcanic shield created by an eruption lasting from 1969 to 1974. Lava poured out of several vents and later merged to form a lava lake at the summit. Some of the flows crossed the old Chain of Craters Rd., plunged spectacularly over Hōlei Pali, and entered the ocean.

Next in line down the rift zone is Makaopuhi Crater, our destination. It used to be split level, but in 1973 a lava flow from Mauna Ulu filled the deep western pit and partially covered the eastern pit. The forested hill to the north is Kāne Nui o Hamo, a volcanic shield formed about 600 years ago.

Extending from the rim of Makaopuhi Crater is the lush native rain forest. It is dominated here by hāpu'u tree ferns and 'ōhi'a trees. 'Ōhi'a colonizes recent lava flows and reaches maturity on older flows, such as this one. The trees have oval leaves and clusters of delicate red flowers. Native birds, such as the 'apapane and 'i'iwi, feed on the nectar and help in pollination.

With their sweeping fronds the hāpu'u tree ferns form a nearly continuous understory in the native forest here. Their trunks consist of roots tightly woven around a small central stem. The brown fiber covering the young fronds of hāpu'u is called *pulu*. From about 1860 to 1885 *pulu* was harvested nearby to become pillow and mattress stuffing. A factory processed the fiber and shipped it to California from Keauhou landing along the Ka'ū coast.

There are several attractive variations to the route as described. For a short novice hike, climb Pu'u Huluhulu and then turn around. For a longer hike continue to the end of the trail at Nāpau (the endings) Crater. The overlook there provides a closer view of the Pu'u 'Ō'ō cone. Total distance round trip is 14 miles.

You can also hike the route one way if you have two cars. Park the second one at Kealakomo (the entrance path) overlook, farther down Chain of Craters Rd. On the trail continue around the rim of Makaopuhi Crater. At the first junction turn right on the Kalapana (announce noted place) Trail. At a second junction bear right on the Nāulu (the groves) Trail. Total one-way distance is 8.2 miles, and it's all downhill.

5 Ka'aha

Length:	8.2-mile round trip
Elevation Gain:	2,300 feet
Suitable for:	Intermediate, Expert
Location:	Hawai'i (the Big Island): Hawai'i Volcanoes National Park
Topo Map:	Ka'ū Desert

Highlights:

This hike descends to Ka'aha, an oasis along the stark, windswept Ka'ū coast. At a nearby cove is a small, black-sand beach with good swimming and snorkeling. Both coming and going, you must negotiate Hilina Pali, a spectacular 1,500-foot-high cliff.

Trailhead Directions:

Distance: *(Hilo to Hilina Pali overlook) 45 miles*
Driving Time: *1 1/2 hours*

From Hilo take Kanoelehua Ave. (Rte 11) toward Volcano.
Kanoelehua Ave. becomes Hawai'i Belt Rd. (still Rte 11).
Just past Kea'au, the road narrows to two lanes.
Ascend gradually, passing the villages of Kurtistown and Mountain View.
Pass turnoffs to the village of Volcano on the right.
Enter Hawai'i Volcanoes National Park.
Shortly afterward turn left at the sign for the park entrance.
Pay the fee at the entrance station.
Almost immediately reach an intersection. Turn left on Crater Rim Dr. (Straight ahead on the right is Kīlauea Visitor Center with restrooms, drinking water, and trail information.)
At the stop sign turn left again, still on Crater Rim Dr.
Pass Kīlauea Iki overlook on the right and Thurston (Nāhuku) lava tube on the left.
Wind through a tree fern and 'ōhi'a forest.

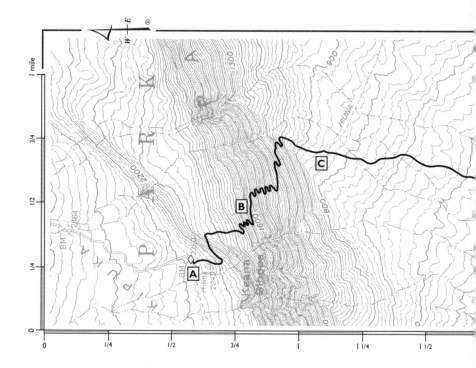

Pass the turnoff to Pu'u Pua'i on the right.

At the next intersection turn left on Chain of Craters Rd.

Pass turnoffs to Puhimau Crater on the left and Ko'oko'olau Crater on the right.

Turn right on Hilina Pali Rd.

Pass Kīpuka Nēnē campground on the left.

Reach the end of the road at Hilina Pali overlook (elevation 2,280 feet) (map point A). Park in the lot next to the picnic shelter. Behind the shelter is a pit toilet.

If you are starting from Kailua (Kona), you have a considerably longer drive. Take Hawai'i Belt Rd. (Rte 11) and follow it around the southern tip of the island to the National Park. Turn right at the park entrance sign and pick up the directions above. The distance to the trailhead is 118 miles, and the driving time is about 3 1/4 hours.

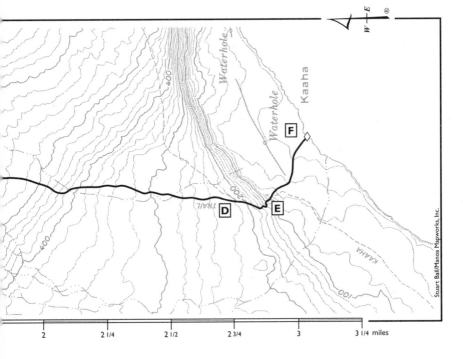

Route Description:

From the picnic shelter take the Hilina Pali Trail. As you face the ocean, it's the trail straight ahead, marked by a small wooden bulletin board. (The trail to the right, also marked by a bulletin board, is the Ka'ū Desert Trail, leading to Pepeiao Cabin.)

Descend gradually to the cliff edge and bear right along it.

Switchback twice and then go straight down as the slope angle eases momentarily.

Continue descending on a series of short switchbacks.

Cross an 'a'ā lava flow made up of rough, loose rock. Watch your footing.

Pass a native lama and an 'ōhi'a tree on the right.

Recross the 'a'ā flow several times on longer switchbacks (map point B).

On the right pass a lone lama tree. It's a shady spot to rest your legs.

Switchback one more time and then descend straight down to the base of the *pali.*

Reach a signed junction (map point C). Keep right on the Ka'aha Trail. (To the left the Hilina Pali Trail heads down to the coast at Halapē.)

Parallel Hilina Pali briefly and then swing left toward the coast.

Descend gradually on old *pāhoehoe* covered with grass. Follow the *ahu* (cairns) marching into the distance.

Reach a signed junction (map point D). Keep right on the Ka'aha Trail. (The trail to the left heads along the coast to Halapē.)

Pass the entrance to a lava tube on the left.

Descend a short but steep *pali.*

The trail curves left past a pit toilet.

Reach the shelter at Ka'aha (elevation 80 feet) (map point E). From the shelter pick up a spur trail heading down to the ocean. Look for the low-lying native shrub naupaka kahakai along the way.

Reach the shore at a cove with a small, black-sand beach (map point F).

Notes:

The route to Ka'aha (the assembly) traverses the hot, dry, and rugged coastal section of the National Park. Winter (November–April) is the most comfortable time of year to take this hike. If you do go in summer, be prepared for high temperatures and intense sun. The only shade along the coast is in the Ka'aha Shelter. Regardless of the season, start hiking early to beat the heat. Wait until well after lunch to start back. Late afternoon usually brings strong trade winds and heavy cloud buildup *mauka* (inland). The air then becomes much cooler for the final climb up the *pali* (cliff).

Before starting the hike, spend a few minutes at the Hilina Pali (cliff struck by wind) overlook. It is a quiet, remote spot, even though accessible by car. From the overlook you can see some of the route directly below. Ka'aha, however, is hidden by a *pali* near the coast. Along the coast to the left are the hump of Pu'u Kapukapu (regal hill) and Keauhou (the new era) and 'Āpua (fish basket)

Points. To the right are the villages of Punalu'u (coral dived for) and Nā'ālehu (the volcanic ashes). In back is massive Mauna Loa (long mountain).

Hilina Pali is a fault scarp, 12 miles long. The cliff formed when the coastal section suddenly dropped 1,500 feet. The Hilina fault system is still active, producing many small earthquakes.

Initially the route descends Hilina Pali on 22 switchbacks. Watch your step because the rock underfoot is often unstable. The remainder of the hike is over old *pāhoehoe* lava covered with grass. The trail is frequently rough and uneven, and the grass hides loose rock and potholes. Again, watch your footing.

The trees on Hilina Pali with dark green, leathery leaves are native lama. Its fruits are green, then yellow, and finally bright red when fully ripe. Lama was sacred to Laka, goddess of the hula. The early Hawaiians used the hard, light-colored wood in temple construction and in hula performances.

After descending Hilina Pali, the route passes several lava tubes. They are usually formed in *pāhoehoe* flows that are confined, such as in a gully. The top and edges of the flow cool and crust over. The lava inside continues to flow through the resulting tunnel. Eventually the flow diminishes and stops, leaving a tube. Do not enter any of the lava tubes, because their fragile ecosystems are extremely vulnerable to unintentional damage.

Ka'aha stands out as the only patch of green along the otherwise barren coast. Fresh water seeping close to the surface of the lava enters the ocean here. The green is mostly naupaka kahakai, a spreading, succulent native shrub. Its flowers are white with purple streaks and appear half-formed. Its white, fleshy fruits float on the ocean, helping to spread the species to remote areas.

Ka'aha Shelter is located about 0.25 mile inland at the foot of a small *pali*. The shelter has three sides, a sandy floor, and a pit toilet nearby. Built into the back of the shelter is a water tank that is fed by rainfall collected on the roof. Filter or treat the water chemically before drinking it.

From the shelter take the makeshift trail that leads down to a small cove with the beginnings of a black-sand beach. Go swimming or snorkeling, explore the tide pools, walk along the coast toward Kālu'e (hanging loose), or just sit on the beach and take in the wild beauty of the area.

The snorkeling at Ka'aha is good, but not great. The fresh water entering the cove causes some temperature fluctuations and fuzzy viewing. There are some colorful coral and a good variety of reef fish. The best area is the ocean side of the cove near the wave break.

Now that you are totally relaxed, are you ready for the climb out?

KONA

6 Kealakekua Bay

Length:	4.2-mile round trip
Elevation Gain:	1,300 feet
Suitable for:	Intermediate
Location:	Hawai'i (the Big Island): below the town of Captain Cook
Topo Map:	Hōnaunau

Highlights:
The great English explorer Captain James Cook met his death at Kealakekua Bay on 14 February 1779. This hot, dry hike descends a dirt road to his monument by the shore. In the bay is some of the best snorkeling in the Islands.

Trailhead Directions:
Distance: *(Kailua [Kona] to Captain Cook) 12 miles*
Driving Time: *1/2 hour*

From Kailua (Kona) take Kuakini Hwy (Rte 11) toward Volcano.
Pass the junction with Rte 180 on the left.
Drive through the towns of Kainaliu and Kealakekua.
Kuakini Hwy becomes Māmalahoa Hwy (still Rte 11).
Enter the town of Captain Cook and look for a Chevron gas station on the left.
Just past it, turn right on Nāpō'opo'o Rd. On the right a sign to Kealakekua Bay marks the intersection. Across the highway from the sign is Shiraki Dry Cleaners.
Drive 0.1 mile down the road. Look for a rock wall and three tall

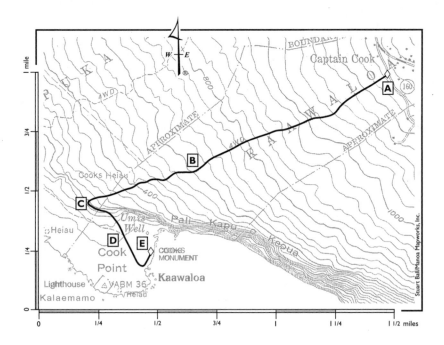

palm trees on the left. Just beyond is a white house on the slope
above.

Park on the shoulder of the road near the wall (elevation 1,290
feet) (map point A).

If you are starting from Hilo, you have a considerably longer
drive. Take Hawaiʻi Belt Rd. (Rte 19) to Waimea. Continue on the
belt road (now Rte 190) to Kailua (Kona) and pick up the directions above. The distance to the trailhead is 106 miles, and the
driving time is about 2 3/4 hours.

Route Description:
Take the dirt road across the street from the wall and the palms. At
the start of the road is an avocado tree on the left as you face the
ocean.

Descend along the dirt road, known as Kaʻawaloa Rd. On the
right are a rock wall and a fence enclosing a small coffee field.

Walk under a spreading mango tree.

Pass a gate on the right.

As the road curves right, reach a junction. Continue straight and down on a dirt road. (The more traveled road to the right leads to a private residence.)

Descend steadily toward the coast. On the left are a rock wall and a fence. Monkeypod trees provide some shade.

The road becomes rockier and is lined with koa haole trees (map point B). On the right is an old 'a'ā lava flow.

Break out into the open. You can look out across Kealakekua Bay to Ke'ei Beach and Palemanō Point. To the right along the coast is Keawekāheka Point and Bay.

On the right pass a rock-walled enclosure with a wire gate. In the middle is a rock mound and a rotted wooden post.

The road bends sharply to the left toward Kealakekua Bay (map point C). Way below on the right is a dirt road following the coast.

Pass a dilapidated wooden gate.

Descend steeply over loose rock. Watch your footing.

Enter a forest of koa haole and kiawe trees. The angle of descent eases as you approach the bay.

The dirt road along the coast comes in on the right (map point D). Keep left.

The road is flanked by magnificent rock walls, all that remains of the ancient Hawaiian village of Ka'awaloa.

Reach a junction. For now, continue straight toward the water. (The path to the left through a break in the rock wall leads to the Cook monument.)

Reach the water's edge. On the left is a small plaque marking the spot where Captain Cook met his death.

Retrace your steps back to the last junction and turn right through the break in the rock wall.

The path swings right and then left to parallel the shore.

Go around the huge trunk of a kiawe tree.

Reach the Cook monument at Ka'awaloa Point (map point E).

Notes:

Most people arrive at Kealakekua (pathway of the god) Bay in a kayak or tour boat. If you are a landlubber or just enjoy reaching remote places the hard way, take this hot, dry hike down to the bay. Spend some time at the monument to the great English explorer Captain James Cook. Then jump in the ocean for a cooling dip and some terrific snorkeling.

Start early in the morning or late in the afternoon to avoid the sweltering heat. For clear water and good lighting, go snorkeling in the early morning. Later in the day the water near the monument is crowded with kayakers from Nāpō'opo'o and tour boats from Kailua (Kona).

Just before reaching the shore, the road passes through the site of Ka'awaloa (the distant kava), an ancient Hawaiian village. All that remains are rock walls and house platforms. At the time of Cook's visit, Ka'awaloa was the royal seat of Kalani'ōpu'u, the chief of Kona, Ka'ū, and Puna. The village consisted of thatched houses shaded by palm trees, and enclosed gardens for growing fruits and vegetables.

In the shallows at Ka'awaloa Point is a small metal plaque mark-ing the spot where Captain Cook died on 14 February 1779. That morning he came ashore with an armed party to retrieve a stolen ship's boat. Cook had planned to take Kalani'ōpu'u hostage and trade him for the boat. The captain, however, was unsuccessful in persuading the chief to come on board his flagship. Meanwhile, a large group of native Hawaiians had gathered to watch the goings-on. Initially peaceful, the crowd turned hostile upon hearing that Cook's sailors had just killed a chief across the bay. Cook's party fired shots, and the natives threw stones. In the ensuing melee Cook was clubbed and stabbed to death.

Along the shore is the Cook monument, erected in the 1870s. It is a white obelisk, surrounded by upright cannons linked with anchor chain. The land underneath the monument belongs to Great Britain. In the pavement are plaques commemorating visits by ships of the British Commonwealth.

From the pier in front of the monument you can look across the bay to the town of Nāpō'opo'o (the holes). On the left is Pali Kapu o Keōua, a sheer cliff that contains ancient burial caves. Keep your eyes open for koaʻe kea, the white-tailed tropicbird, soaring near the cliffs.

The snorkeling at Kealakekua Bay is superb, with a good variety of reef fish and coral. The monument pier offers easy access to the water. You can also get in from the fingers of lava near the site of Cook's death. If you decide to swim or snorkel, you are on your own. There are no lifeguards at Kealakekua Bay.

After snorkeling, walk along the shore to Kalaemamo Point and the small Nāpōʻopoʻo lighthouse. Along the way is a native wiliwili tree. It has heart-shaped, leathery leaflets in groups of three. Flowers appear in the spring and are usually orange. Early Hawaiians used the soft, light wood for surfboards, canoe outriggers, and fishnet floats. The red seeds were strung together to form *lei hua* (seed or nut garlands).

The return trip upslope is relatively painless, especially after an invigorating swim. Keep a steady pace and drink lots of water. Before you know it, the avocado tree at the trailhead comes into view.

HĀMĀKUA

7 Waipiʻo Valley

Length:	5.7-mile round trip
Elevation Gain:	2,100 feet
Suitable for:	Intermediate
Location:	Hawaiʻi (the Big Island): Hāmākua and Kohala Forest Reserves near Honokaʻa
Topo Map:	Kukuihaele

Highlights:
Waipiʻo is a deep, lush valley on the rugged Kohala coast. This up-and-down hike descends one side of the valley and climbs the other. In between is a windswept black-sand beach, framed by sheer sea cliffs.

Trailhead Directions:

Distance: *(Hilo to Waipiʻo Valley lookout) 51 miles*
Driving Time: *1 1/4 hours*

From Hilo take Hawaiʻi Belt Rd. (Rte 19) toward Waimea.
Proceed along the Hāmākua Coast past a series of villages.
Drive through Laupāhoehoe village.
Cross Laupāhoehoe and Kaʻawaliʻi Gulches.
Turn right on Rte 240 to Honokaʻa.
Drive through Honokaʻa town.
The road jogs right and then left.
Shortly afterward reach Waipiʻo Valley lookout (elevation 904 feet) (map point A). Turn around and park on the side of the road. Leave the small parking lot at the lookout for short-term sightseers. The lookout has restrooms and picnic tables but no drinking water.

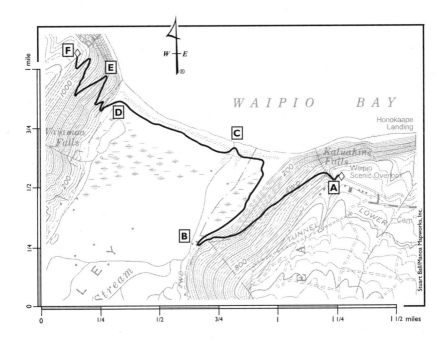

If you are starting from Kailua (Kona), you have a somewhat longer drive. Take Hawai'i Belt Rd. (Rte 190) to Waimea. Continue on the belt road (now Rte 19) toward Honoka'a. Turn left into Honoka'a and pick up the directions above. The distance to the trailhead is 64 miles, and the driving time is about 1 3/4 hours.

Route Description:

Take the one-lane paved road leading into Waipi'o Valley.

Initially, the road switches back twice and crosses a narrow, fast-flowing stream.

Descend very steeply down the side of the valley. Watch out for four-wheel-drive vehicles. Look for the lavender and purple blossoms of the maunaloa shrub on the cliff to the left.

At the bottom reach a junction (map point B). Turn sharp right toward the beach. (Do not take the private road to the left that heads farther into the valley.)

The road becomes dirt and then sand. Huge monkeypod and

kukui trees shade the route. Look for 'ape with its huge, heart-shaped leaves and noni with its warty fruit.

Before reaching the shore, enter a grove of ironwood trees.

The road curves left and parallels the black-sand beach.

Reach Wailoa Stream and ford it (map point C). There is no official crossing. The stream is narrower and shallower at its mouth near the ocean; however, the current there can be very strong. As an alternative, ford the stream to the left at its widest point. The current is less noticeable there, but the water is waist deep.

On the opposite bank pick up a wide path paralleling the beach.

Stroll through stands of ironwood and kamani haole. Near the shore is the low-lying native shrub naupaka kahakai with its white half-flowers. There is a picturesque view of Hi'ilawe Falls through the trees.

In a break in the ironwoods halfway down the beach, pass Paka'alana *heiau*, a *pu'uhonua* (sacred place of refuge).

At the far end of the beach, pass some standing water on the left.

Just past the water, the path becomes rocky and then bears left *mauka* (inland).

On the left pass a small plot surrounded by barbed wire.

Almost immediately reach a junction marked by a hand-painted sign (map point D). Keep right on the Waimanu Trail, which is the less-traveled route uphill. (Do not take the trail to the left that crosses private property in the valley.)

Climb the valley wall on seven long switchbacks. Look for the native shrubs 'ilima and 'ūlei in the sunny sections.

At the fourth switchback is a superb view point (map point E). The beach and ocean are directly below. You can see well into Waipi'o Valley. The waterfall *makai* (seaward) of the road you descended is called Kaluahine.

After the fifth switchback go through an ironwood grove. The upper switchbacks are less steep and more shady than the lower ones.

After the seventh switchback reach the top of the ridge at a small clearing in the ironwoods (elevation 1,150 feet) (map point F). (The trail continues across 13 gulches to Waimanu Valley.)

Notes:

This very scenic hike is mostly ups and downs. Initially, you descend steeply into Waipiʻo (curved water) Valley on a paved road. After a stream crossing and a pleasant beach walk, the route climbs steeply out of the valley on the narrow switchbacks of the Waimanu (bird water) Trail. You then repeat the process in reverse on the return trip. A very attractive option is to turn around at the far end of the beach, thus eliminating over half the elevation gain.

Before starting the hike, enjoy the marvelous view from Waipiʻo lookout. The valley lies about 1,000 feet below and extends deep into the Kohala Mountains. A series of waterfalls cascades down the far wall. You can make out the Waimanu Trail as it zigzags up the cliffs near the ocean.

In ancient times Waipiʻo Valley was one of the major population centers on the Big Island. The fertile valley supported a thriving community based on taro farming and fish raising. Waipiʻo Valley was said to be a favorite haunt of Hawaiian royalty. Today only a few taro farmers remain.

In Waipiʻo Valley you must cross wide Wailoa (long water) Stream. The route narrative describes the best places to ford. The rocks on the bottom are very slippery. If possible, wear tabis (Japanese reef walkers) or strapped sandals. Do not attempt the crossing if the stream is obviously swollen from heavy rain in the back of the valley.

Once across the stream you can really enjoy the setting. Take in the broad sweep of the bay, framed by sheer sea cliffs. Listen for the wind sighing through the ironwoods. Watch the surf pound the black boulders and roll up the beach. Look back into the valley for lovely Hiʻilawe (lift and carry) Falls, the highest free fall in Hawaiʻi.

According to legend, a terrible whirlwind once lived in Waipiʻo Valley. He frequently flattened the houses and destroyed the crops of the Hawaiian people living there. Hiʻiaka, sister of Pele, goddess of the volcano, went on a quest to rid the Big Island of evil beings. She found the whirlwind and struck him again and again with a sacred *pāʻū* (skirt) as powerful as lightning. But the whirlwind proved elusive, twisting and turning to avoid her blows. Hiʻiaka then called upon her mighty sister for help. Pele unleashed thunder, lightning, rain, and hail to subdue the whirlwind. He crawled back to his cave and never bothered the people of Waipi'o again.

The climb up the far wall of the valley is hot, and narrow and rocky in spots. Go at least as far as the fourth switchback with its splendid view. On the way up look for the sprawling native shrub 'ūlei in the sunny sections. It has small, oblong leaves arranged in pairs; clusters of white, roselike flowers; and white fruit. Early Hawaiians ate the berries and used the tough wood for making digging sticks, fish spears, and 'ūkēkē (the musical bow).

The end of the hike, at the ridge top, is somewhat an anticlimax. Ironwoods block much of the view, and the mosquitoes there encourage you to leave. From the top you can continue along the Waimanu Trail. It winds through 13 gulches and then descends steeply to Waimanu Valley in 6.7 miles. The whole trail should really be done as an overnight trip.

8 Kalōpā Gulch

Length:	2.8-mile loop
Elevation Gain:	600 feet
Suitable for:	Novice
Location:	Hawai'i (the Big Island): Kalōpā Native Forest State Park and Forest Reserve near Honoka'a
Topo Map:	Honoka'a

Highlights:
This short loop explores a remnant native forest above the Hāmākua Coast. The trail initially follows a rocky gulch cut into the slopes of Mauna Kea, a dormant volcano. Along the way is a good variety of native rain forest plants.

Trailhead Directions:

Distance: *(Hilo to Kalōpā State Park) 42 miles*

Driving Time: 1 1/4 hours

From Hilo take Hawai'i Belt Rd. (Rte 19) toward Waimea.
Proceed along the Hāmākua Coast past a series of villages.
Drive through Laupāhoehoe village.
Cross Laupāhoehoe and Ka'awali'i Gulches.
Between mile markers 38 and 39, turn left on Kalōpā Rd. Look for the sign to Kalōpā State Park.
Cross two wooden bridges and pass a cemetery on the left.
Turn left on Kalaniai Rd.
Turn right, still on Kalaniai Rd.
Turn left, still on Kalaniai Rd.
Enter Kalōpā Native Forest State Park and Recreation Area.
The road forks. Keep right to the cabins and picnic area. (The left fork goes to the campground.)
Take the second right and park in the lot near the picnic pavil-

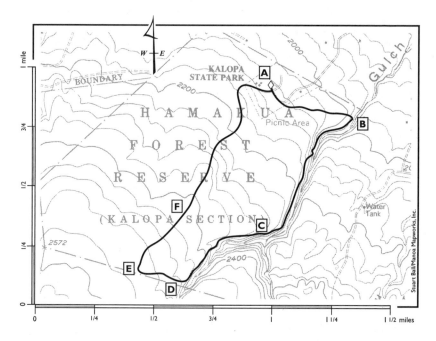

ion (elevation 2,000 feet) (map point A). The pavilion has drinking water and restrooms.

If you are starting from Kailua (Kona), you have a somewhat longer drive. Take Hawai'i Belt Rd. (Rte 190) to Waimea. Continue on the belt road (now Rte 19) past Honoka'a. Between mile markers 39 and 38 turn right on Kalōpā Rd. and pick up the directions above. The distance to the trailhead is 60 miles, and the driving time is about 1 3/4 hours.

Route Description:
Walk back along the road toward the park entrance.

Just past the fork to the campground, reach a signed junction. Turn right onto a trail, known as Robusta Lane.

Reach a signed four-way junction. Continue straight across. (To the left and right is the Perimeter Horse Trail.)

Descend gradually through a grove of tall eucalyptus trees. Kōpiko and guava make up the understory.

Robusta Lane ends at the edge of Kalōpā Gulch (map point B). Turn right, up the gulch on the Gulch Rim Trail.

Climb very gradually along the gulch. Look for the native trees hame, which grows in clumps, and kōlea, whose new leaves are bright pink.

The trail forks. Bear left and cross a rocky gully under two downed trees.

Enter a grove of blue gum trees.

Reach a signed junction. Keep left on the rim trail. (To the right, Blue Gum Lane leads to the Old Road.)

Continue the gradual ascent along the edge of the gulch.

Pass the point where the gulch splits. The trail climbs up the right gulch, called Hanaipoe.

Pass a small waterfall and pool well below in the gulch. Watch for 'ie'ie with its tangled stems.

Reach another signed junction (map point C). Continue straight on the rim trail. (To the right, Silk Oak Lane leads to the Old Road.)

Pass a small pool in a gully on the right.

Climb steeply, but briefly along the gully. The trail is lined with native hāpu'u tree ferns.

Reach an obscure junction marked by a metal pole. Turn right, away from the gulch on Ironwood Lane (map point D).

Cross the gully.

Jog left and then right, paralleling the forest reserve boundary fence.

After crossing a second gully, the trail becomes obscure. Keep left, following the fence.

The trail becomes better defined through a grassy area.

Enter a grove of ironwood trees.

Reach a four-way junction (elevation 2,570 feet) (map point E). Turn right on an overgrown road, known as the Old Road. (To the left the road is closed off by a metal gate in the boundary fence. Beyond is private pasture land. Straight ahead is the Perimeter Horse Trail.)

Descend gradually along the road, which is heavily overgrown with Jamaica oī and other introduced shrubs.

In a stand of ironwoods, reach an obscure junction marked by a metal pole (map point F). Continue descending on the road. (To the right, Silk Oak Lane leads to the Gulch Rim Trail.)

Reach another obscure junction. Continue straight on the road. (To the right, Blue Gum Lane leads back to the Gulch Rim Trail.)

The trail opens up briefly and actually becomes a road.

Reach an obscure four-way junction. Continue straight on the road. (To the left and right is the Perimeter Horse Trail.)

After entering the developed area of the park, bear left on a trail toward the rental cabins.

The trail becomes a paved road.

On the right pass a bulletin board with park information posted and brochures for sale.

Turn left by the picnic pavilion to reach your car (map point A).

Notes:

Kalōpā (tenant farmer) Gulch is a short, damp hike through a remnant native rain forest surrounded by pasture land. Expect to get wet, because the area receives about 100 inches of rainfall a year. After all, a rain forest should be experienced in the rain, right? If by some chance the weather is sunny, enjoy it while it lasts.

Before starting the hike, pick up the excellent trail guide at the information board across from the rental cabins. That inexpensive pamphlet has a map of the area and notes on its history and native plants.

Unfortunately, the condition of the trail system does not match the high quality of the guide. The trails are overgrown and obscure in spots. Look for surveyor's ribbon marking the route and key junctions. Follow the description above closely, and you should have no problem. Although rated novice because of its short length and low elevation gain, the loop may prove challenging for a real beginner.

On the way to the gulch, the forest understory consists of introduced guava and native kōpiko trees. In the 1800s cattle grazing destroyed much of the native understory and allowed guava to come in. In 1903 the Kalōpā area became a forest reserve. With the cattle gone, the kōpiko seedlings thrived under the shady guava.

Now the kōpiko trees are shading the sun-loving guava seedlings. The remaining guava trees are aging and gradually dying out.

Kōpiko is a native member of the coffee family. It has leathery, oblong leaves with a light green midrib. Kōpiko produces clusters of tiny, white flowers and fleshy, orange fruits.

Along Kalōpā Gulch are two other native trees, hame and kōlea. Hame grows in clumps, with young trees typically ringing an old one. Its leaves are oval and glossy. Early Hawaiians used the red purple berries as a dye for *kapa* (bark cloth). Kōlea has narrow, oval leaves growing at the branch tips. The leaves are bright pink when young, gradually turning dark green with age. Early Hawaiians used the light-colored wood in outrigger canoe construction and, as charcoal, to dye *kapa*.

Although the forest reserve is not large enough to support large numbers of native birds, you may catch a glimpse of an 'elepaio. It is brown on top with a chestnut-colored breast and a dark tail, usually cocked. 'Elepaio are very curious, which is why you can often see them.

If you are really lucky, you may spot an 'io, the native Hawaiian hawk. It may be dark brown all over or dark brown above and white below. The hawk soars above field and forest, looking for insects, rodents, and small birds. The 'io is an endangered species found only on the Big Island and is a symbol of royalty in Hawaiian legend.

There are several variations to the route as described. You can, of course, do the loop in reverse. For a shorter hike, take the Gulch Rim Trail and then turn right on either Blue Gum or Silk Oak Lanes. Turn right again to complete the loop. The park also has a 0.7-mile nature trail and a small arboretum of native plants.

SADDLE ROAD

9 Puʻu ʻŌʻō Trail

Length:	10.0-mile round trip
Elevation Gain:	200 feet
Suitable for:	Intermediate
Location:	Hawaiʻi (the Big Island): Mauna Loa and Upper Waiākea Forest Reserves off the Saddle Rd.
Topo Map:	Puʻu ʻŌʻō, Upper Piʻihonua

Highlights:

This pleasant hike follows the historic Puʻu ʻŌʻō–Volcano Trail, used by cattle ranchers in the 1800s and early 1900s. Along the way are *kīpuka*, islands of lush native forest surrounded by barren lava flows. You may catch a glimpse of some native birds, such as the red ʻapapane or ʻiʻiwi.

Trailhead Directions:

Distance: **(Hilo to Puʻu ʻŌʻō trailhead) 23 miles**
Driving Time: *3/4 hour*

From Hilo take Waiānuenue Ave. (Rte 200).
The road forks. Keep left on Kaūmana Dr. (still Rte 200).
Kaūmana Dr. becomes Saddle Rd.
Climb gradually up the broad saddle between Mauna Loa and Mauna Kea through scrub ʻōhiʻa forest.
Pass mile marker 22.
Begin looking for the signed trailhead on the left. It is 0.4 mile farther along the road at the top of a small rise near a utility pole.

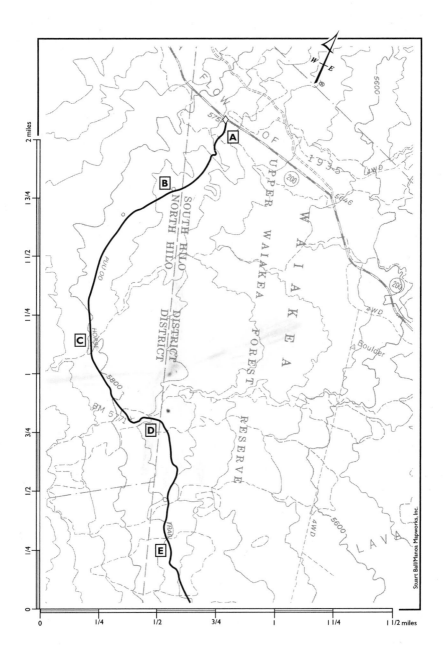

Turn left into a small cleared area and park there (elevation 5,757 feet) (map point A).

If you are starting from Kailua (Kona), you have a considerably longer drive. Take Hawai'i Belt Rd. (Rte 190) toward Waimea. Turn right on Saddle Rd. (Rte 200). Drive up the saddle to mile marker 23. Look for the signed trailhead 0.6 miles farther on the right. The distance to the trailhead is 65 miles, and the driving time is about 1 3/4 hours.

Route Description:

At the back of the cleared area pick up the Pu'u 'Ō'ō Trail, which heads away from the road across a rough 'a'ā lava flow.

Enter a forest of scrub 'ōhi'a trees. Look for the native shrubs pūkiawe, 'ōhelo, and kūkaenēnē. Watch for the native birds 'apapane and 'i'iwi.

Go through a dilapidated fence marking the boundary of the Upper Waiākea Forest Reserve.

Emerge onto a grassy, lumpy area lined with native koa trees (map point B). Water stands in some of the depressions along the trail.

Reenter the 'ōhi'a forest, now more open. The route is marked with small ahu (cairns). Look for the native shrub 'a'ali'i.

Cross another grassy area. Watch for 'ākala, the thornless Hawaiian raspberry.

Go through a stand of koa trees and then emerge back into the open. On the left is a barren 'a'ā lava flow from the 1855 eruption of Mauna Loa.

Enter a kīpuka with magnificent 'ōhi'a and koa trees, and huge hāpu'u tree ferns (map point C).

Traverse the jagged 'a'ā flow of 1855. Mauna Loa, the source of the lava, is in the distance to the right; Mauna Kea is to the left.

Enter an open 'ōhi'a forest on old pāhoehoe lava (map point D).

Descend very gradually along a wide corridor through the woods.

The trail curves right and then crosses an arm of the 1855 flow. Small 'ōhi'a and 'ama'u ferns are starting to colonize the pāhoehoe lava. Watch for the ahu.

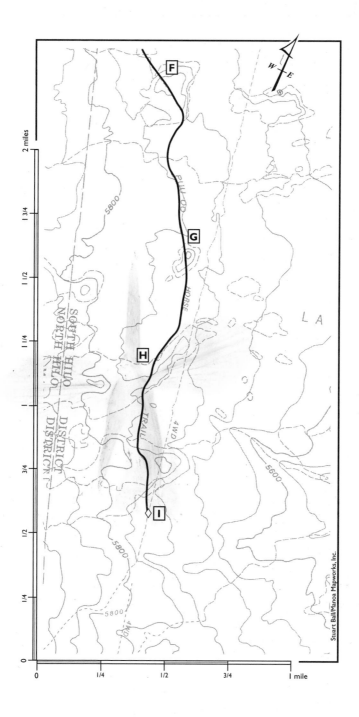

Keep left to reenter the forest (map point E).

Cross another arm of the 1855 flow.

Enter another lush *kīpuka* with old-growth 'ōhi'a and koa (map point F).

Traverse the partially vegetated lava flows of 1855 and 1881.

Skirt the right edge of a small *kīpuka* before entering it (map point G).

Emerge onto the 1881 lava flow again.

Parallel the border of the forest and then bear left to enter it (map point H).

Climb gradually and then descend.

Cross an arm of the 1855 flow once more.

Enter the last *kīpuka*. On the far side the forest thins out.

Reach the dirt Kūlani Powerline Rd. (elevation 5,740 feet) (map point I). The junction is marked by two large *ahu* and the stump of a utility pole.

Notes:
The Pu'u 'Ō'ō Trail is not a popular hike, probably because of the poor access and weather. If you like walking through wild, remote country, however, this hike is for you. If you enjoy identifying native plants and birds, take this hike. You may have it all to yourself.

Start early for the best weather. In the afternoon, clouds frequently ride up the saddle and blanket the slopes in mist and cold rain. While crossing the lava flows, watch closely for the next *ahu* (cairn). Some are quite small and thus easily missed, especially when the fog rolls in. Keep at least one *ahu* in sight at all times.

Access to the Pu'u Ō'ō Trail is over the notorious Saddle Rd. with its winding route and sometimes foggy conditions. Drive carefully, turn your headlights on, and you should have no problem. Unfortunately, some rental car companies do not allow you to drive on the Saddle Rd.

The hike follows a portion of the historic Pu'u 'Ō'ō–Volcano Trail. Cattle ranchers developed that roundabout route in the 1800s to avoid the jagged *'a'ā* lava flows lying directly between the saddle area and Hilo. The ranchers drove their cattle from pasture on Mauna Kea (white mountain) over the trail to Volcano and then down the road to market in Hilo. In earlier times the route continued south from Volcano to Keauhou (the new era) landing along the Ka'ū coast. There the cattle were driven into the ocean and hauled on board ships bound for Hilo and Honolulu.

The first section of the trail goes through a scrub native 'ōhi'a forest with pūkiawe and 'ōhelo shrubs. Pūkiawe has tiny, rigid leaves and small white, pink, or red berries. 'Ōhelo has rounded leaves and delicious red yellow berries, about the size of blueberries. 'Ōhi'a trees have oval leaves and clusters of delicate red flowers. Native birds, such as the 'apapane, feed on the nectar and help in pollination.

If you're lucky, you may catch a glimpse of an 'apapane or 'i'iwi in the forest canopy. They are easier to see here because the tree tops are so low. Both birds have a red breast and head, and black wings and tail. The 'i'iwi has a long, curved, salmon-colored bill for sipping 'ōhi'a nectar. The 'apapane has a slightly curved black bill. In flight the 'apapane makes a whirring sound as it darts from tree to tree searching for insects and nectar.

In the more open forest you can see two other native shrubs, 'a'ali'i and 'ākala. 'A'ali'i has narrow, dull green leaves and red seed capsules. 'Ākala, the Hawaiian raspberry, has light green, serrated leaves and few or no thorns. The flowers are pink to red, and the edible berries are red to purple.

The trail repeatedly crosses the 1855 and 1881 lava flows from Mauna Loa (long mountain). Both eruptions started at vents along the northeast rift zone at the 9,500-foot level. As you can see, small 'ōhi'a trees and 'ama'u ferns are beginning to colonize the lava. 'Ama'u has a short trunk and fronds that are bright red when young and green when mature.

Alternating with the bare lava are wooded islands of older lava, known as *kīpuka*. They contain magnificent old-growth 'ōhi'a and koa trees and hāpu'u tree ferns. Koa has sickle-shaped foliage and pale yellow flower clusters. Hāpu'u has sweeping, delicate fronds and a trunk consisting of roots tightly woven around a central stem.

If the weather has turned bad, Kūlani Powerline Rd. makes a good option for the return trip. The road is rough and boring, but it is easier to follow than the trail and somewhat shorter. When you reach the Saddle Rd., turn left and walk 0.7 mile back to your car.

10 Mauna Loa
(via the Observatory Trail)

Length:	12.6-mile round trip
Elevation Gain:	2,700 feet
Suitable for:	Expert
Location:	Hawai'i (the Big Island): Mauna Loa Forest Reserve and Hawai'i Volcanoes National Park off the Saddle Rd.
Topo Map:	Ko'oko'olau, Mauna Loa

Highlights:

Mauna Loa is the largest active volcano in the world. This demanding hike climbs to its summit, past spatter cones, pit craters, and wide expanses of barren lava. At the top is Moku'āweoweo, a huge, desolate caldera with steaming vents and fissures.

Trailhead Directions:

Distance: **(Hilo to Observatory trailhead) 45 miles**

Driving Time: **1 1/2 hours**

From Hilo take Waiānuenue Ave. (Rte 200).
The road forks. Keep left on Kaūmana Dr. (still Rte 200).
Kaūmana Dr. becomes Saddle Rd.
Climb gradually up the broad saddle between Mauna Loa and Mauna Kea. The road winds through scrub 'ōhi'a forest and then barren lava flows.
Around mile marker 27 look for Pu'u Huluhulu, a wooded hill on the left near the road.
Just before reaching the hill, turn left on an unmarked one-lane paved road.
Ascend gradually up the lower slopes of Mauna Loa. The paved road jogs once to the left and, later on, once to the right.
Follow a power line leading up to Mauna Loa Observatory.

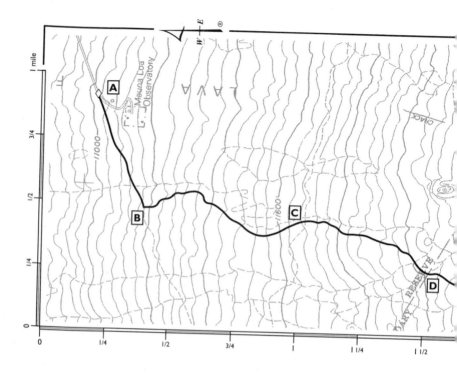

Park in the small public lot on the left below the observatory (elevation 11,020 feet) (map point A).

If you are starting from Kailua (Kona), you have a somewhat longer drive. Take Hawai'i Belt Rd. (Rte 190) toward Waimea. Turn right on Saddle Rd. (Rte 200). Drive up the saddle to mile marker 28. Turn right on the unmarked road just past Pu'u Huluhulu and pick up the directions above. The distance to the trailhead is 77 miles, and the driving time is about 2 1/2 hours.

Route Description:

Just beyond the parking lot is a signed junction. Take the rocky dirt road straight ahead. (To the left the paved road climbs to the observatory.)

Cross two 'a'ā lava flows.

Reach a second signed junction (map point B). Turn left and up

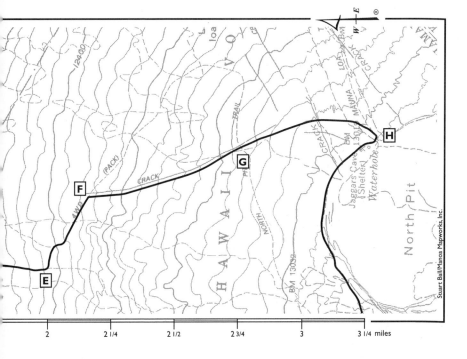

on the Observatory Trail. (The dirt road continues straight and then switchbacks up the mountain, crossing the trail several times.)

Climb steadily on a gray prehistoric *pāhoehoe* flow. The route is marked with *ahu* (cairns) and splotches of yellow paint on the rock. To the left is a jagged, brown *'a'ā* flow, also prehistoric.

Cross the rocky dirt road (map point C).

Reach a lava tube, indicated by two tall *ahu*. A rock windbreak across the tube provides some shelter.

The trail works right and then traverses an old *'a'ā* lava flow.

Resume steady climbing on gray *pāhoehoe* lava (map point D). On the left is a prehistoric red spatter cone.

At a trail sign turn left along the edge of the *'a'ā* flow (map point E). (The old route of the Observatory Trail continues straight up.)

At another trail sign reach a junction. Turn right on the rocky dirt road.

The road swings left, crossing an *'a'ā* flow.

At the third trail sign reach another junction (map point F). Turn right off the road onto the Observatory Trail. (The road continues straight, through a locked gate.)

Climb alongside a brightly colored fissure. Underfoot is green pumice. To the right is the shiny black *pāhoehoe* of the 1942 flow.

Cross the 1942 lava flow.

Reach a second junction with the road (map point G). Continue straight across on the trail. (To the right the road leads to the original site of the Mauna Loa Observatory.)

The trail curves left and crosses the 1942 fissure.

On the right pass a primitive toilet, strategically situated above a crack.

Reach the end of the Observatory Trail at a signed junction (map point H). Turn right on the Summit Trail. (To the left the Cabin Trail leads to the Mauna Loa Trail and Cabin.)

Shortly afterward pass Jaggar's Cave (elevation 13,019 feet), marked by a monumental *ahu* on the left. The cave provides shelter from the wind and has a water hole next door.

Follow the rim of North Pit. Beyond is the summit caldera, Moku'āweoweo.

Jump over the multicolored fissure from the 1942 eruption.

Traverse prehistoric *'a'ā* and *pāhoehoe* lava flows.

Angle away from the rim and begin climbing.

Reach a signed junction (map point I). Continue straight on the Summit Trail. (To the right the old route of the Observatory Trail heads downhill.)

Climb more steeply on old *pāhoehoe* lava.

Pass a seismic station with its antenna.

Pass the original site of the observatory, downslope to the right (map point J).

Angle left toward the crater rim.

Reach the summit of Mauna Loa (elevation 13,679 feet) (map point K).

Notes:

The climb to the summit of Mauna Loa (long mountain) has nothing in common with beaches, palm trees, and the rest of tourist

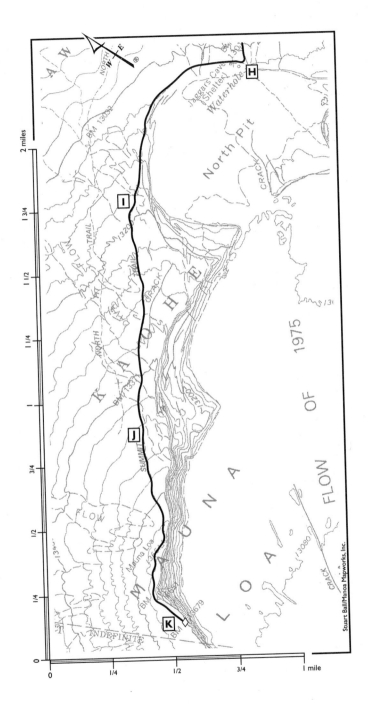

Hawai'i. This is alpine hiking at elevations well above 10,000 feet. The thin air, long distance, high wind, and rough footing make this a climb to be reckoned with, and remembered. Take this mountain seriously.

Summer (May–August) is the best time of year to climb Mauna Loa. The days are long, and the weather is usually settled. Midday temperatures range from 50 to 70 degrees F.; it can feel hotter because of the intense sun or colder because of wind chill. During winter (December–March) the days are shorter and the wind stronger. A sudden storm can blanket the summit area with several inches or feet of snow, burying the trail. Whatever the season, start early and bring extra layers of clothing and plenty of water and sunscreen.

Access to the Observatory Trail is over the notorious Saddle Rd. with its winding route and sometimes foggy conditions. Drive carefully, turn your headlights on, and you should have no problem. Unfortunately, some rental car companies do not allow you to drive on the Saddle Rd.

In view from the parking lot are three dormant volcanoes. Across the saddle to the north is Mauna Kea (white mountain), the highest peak in the state at 13,796 feet. You can see several observatories clustered near its summit. To the left and well below is Hualālai at 8,271 feet. In the distance between those two is Haleakalā (house of the sun), the highest point on the island of Maui at 10,023 feet.

The mountain you are about to climb is a shield volcano, the largest in the world. Mauna Loa sits astride a hot spot in the earth's crust where molten rock lies close to the surface. Eruptions over many years have built the volcano from its base deep in the ocean to its current height of 13,679 feet. The latest eruption in 1984 started at the summit caldera, Moku'āweoweo (red fish section), and then shifted to the rift zone extending to the northeast above you. The resulting lava coursed down the saddle to within 5 miles of the outskirts of Hilo.

Once on the trail, watch closely for the *ahu* (cairns) marking the route. They are sometimes difficult to spot against a background of black lava. Keep at least one *ahu* in sight at all times, especially in bad weather. While climbing, walk at a slow, but steady pace to minimize the effect of altitude. Breathe deeply, take frequent breaks, and drink plenty of water. If you have a headache, nausea, or difficulty breathing, slow down even more. Turn around if the symptoms get worse.

Before reaching Jaggar's Cave, the trail crosses a fissure and lava flow from the 1942 eruption. Volcanic activity began on the evening of 26 April. A fissure opened up in the summit crater across the North Pit and along the northeast rift zone. For two days lava cascaded from small fountains in the fissure and flowed down toward the saddle. Because World War II had started, the government tried to keep the eruption secret. Some officials feared that the Japanese might use the volcano as a beacon for navigation. The effort was largely unsuccessful because Tokyo Rose soon broadcast news of the eruption over Japanese radio.

Jaggar's Cave makes a good rest stop or turnaround point. The cave is actually an open pit, but it is sheltered from the wind and does have a water hole next door. (Treat the water before drinking it.) Thomas Jaggar, pioneering volcanologist and founder of the Hawaiian Volcano Observatory, used the cave on his field trips to study the mountain.

After Jaggar's Cave the Summit Trail initially hugs the rim of North Pit. It is a shallow, circular depression covered with smooth lava from the 1984 eruption. The route then veers away from the rim and begins a rough, seemingly endless climb to the summit. Because nothing is forever, the top eventually heaves into sight.

The view from the summit of Mauna Loa is breathtaking. Directly below is the summit caldera, Moku'āweoweo, 2.7 miles long, 1.6 miles wide, and 600 feet deep in places. Steam still seeps from a fissure that opened the length of the crater in 1984. Lava from that eruption covers much of the floor. The tall cone in the center of the crater was built in 1940. Along the near rim to the right is the 1949 cone, colored red and green. On the far right a gap in the crater wall leads to South Pit. North Pit is through a gap in the rim on the left. Across the crater on the far rim is Mauna Loa Cabin.

The hike down is quite pleasant, at least compared with the hike up. Just put one foot in front of the other and let gravity carry you down the slopes. Watch your footing, though, on the rough *'a'ā* flows and the steep *pāhoehoe* sections. On the way down enjoy the expansive views as the mountain unfolds in front of you.

11 Mauna Kea

Length:	12.0-mile round trip
Elevation Gain:	4,600 feet
Suitable for:	Expert
Location:	Hawai'i (the Big Island): Mauna Kea Forest Reserve and Mauna Kea Ice Age Natural Area Reserve off the Saddle Rd.
Topo Map:	Mauna Kea

Highlights:

The dormant volcano Mauna Kea is the highest mountain in Hawai'i. This challenging climb follows a steep, rough trail and then a paved road to the observatories at the summit. Along the way are colorful cones, an early Hawaiian quarry, and even a glistening lake.

Trailhead Directions:

Distance: *(Hilo to Visitor Information Station) 35 miles*

Driving Time: *1 hour*

From Hilo take Waiānuenue Ave. (Rte 200).

The road forks. Keep left on Kaūmana Dr. (still Rte 200).

Kaūmana Dr. becomes Saddle Rd.

Climb gradually up the broad saddle between Mauna Loa and Mauna Kea. The road winds through scrub 'ōhi'a forest and then barren lava flows.

Around mile marker 27 look for Pu'u Huluhulu, a wooded hill on the left near the road.

Across from Pu'u Huluhulu and a hunter check-in station, turn right on the paved access road to Mauna Kea.

Ascend through pasture land, gradually at first and then more steeply.

Enter Mauna Kea Forest Reserve.

Reach the Visitor Information Station of the Onizuka Center for

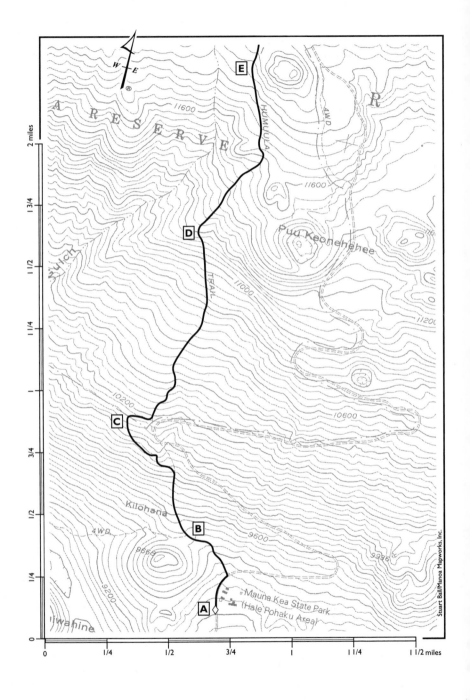

International Astronomy (elevation 9,200 feet) (map point A). Turn right into the lot and park there.

Before starting, fill out a hiker registration form in the box near the front door. The box also contains trail maps and a cautionary pamphlet. The visitor station has restrooms and drinking water.

If you are starting from Kailua (Kona), you have a somewhat longer drive. Take Hawaiʻi Belt Rd. (Rte 190) toward Waimea. Turn right on Saddle Rd. (Rte 200). Drive up the saddle to mile marker 28. Turn left on the unmarked road across from Puʻu Huluhulu and pick up the directions above. The distance to the trailhead is 66 miles, and the driving time is about 1 3/4 hours.

Route Description:

Walk back out to the main road and turn right uphill.

Pass two turnoffs to Hale Pōhaku on the right.

Reach a junction across from the road maintenance yard. Turn left on a dirt road. (The access road to the summit continues straight and becomes unpaved. Only four-wheel-drive vehicles are allowed beyond this point.)

Climb steadily through scattered native māmane trees. On the left is a red brown cinder cone.

The road forks (map point B). Keep right and up.

Pass two concrete slabs on the right.

As the road curves right, bear left on the Mauna Kea Trail. The junction is marked by three wooden posts and a hunting warning sign.

Ascend almost straight up on brown sand and cinders.

The trail swings left and levels off, briefly.

Climb very steeply and then more gradually on black sand and cinders. Look for the native shrubs pūkiawe and ʻōhelo among the lava outcrops.

Enter Mauna Kea Ice Age Natural Area Reserve (map point C).

Ignore several side trails on the right leading to a switchback on the access road.

Resume serious climbing on gray brown cinders. The trail is marked with rusty metal stakes.

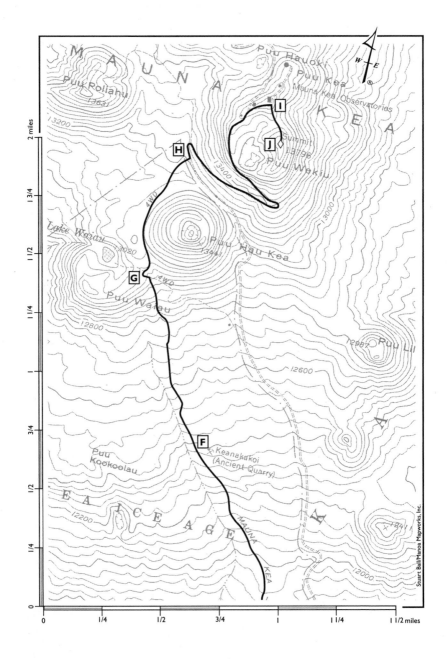

Reach "White Rock," a large boulder covered with paint and graffiti (elevation 11,200 feet) (map point D). Take a breather and look at the panoramic view.

Climb steadily on red cinder and loose rock. To the right is Keonehehe'e, a large red cinder cone. To the left is dry Waikahalulu Gulch.

Work around the base of an unnamed cone on the right (map point E).

Climb steadily up the light-colored, boulder-strewn slopes. The trail is now marked by *ahu* (cairns) and splotches of yellow paint, as well as the metal stakes. A line of three red cinder cones on the right allows tracking of your progress toward Lake Waiau.

The angle of ascent steepens briefly and then eases.

On the right is Keanakāko'i, an ancient adze quarry (elevation 12,400 feet) (map point F).

Continue the steady ascent up the desolate slopes.

Climb steeply on loose sand and rock. The cinder cone on the left is Pu'u Waiau, and the one on the right across the access road is Pu'u Līlīnoe.

Reach a junction (map point G). Turn left uphill. (The side trail to the right leads to a parking lot on the access road.)

Shortly afterward reach another junction. This time turn right. (The side trail to the left leads a short distance to Lake Waiau.)

Climb around the base of Pu'u Haukea on the right. To the left is a striking red orange cone called Pu'u Poli'ahu, named after the goddess of snow.

Reach the end of the Mauna Kea Trail at a junction with the access road (map point H). Turn left and up on the paved road.

Almost immediately switchback to the right. On the left is a side road leading to several observatories.

Switchback to the left and climb the slopes of Pu'u Wēkiu, the summit cone.

On the left another side road leads to more observatories.

Pass the United Kingdom infrared telescope and the University of Hawai'i 88-inch telescope (map point I). Across from the latter, climb over the guardrail to the right by a yellow ice warning sign.

Descend briefly on a makeshift trail and then climb once more.

Reach the summit of Mauna Kea (elevation 13,796 feet) (map point J).

Notes:
The ascent to the summit of Mauna Kea (white mountain) is the toughest day hike in the Islands. The air is thin; the trail, rough; the route, long; and the climbing, relentless. Take this mountain seriously. Come prepared for alpine hiking at elevations well above 10,000 feet.

Summer (May–August) is the best time of year to climb Mauna Kea. The days are long, and the weather is usually settled. Midday temperatures range from 50 to 70 degrees F.; it can feel hotter because of the intense sun or colder because of wind chill. During winter (December–March) the days are shorter and the wind stronger. A sudden storm can blanket the summit area with several inches or feet of snow, burying the trail. Whatever the season, start early and bring extra layers of clothing and plenty of water and sunscreen.

Access to the Mauna Kea Trail is over the notorious Saddle Rd. with its winding route and sometimes foggy conditions. Drive carefully, turn your headlights on, and you should have no problem. Unfortunately, some rental car companies do not allow you to drive on the Saddle Rd.

The mountain you are about to climb is a shield volcano, the highest in the state. Mauna Kea sits astride a hot spot in the earth's crust where molten rock lies close to the surface. Eruptions over many years have built the volcano from its base deep in the ocean to its current height of 13,796 feet. Mauna Kea has lain dormant for over 2,000 years. The last series of eruptions filled the summit caldera and created a broad cap, now dotted with cinder cones.

Once on the trail, watch closely for the three types of route markers: metal stakes, *ahu* (cairns), and yellow paint splotches on the rock. The stakes and *ahu* are sometimes difficult to spot against a background of like-colored cinders or boulders. Keep at least one marker in sight at all times, especially in bad weather. While climbing, walk at a slow, but steady pace to minimize the effect of altitude. Breathe deeply, take frequent breaks, and drink plenty of water. If you have a headache, nausea, or difficulty breathing, slow down even more. Turn around if the symptoms get worse.

The initial climb is incredibly steep. Take a breather at the well-known landmark "White Rock." Look down for a last view of the Hale Pōhaku area. Look around for a last view of anything green. Across the saddle is massive Mauna Loa (long mountain), an active volcano with an elevation of 13,679 feet. You can clearly see the walls of its summit caldera, Mokuʻāweoweo (red fish section). To the right and well below is Hualālai, another dormant volcano at 8,271 feet.

At the 12,400-foot level, look for Keanakākoʻi (the adze-making cave), an ancient quarry. The cave is located partway up the line of cliffs on the right. Early Hawaiians mined the dense basalt in the cave and shaped it into stone tools.

If you have the energy, take the short side trip to Lake Waiau (swirling water). It is a brilliant blue tarn nestled among red cinder hills. According to legend, the lake is bottomless, leading to the very heart of the volcano.

After leaving Lake Waiau, the trail passes a colorful cone called Puʻu Poliʻahu. It is named after the legendary snow goddess of Mauna Kea. One day she and a group of friends were sledding down the slopes on the Hāmākua side of the mountain. Out of nowhere a beautiful woman appeared and was invited to join the games. After Poliʻahu proved the faster of the two in a sled race, she noticed the ground getting warm. The beautiful stranger, now very angry, turned out to be Pele, the goddess of fire. She stoked her subterranean fires, and hot lava burst to the surface on Mauna Kea. Poliʻahu quickly retreated to the summit and then threw her mantle of snow over the whole mountain. Gradually the fires died down, and the lava cooled and hardened. Pele was forced to withdraw to her home in Kīlauea Volcano, where she lives to this day. And each winter Poliʻahu cloaks the summit of her mountain with a blanket of snow.

The summit area with its paved road and clusters of observatories is somewhat of an anticlimax, but not for long. Creep up the last cinder mound to the true summit, flop down by the benchmark, and look around. Mauna Kea is not Mount Everest, but it's definitely the top of the world in these parts.

The hike down is quite pleasant, at least compared with the hike up. Just put one foot in front of the other and let gravity carry you down the slopes. Watch your footing, though, on the loose rock and cinders. On the way down enjoy the expansive views as the mountain unfolds in front of you.

The access road to the summit provides several unappealing variations to the route as described. You can walk the road one way and the trail the other, or the road both ways. The road is well graded and easy to follow, but it is longer and less interesting than the trail. Use the road as an alternate route only if the weather turns bad.

A more attractive option is to hitchhike one way. Past the visitor station, traffic is light on the access road, but your chance of getting a ride is usually good. If you have two four-wheel-drive vehicles, park one at the visitor station and the other at the lot near Lake Waiau. Hike up or down the mountain as you choose.

KAUA'I

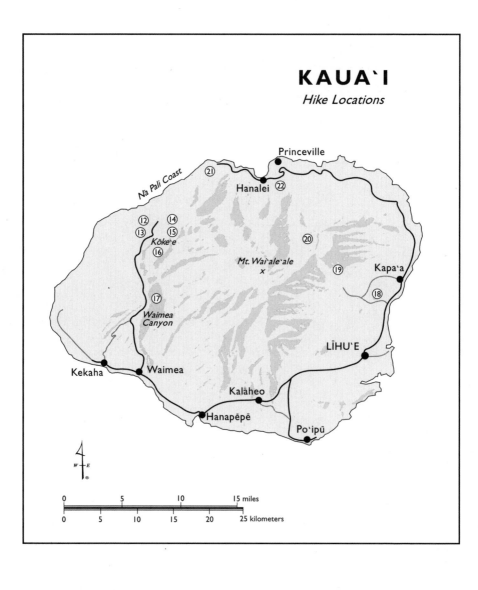

KAUA‘I

Hike Locations

Princeville

㉑

Na Pali Coast

Hanalei ㉒

⑫ ⑭
⑬ ⑮
Kōke‘e
⑯

⑳

Mt. Wai‘ale‘ale
x

⑲

Kapa‘a

⑱

⑰

*Waimea
Canyon*

LĪHU‘E

Kekaha ● Waimea

Kalāheo

Hanapēpē

Po‘ipū

W—E

| 0 | | 5 | | 10 | | 15 miles |

| 0 | 5 | 10 | 15 | 20 | 25 kilometers |

KŌKEʻE

12 Awaʻawapuhi

Length:	6.5-mile round trip
Elevation Gain:	1,600 feet
Suitable for:	Intermediate
Location:	Kauaʻi: Kōkeʻe State Park and Nā Pali–Kona Forest Reserve
Topo Map:	Hāʻena, Mākaha Point

Highlights:
This hike descends to an awesome overlook of the Nāpali Coast. Far below lies Awaʻawapuhi, a slot canyon leading to the ocean. Along the route are many varieties of native rain forest and dry-land plants.

Trailhead Directions:

Distance: *(Līhuʻe Airport to Awaʻawapuhi trailhead) 42 miles*
Driving Time: 1 1/2 hours

From Līhuʻe take Kaumualiʻi Hwy (Rte 50) toward Waimea.
Pass a sugar mill on the left and then Kauaʻi Community College on the right.
Drive through the towns of Lāwaʻi and Kalāheo.
Pass the Hanapēpē River overlook on the right.
Drive through the towns of ʻEleʻele and Hanapēpē.
Pass the Russian fort on the left and then enter Waimea town.
Look for the Waimea Baptist Church on the right. It's beige with a white steeple.
Just past the church, turn right on Waimea Canyon Rd.
Ascend gradually along the rim of Waimea Canyon.

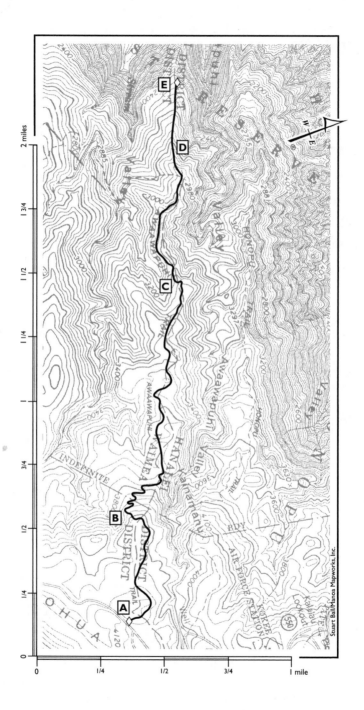

At the stop sign turn right on Kōke'e Rd.

Pass the Kōke'e Hunter Check-in Station on the right.

Pass turnoffs to Waimea Canyon and Pu'u Hinahina lookouts on the right.

Enter Kōke'e State Park.

On the left drive by the turnoff to Kōke'e Lodge and Museum. The lodge has restrooms and drinking water, and the museum has trail maps and a short pamphlet on the hike.

Pass Kōke'e campground on the left and then ascend gradually on three switchbacks.

Just after mile marker 17, look for a parking lot on the left. Across from the lot is a dirt road with a yellow gate.

Turn into the lot and park there (elevation 4,120 feet) (map point A).

Route Description:

Take the Awa'awapuhi Trail from the left side of the parking lot.

Climb briefly and then descend gradually.

The trail levels off through native rain forest recovering from hurricanes 'Iwa and 'Iniki. Look for small 'ōhi'a trees and naupaka kuahiwi shrubs with their white half-flowers.

Descend steeply on a series of switchbacks (map point B).

The angle of descent eases. The trail is wide and covered with roots in some spots. On the forest floor are huge koa trunks downed by the hurricanes.

Leave the ridge line and switchback once. The vegetation gradually changes from rain forest to dry-land scrub. Predominating are the native shrubs pūkiawe and 'a'ali'i.

Go around to the left of an eroded knob.

Regain the crest of the ridge and continue to descend. Views of Nu'alolo Valley open up on the left.

Bear left off the ridge line and switchback twice (map point C).

Descend steadily along the left side of the ridge. Watch for native 'iliahi (sandalwood) as well as the other dry-land shrubs mentioned earlier.

Reach a signed junction (map point D). Continue straight on the Awa'awapuhi Trail. (To the left the Nu'alolo Cliff Trail leads to the Nu'alolo Trail.)

Reach the end of the Awa'awapuhi Trail at a double overlook (elevation 2,520 feet) (map point E).

Notes:
If you have time for only one hike in the Kōke'e (to bend) area, make it Awa'awapuhi. The trail is straightforward, well graded, and of reasonable length. On the way down you start in native rain forest and finish in dry-land scrub. At the end is a view worth sweating for. The only catch is the climb back up.

Along the trail are well over 50 different species of native rain forest and dry-land plants. All are identified and illustrated in the Awa'awapuhi Botanical Trail Guide, a pamphlet available from the State Division of Forestry and Wildlife in Līhu'e. The address is listed in the appendix. Numbers in the guide are keyed to markers on the route, although some are missing. The notes below describe a few of the more easily identified native plants.

'Ōhi'a trees predominate in the wet upper section of the trail. They have oval leaves and clusters of delicate red flowers. Native birds, such as the 'apapane, feed on the nectar and help in pollination. Early Hawaiians used the flowers in *lei* (garlands) and the wood in outrigger canoes. The hard, durable wood was also carved into god images for *heiau* (religious sites).

In the drier middle section of the trail, koa gradually replaces 'ōhi'a as the dominant tree. Koa has sickle-shaped foliage and pale yellow flower clusters. Early Hawaiians made surfboards and outrigger canoe hulls out of the beautiful red brown wood. Today it is made into fine furniture.

To build a canoe, the master canoe maker (*kahuna kālai wa'a*) first selected a tall, straight koa tree, preferably near water. After felling the tree, he waited for Lea, the goddess of canoe builders, to appear in the form of a small native bird, the 'elepaio. If the bird walked along the entire trunk without stopping, the wood was sound and could be used for the canoe. If, however, the 'elepaio stopped and pecked at the bark, the master knew that the tree was riddled with insects and must be discarded.

Farther down the ridge the native dry-land shrubs pūkiawe and 'a'ali'i make their appearance. Pūkiawe has tiny, rigid leaves and small white, pink, or red berries. 'A'ali'i has narrow, shiny leaves and red seed capsules that early Hawaiians used in *lei* making and for *kapa* (bark cloth) dye.

Before the junction with the Nu'alolo Cliff Trail, look for 'iliahi, the sandalwood tree. Its small leaves are dull green and appear wilted. 'Iliahi is partially parasitic, with outgrowths on its roots that steal nutrients from nearby plants. Early Hawaiians ground the fragrant heartwood into a powder to perfume their *kapa*. Beginning in the late 1700s, sandalwood was indiscriminately cut down and exported to China to make incense and furniture. The trade ended around 1840 when the forests were depleted of 'iliahi.

The view from the double overlook at the end of the trail is truly awesome. On the left are the sheer cliffs of Nu'alolo Valley. Far below on the right is Awa'awapuhi (ginger valley), a narrow canyon with a meandering stream leading to the ocean. Between the overlooks is a knife-edge ridge dividing the two valleys. Look for feral goats perched on the cliffs and koa'e kea, the white-tailed tropicbird, soaring above them. Spend some time watching the interplay of sun and clouds on ocean, ridge, and canyon. Life doesn't get much better than this.

The Hawaiian name for the valley may be Awawāpuhi (eel valley), rather than Awa'awapuhi (ginger valley). Nearby is Kaluapuhi (eel pit), whereas there is no ginger in the valley.

The Awa'awapuhi Trail is also the return leg of the Nu'alolo Cliff loop. If you have a whole day and are an experienced hiker, try that 11.4-mile loop instead.

13 Nu'alolo Cliff

Length:	11.4-mile loop
Elevation Gain:	2,200 feet
Suitable for:	Expert
Location:	Kaua'i: Kōke'e State Park and Nā Pali– Kona Forest Reserve
Topo Map:	Hā'ena, Mākaha Point

Highlights:

This splendid loop hike winds above the sheer cliffs in back of Nu'alolo, a deep canyon descending to the Nāpali Coast. Along the way are cascading waterfalls, awe-inspiring lookouts, and some narrow trail sections. You may also encounter nēnē, the endangered Hawaiian goose, and iliau, a distinctive shrub found only on Kaua'i.

Trailhead Directions:

Distance: *(Līhu'e Airport to Kōke'e Museum) 40 miles*

Driving Time: *1 1/2 hours*

From Līhu'e take Kaumuali'i Hwy (Rte 50) toward Waimea.

Pass a sugar mill on the left and then Kaua'i Community College on the right.

Drive through the towns of Lāwa'i and Kalāheo.

Pass the Hanapēpē River overlook on the right.

Drive through the towns of 'Ele'ele and Hanapēpē.

Pass the Russian fort on the left and then enter Waimea town.

Look for the Waimea Baptist Church on the right. It's beige with a white steeple.

Just past the church, turn right on Waimea Canyon Rd.

Ascend gradually along the rim of Waimea Canyon.

At the stop sign turn right on Kōke'e Rd.

Pass the Kōke'e Hunter Check-in Station on the right.

Pass turnoffs to Waimea Canyon and Pu'u Hinahina lookouts on the right.

Enter Kōke'e State Park.

Pass the Kōke'e cabins on the left.

By Park Headquarters turn left to Kōke'e Lodge and Museum (elevation 3,680 feet) (map point A). The lodge has restrooms and drinking water, and the museum has trail maps and a short pamphlet on the hike. If you have only one car, park in the lot in front of the museum and start hiking. If you have two cars, drop off people, if necessary, and continue along Kōke'e Rd.

Pass Kōke'e campground on the left and then ascend gradually on three switchbacks.

Just after mile marker 17 is the Awa'awapuhi trailhead. Look for a parking lot on the left. Across from the lot is a dirt road with a yellow gate.

Turn into the lot and park one car there (elevation 4,120 feet) (map point N). Backtrack to the museum parking lot in the other car and leave it there. The distance from the museum to the Awa'awapuhi trailhead is about 1.7 miles.

Route Description:

Walk back to the main road and turn right.

Pass Park Headquarters on the right.

After going by a paved driveway, reach a signed junction. Turn right on a dirt road.

About 25 yards in, turn left off the road onto the Nu'alolo Trail.

Climb steeply on two switchbacks and then more gradually. The forest consists of native 'ōhi'a and koa trees with an understory of introduced strawberry guava and karakanut. On the floor are huge koa trunks downed by hurricane 'Iwa. The pest vine banana poka is much in evidence.

Begin descending. The trail alternately widens and contracts.

Pass a fenced-off area on the left.

Enter a gulch and follow it downhill (map point B).

Go over two hillocks.

Cross a lumpy meadow with scattered lantana shrubs.

Jog right, climb, and then jog left (map point C).

Continue the descent on the narrow, grass-lined trail. Look for the ocean through the trees.

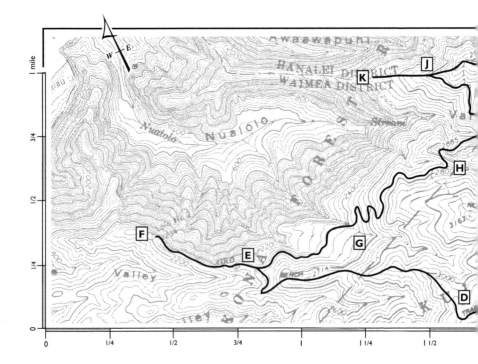

Veer to the left side of the ridge. Along the trail are the native dry-land shrubs pūkiawe, 'a'ali'i, and naupaka kuahiwi with its white half-flowers. You can also see 'iliahi (sandalwood) with its droopy leaves and olomea with its red veins and stems.

The trail descends over a series of small knobs, each with a look-out (map point D). Look for the islands of Ni'ihau and Lehua in the distance.

Pass a small group of native iliau shrubs on the right.

Descend steeply on two switchbacks through strawberry guava.

Reach a signed junction. Keep right on the Nu'alolo Trail. (To the left is the Anaki hunter's route.)

Go around to the left of an eroded hump in the ridge.

Shortly afterward reach a signed junction (map point E). For now continue straight on the Nu'alolo Trail. (To the right is the Nu'alolo Cliff Trail, the return route.)

The ridge becomes narrow and eroded. On the right is a sheer

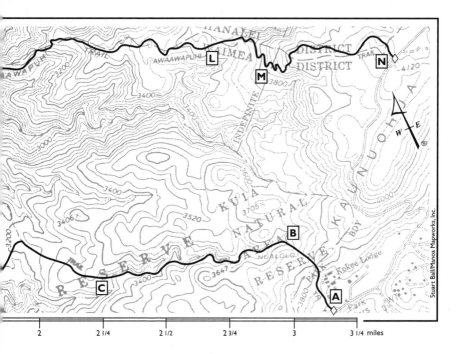

drop to the floor of Nu'alolo Valley. In back is a cascading waterfall. Look for koa'e kea, the white-tailed tropicbird, soaring by the cliffs.

The trail ends at a miniature butte with the Lolo benchmark on top (elevation 2,234 feet) (map point F).

Descend a short distance past a second benchmark for a better view of the awesome Nāpali Coast.

Backtrack to the junction with the Nu'alolo Cliff Trail (map point E) and turn left on it. (Straight ahead is the way you came in.)

Begin contouring around the back of Nu'alolo Valley.

Work into and out of two small, wooded ravines.

Cross an eroded side ridge over loose dirt. Watch your footing. Don't hike and look at the same time!

Work into and out of a double gulch.

Walk along the edge of a wide grassy promontory. Look for nēnē (Hawaiian goose) here.

Pass a covered picnic table on the right.

Enter a lush gulch (map point G). Watch for the native birds 'elepaio and 'apapane in the tall 'ōhi'a trees here.

Climb out of the gulch on five switchbacks.

Amble through a level shady section.

Work into and out of another gulch with a tiny stream (map point H).

Enter the large gulch at the very back of Nu'alolo Valley. Watch for native lama trees. In the cliff above is a nesting area for the tropicbirds.

Cross Nu'alolo Stream below a small waterfall (map point I). The stream becomes the large waterfall you saw from the Lolo benchmark.

Reach a signed junction with the Awa'awapuhi Trail (map point J). For now turn left on it. (To the right is the return route.)

Reach the end of the Awa'awapuhi Trail at the double overlook (elevation 2,520 feet) (map point K).

Retrace your steps to the junction with the Nu'alolo Cliff Trail (map point J). This time continue straight on the Awa'awapuhi Trail. (To the right is the way you came in.)

Ascend steadily along the right side of the ridge.

Climb to the top of the ridge on two switchbacks (map point L).

Follow the ridge line, ascending steadily through native dry-land forest.

Leave the top of the ridge to the right to bypass an eroded knob.

Climb more steeply, switchbacking once to regain the ridge line. The vegetation gradually changes from dry-land shrubs to rain forest.

Descend briefly and then resume climbing. The trail is wide and covered with roots in some spots.

Ascend more steeply on a series of switchbacks (map point M).

The trail levels off in a more open forest.

Climb gradually and then descend briefly.

Reach the parking lot on Kōke'e Rd. (elevation 4,120 feet) (map point N). If your only car is parked at the museum, turn right on the road.

Walk the 1.7 miles along the road back to your car (map point A).

Notes:

Nu'alolo Cliff is certainly the best day hike on Kaua'i, and it may be the best in the Islands. The winding route provides a bird's-eye view of the spectacular Nāpali (the cliffs) Coast. Along the ridges and ravines leading down to Nu'alolo and Awa'awapuhi are some unusual plants and wildlife. The hike also provides a challenge with its down and up, sometimes narrow route. Get an early start because of the high mileage and many points of interest.

Native 'ōhi'a trees predominate in the wet upper section of the Nu'alolo Trail. They have oval leaves and clusters of delicate red flowers. Native birds, such as the 'apapane, feed on the nectar and help in pollination. Early Hawaiians used the flowers in *lei* (garlands) and the wood in outrigger canoes. The hard, durable wood was also carved into god images for *heiau* (religious sites).

In the drier middle section of the trail, native koa gradually replaces 'ōhi'a as the dominant tree. Koa has sickle-shaped foliage and pale yellow flower clusters. Early Hawaiians made surfboards and outrigger canoe hulls out of the beautiful red brown wood. Today it is made into fine furniture.

Farther down the ridge the native dry-land shrubs pūkiawe and 'a'ali'i make their appearance. Pūkiawe has tiny, rigid leaves and small white, pink, or red berries. 'A'ali'i has narrow, shiny leaves and red seed capsules that early Hawaiians used in *lei* making and for *kapa* (bark cloth) dye.

Before reaching the two switchbacks, watch for the native shrub iliau. It has slender, swordlike leaves clustered at the top of a woody stem. After growing for many years, the shrub flowers once during the summer and then dies. The flower stalks are tall and showy with cream-colored petals. Found only on Kaua'i, iliau is a relative of 'āhinahina, the silversword, which occurs on Haleakalā and Mauna Kea.

Past the second benchmark is a magnificent view of the rugged Nāpali Coast. Far below lies Nu'alolo Valley, backed by steep cliffs and a cascading waterfall. To the right (north) is Kalalau (the stray-ing) Beach and Valley. In the distance the Nāpali Coast ends at Kē'ē (avoidance) Beach near Ka'īlio (dog) Point. Look for feral goats perched on the cliffs and white-tailed tropicbirds soaring above them.

Along the cliff trail you may see nēnē, the Hawaiian goose. The nēnē has a black face and head and a gray brown body. It lives in dry upland areas, so has lost much of the webbing on its feet. Like its Canadian counterpart, the nēnē is a strong flyer and often honks in midflight. The nēnē is an endangered species and should be treated with respect.

In the gulches look for the native birds 'elepaio and 'apapane. The 'elepaio is gray brown on top and has a white breast splotched with gray and black. Its dark tail is usually cocked. The 'apapane has a red breast and head, black wings and tail, and a slightly curved black bill. In flight the 'apapane makes a whirring sound as it darts from tree to tree searching for insects and nectar.

At the very back of Nu'alolo Valley is the native tree lama. Its oblong, pointed leaves are dark green and leathery. Its fruits are green, then yellow, and finally bright red when fully ripe. Lama was sacred to Laka, goddess of the hula. Early Hawaiians used the hard, light-colored wood in temple construction and in hula per-formances.

The view from the double overlook at the end of Awa'awapuhi Trail is breathtaking. On the left is the Lolo benchmark ridge extending from the sheer Nu'alolo cliffs. Far below on the right is Awa'awapuhi (ginger valley), a narrow canyon with a meandering stream leading to the ocean. Between the overlooks is a knife-edge ridge dividing the two valleys. Spend some time watching the inter-play of sun and clouds on ocean, ridge, and canyon. Don't get too comfortable, however, because the route is all uphill from here.

Although the loop is described clockwise, you can, of course, walk it in either direction. For a similar but shorter hike, try Awa'awapuhi. It forms the return portion of the Nu'alolo Cliff loop.

14 Alaka'i Swamp

Length:	8.0-mile round trip
Elevation Gain:	1,400 feet
Suitable for:	Novice, Intermediate
Location:	Kaua'i: Kōke'e State Park and Nā Pali–Kona Forest Reserve and Alaka'i Wilderness Preserve
Topo Map:	Hā'ena

Highlights:

A scenic stroll along the rim of Kalalau Valley turns into a wet, wild tramp through the Alaka'i Swamp. Follow the boardwalk to misty Kilohana, a lookout over Hanalei Bay. Along the route is an incredible variety of native rain forest plants and birds.

Trailhead Directions:

Distance: (Līhu'e to Pu'u o Kila lookout) 44 miles

Driving Time: 1 1/2 hours

From Līhu'e take Kaumuali'i Hwy (Rte 50) toward Waimea.

Pass a sugar mill on the left and then Kaua'i Community College on the right.

Drive through the towns of Lāwa'i and Kalāheo.

Pass the Hanapēpē River overlook on the right.

Drive through the towns of 'Ele'ele and Hanapēpē.

Pass the Russian fort on the left and then enter Waimea town.

Look for the Waimea Baptist Church on the right. It's beige with a white steeple.

Just past the church, turn right on Waimea Canyon Rd.

Ascend gradually along the rim of Waimea Canyon.

At the stop sign turn right on Kōke'e Rd.

Pass the Kōke'e Hunter Check-in Station on the right.

Pass turnoffs to Waimea Canyon and Pu'u Hinahina lookouts on the right.

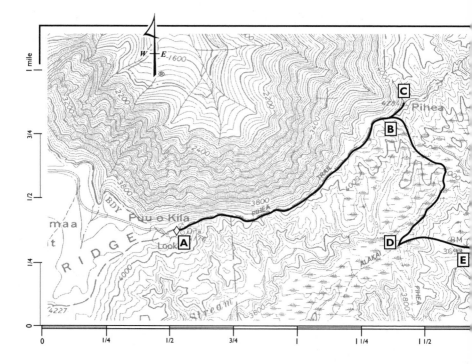

Enter Kōke'e State Park.

On the left pass the turnoff to Kōke'e Lodge and Museum. The lodge has restrooms and drinking water, and the museum has trail maps and a small pamphlet on the hike.

Pass Kōke'e campground on the left and then ascend gradually on three switchbacks.

Pass turnoffs to Headquarters, Hawai'i National Guard, and the Kalalau lookout on the left.

Reach the end of the paved road at Pu'u o Kila lookout (map point A).

Route Description:

From the parking area walk up the paved path to Pu'u o Kila lookout (elevation 4,176 feet).

Pick up the Pihea Trail, an eroded dirt road following the rim of Kalalau Valley.

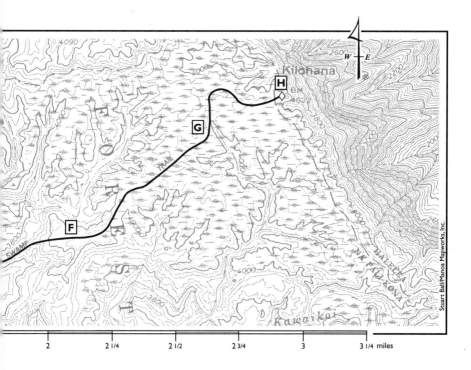

Descend initially through a native 'ōhi'a forest with some 'a'ali'i shrubs. There are several more lookouts on the left. Ahead along the rim is the peak of Pihea.

Traverse a series of small ups and downs. Look for 'ama'u ferns in this section. You may also see some native birds here, such as the 'apapane, 'i'iwi, or 'anianiau.

The road narrows to a rough and rooty trail.

Cross a muddy area and then climb steeply. Watch for native 'ōlapa trees with their fluttering leaves and hāpu'u tree ferns.

Reach a signed junction (map point B). For now continue straight to the Pihea vista. (To the right the Pihea Trail leads into the Alaka'i Swamp.)

Climb steeply to the summit of Pihea (elevation 4,284 feet) (map point C). From the top you can now see the left side of Kalalau Valley. Ringing the lookout are 'ōlapa trees and pū'ahanui (kanawao) shrubs with their delicate pink flowers.

Retrace your steps to the junction (map point B) and turn left on the Pihea Trail. (Straight ahead is the way you came in.)

After descending steeply down a side ridge, the muddy trail becomes a dry boardwalk passing through an amazing assemblage of native rain forest plants. 'Ōhi'a and hāpu'u still predominate; however, look for 'ōhā wai, with its curved purple-and-white flowers and yellow berries.

The boardwalk descends more gradually and then levels off in a flat area. Watch for alani with its curled-up leaves and purple stems. Also, look for the native birds 'elepaio and 'anianiau in the forest canopy.

Reach a signed four-way junction with another boardwalk (map point D). Turn left on the Alaka'i Swamp Trail. (The Pihea Trail continues straight, to Kawaikōī Camp. To the right the Alaka'i Swamp Trail heads back to Camp 10–Mōhihi Rd.)

Descend steeply on wooden stairs. The route follows a telephone line built during World War II. You can still see some poles standing or on the ground.

The boardwalk ends as the angle of descent eases.

Cross a tributary of Kawaikōī Stream (map point E).

Climb steadily up a ridge.

Go around to the right of a hump in the ridge. On the left are views of Pihea peak and the rim of Kalalau Valley. Watch for native 'ohe naupaka with its yellow, tube-shaped flowers.

The boardwalk reappears across a flat swampy area (map point F). Most of the telephone poles are cut off at the base. The vegetation, mostly 'ōhi'a and 'ōlapa, is stunted.

Cross a very wet bog.

Descend into and climb out of a small, lush gully.

Pass two standing telephone poles on the right.

Shortly afterward the boardwalk swings left, away from the phone line (map point G).

Rejoin the phone line.

Descend gradually through a more vegetated section.

Reach Kilohana (elevation 4,022 feet) (map point H).

Notes:
The hike through Alaka'i (to lead) Swamp used to be one of the most difficult on the island. Not any more. An elevated boardwalk now spans the bogs. With a little acrobatic skill you can walk through the swamp without getting your feet wet. Fall off the board-walk, though, and you're up to your knees (or higher) in mud. Good luck.

Summer (May–October) is the best time of year to hike in the swamp. Rainfall is lighter and the temperature higher then. Start early in the morning for the best views and bird watching. Later in the day the clouds usually roll in and blanket the swamp in mist and light rain. Whenever you go, bring a good rain jacket and an extra layer of warm clothing.

Before starting, take in the magnificent view from Pu'u o Kila lookout. Far below lies the broad expanse of Kalalau Valley with its sheer, fluted cliffs. *Mauka* (inland) is our destination, the featureless Alaka'i Swamp. In back the ground slopes upward to cloud-draped Wai'ale'ale (rippling water), the wettest spot on earth.

The hike initially follows a dirt road along the rim of Kalalau Valley. The road is a remnant of an ill-conceived scheme to build a paved highway from Kōke'e (to bend) to Hanalei. A lack of money, and the rough terrain and wet conditions soon forced the project to a halt.

Because the forest canopy is at eye level, the road is a good place to spot native birds, such as the 'apapane and 'i'iwi. Both of these birds have a red breast and head, and black wings and tail. The 'i'iwi has a long, curved, salmon-colored bill, whereas the 'apapane has a slightly curved black bill. In flight the 'apapane makes a whirring sound as it darts from tree to tree searching for insects and nectar.

Along the trail are well over 50 different species of native plants that prefer a wet mountain habitat. All are identified and illustrated in the Pihea Trail Plant Guide, a pamphlet available from the State Division of Forestry and Wildlife in Līhu'e. The address is listed in the appendix. The notes below describe a few of the more distinctive native plants.

Ringing the Pihea vista are native 'ōlapa trees. The leaves are opposite, oblong, and flutter in the slightest wind. In a special hula stance named after the tree, dancers mimic the exquisite movements of the leaves. Early Hawaiians used the bark, leaves, and purple fruit to make a blue black dye to decorate their *kapa* (bark cloth).

On the initial boardwalk section look for the native lobelia 'ōhā wai. It has narrow, serrated leaves and branches arranged like a candelabra. The showy, curved flowers are purple outside and cream colored within. Native honeycreepers, such as the 'apapane and 'i'iwi, use their curved bill to feed on the nectar.

Around the four-way boardwalk junction you may catch a glimpse of two other native birds, 'elepaio and 'anianiau. The 'elepaio is gray brown on top and has a white breast splotched with gray and black. Its dark tail is usually cocked. Found only on Kaua'i, the 'anianiau is yellow green on top and bright yellow underneath with a short, slightly curved bill. Both birds are very curious, which is why you can often see them.

After the short ridge section, watch for the native shrub 'ohe naupaka. It has narrow, pointed leaves growing in clumps at the end of the branches. The distinctive tube-shaped flowers are bright yellow orange.

The route through the swamp follows a telephone line put up by the U.S. Army in World War II. Most of the poles have fallen over or been cut down at the base. In the bog the vegetation is stunted because of the high wind and soggy soil. In some areas the rain has washed away the colorful minerals, leaving a gray clay, rich in titanium.

Walking in the swamp is a dark, eerie experience. Clouds blot out the sun. Mist settles over the bog and swirls among the dwarf trees. Then the rain begins to fall, every day of the year.

The boardwalk ends at Kilohana (lookout point). If you are very, very lucky, you may get a spectacular, if fleeting, view. Wainiha (unfriendly water) Valley and Bay lie 4,000 feet below. Along the coast are Hanalei (crescent) Bay and Kīlauea (spewing) Point. Along the ridge to the left is Pali 'Ele'ele (black cliff). To the right Wainiha Pali leads to Wai'ale'ale.

There is an attractive option combining portions of the Alaka'i Swamp and Kawaikōī Stream hikes. Follow the initial route description of this hike. At the four-way boardwalk junction continue straight on the Pihea Trail. Cross Kawaikōī Stream and take the loop portion of that hike. Walk along Camp 10–Mōhihi Rd. and then turn right on the Alaka'i Swamp Trail. At the familiar four-way junction turn left back onto the Pihea Trail. Total distance is 8.2 miles.

15 Kawaikōī Stream

Length:	9.1-mile round trip
Elevation Gain:	1,200 feet
Suitable for:	Intermediate
Location:	Kaua'i: Kōke'e State Park and Nā Pali–Kona Forest Reserve
Topo Map:	Hā'ena

Highlights:

This hike is perhaps the loveliest stream walk in the Islands. Deep, serene pools alternate with shallow, noisy rapids. By the stream you may encounter two native waterfowl, the Hawaiian coot and Hawaiian duck.

Trailhead Directions:

Distance: *(Līhu'e to Kōke'e campground) 40 miles*

Driving Time: *1 1/2 hours*

From Līhu'e take Kaumuali'i Hwy (Rte 50) toward Waimea.

Pass a sugar mill on the left and then Kaua'i Community College on the right.

Drive through the towns of Lāwa'i and Kalāheo.

Pass the Hanapēpē River overlook on the right.

Drive through the towns of 'Ele'ele and Hanapēpē.

Pass the Russian fort on the left and then enter Waimea town.

Look for the Waimea Baptist Church on the right. It's beige with a white steeple.

Just past the church, turn right on Waimea Canyon Rd.

Ascend gradually along the rim of Waimea Canyon.

At the stop sign turn right on Kōke'e Rd.

Pass the Kōke'e Hunter Check-in Station on the right.

Pass turnoffs to Waimea Canyon and Pu'u Hinahina lookouts on the right.

Enter Kōkeʻe State Park.

On the left pass the turnoff to Kōkeʻe Lodge and Museum. The lodge has restrooms and drinking water, and the museum has trail maps and a small pamphlet on the hike.

Take the next left to Kōkeʻe campground and park in the lot there (elevation 3,680 feet) (map point A).

Route Description:

Walk back to Kōkeʻe Rd. and turn left on it.

Almost immediately turn right on a dirt road that splits three ways. Take the middle fork, which is Camp 10–Mōhihi Rd. (The left fork goes to a private cabin, and the right to a water tank.)

Descend gradually under a canopy of native koa and ʻōhiʻa trees. Look for kāhili ginger by the roadside.

A well-used dirt road comes in on the right (map point B). Keep left.

The road is lined with eucalyptus trees. On both sides are driveways leading to private cabins.

The road forks. Take the right fork, still on Camp 10–Mōhihi Rd. (The left fork leads to the Puʻu Kaʻōhelo–Berry Flat Trail.)

Climb gradually and go through an open yellow gate.

At the next fork, keep left on Camp 10–Mōhihi Rd. (map point C). (To the right is Kumuwela Rd., leading to the Canyon and Ditch Trails.)

Cross a flat area. The Puʻu Kaʻōhelo–Berry Flat Trail comes in on the left.

The road forks again. Keep left on the main route.

Shortly afterward the road turns right and begins to descend. Native ʻaʻaliʻi shrubs and hāpuʻu tree ferns line the road.

Parallel a tributary of Kauaikananā Stream.

As the road turns sharp left, it splits. Keep left on the main route. (The road to the right leads down to Kauaikananā Stream and the Ditch Trail.)

Cross Kauaikananā Stream on a bridge (map point D).

Cross a tributary of Kauaikananā Stream on another bridge.

After climbing steadily, reach a signed junction (elevation 3,695

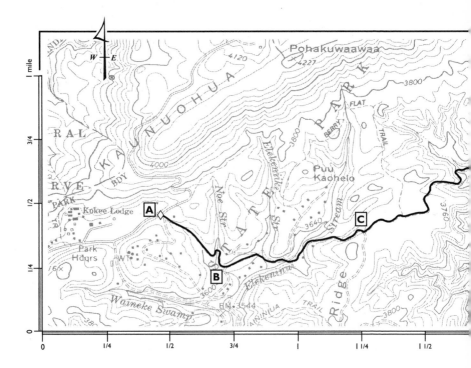

feet). Continue straight on Camp 10–Mōhihi Rd. (The grassy road to the left is the start of the Alakaʻi Swamp Trail that leads to the swamp and the Pihea Trail. The grassy road to the right leads a short distance to the Alakaʻi Picnic Area. It has a covered table, pit toilet, and a superb view down Poʻomau Canyon.)

Descend gradually toward Kawaikōī Stream.

Pass Kawaikōī Camp and picnic area on the left. The Pihea Trail ends in back of the camp.

Ford Kawaikōī Stream.

Shortly afterward reach a signed junction (elevation 3,440 feet) (map point E). Turn sharp left off the road on the Kawaikōī Stream Trail. (To the right a side road leads to Sugi Grove and camp. The Camp 10–Mōhihi Rd. continues straight.)

Swing right, through a stand of sugi (Japanese) cedars.

Cross two wet gullies on plank bridges.

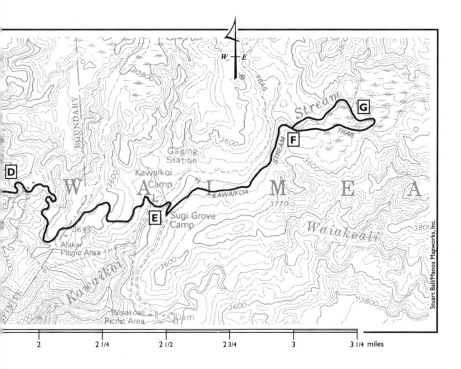

The trail parallels Kawaikōī Stream well above it.

Enter another grove of sugi cedars. Look for the native forest bird 'elepaio.

Descend to the stream and stroll alongside it. 'Ama'u ferns line the banks. Watch for the Hawaiian coot and Hawaiian duck.

Cross a tiny stream on a plank. Look for native olomea shrubs with their red-veined leaves in this area.

Reach a signed junction. Continue straight on the stream trail. (To the left a side trail crosses the stream to connect with the Pihea Trail.)

Reach another junction with the loop portion of the trail (map point F). Keep right and up. (The trail on the left along the stream is the return route.)

The trail climbs away from the stream and then levels off. Look for the native shrub naupaka kuahiwi with its white half-flowers.

Cross a tributary of the main stream.

Climb steadily, working back toward the stream.

On the left pass two stream overlooks. Near the first one is a native lapalapa tree with its round, fluttering leaves.

Descend to the stream on one switchback and cross it (map point G). On the left is a deep pool for swimming.

Proceed downstream right next to the water.

Traverse a narrow, slippery ledge just above the stream. Watch your footing.

Contour above the stream. Watch for native pūʻahanui (kanawao) shrubs with their large serrated and creased leaves.

Cross two marshy areas on a series of planks. Water drips from the cliff on the right.

Recross Kawaikōī Stream.

Shortly afterward reach the familiar loop junction (map point F). Keep right, downstream.

Retrace your steps on the stream trail and then on the Camp 10–Mōhihi Rd. back to the campground.

Notes:

Kawaikōī (flowing water) Stream is for lovers—plant lovers, bird lovers, lovers of solitude, and lovers of softly murmuring streams. All the hikes in the Kōkeʻe area are superb, but this one is special. Don't miss it.

Unfortunately, the hike includes a long walk on a hilly dirt road. Luckily, the traffic is light, and the scenery is outstanding, so the miles pass quickly. With a four-wheel-drive vehicle you may be able to get to the start of the stream trail near Sugi Grove. The hike then becomes a short novice loop of 1.7 miles. The dirt road is not recommended for two-wheel-drive vehicles because of the steep, often slippery grades.

While hiking on the road near Kauaikananā Stream, consider this humorous Hawaiian story. Two men were walking along the stream in a rainstorm. One found shelter in a small cave. His companion went under a tree and shouted "Rain on, O rain, a rain defied is this." The man in the cave figured his friend had found better shelter and so came out to take a look. The man under the tree then quickly slipped into the cave. Kauaikananā means the rain defied.

On the stream trail you may catch a glimpse of the small native bird 'elepaio in the sugi (Japanese) cedar groves. It is gray brown on top and has a white breast splotched with gray and black. Its dark tail is usually cocked. 'Elepaio are very curious, which is why you can often see them. The cedar groves were planted in the 1930s by the Civilian Conservation Corps for watershed restoration.

The walk beside Kawaikōī Stream is lovely and serene. Deep, placid pools alternate with shallow, noisy riffles. The water flowing by is dark and mysterious and comes from deep in the Alaka'i (to lead) Swamp. Soft grass and native ferns line the banks of the stream. Savor this walk; don't rush it.

While strolling quietly along the stream, watch for two native waterfowl, 'alae ke'oke'o, the Hawaiian coot, and koloa, the Hawaiian duck. The coot is black, except for a white bill and forehead. The duck is mottled brown, similar to a female mallard. Both birds eat freshwater vegetation, mollusks, and insects. 'Alae ke'oke'o is prominent in Hawaiian mythology.

At a secluded overlook before the stream crossing is a large native lapalapa tree. Its roundish leaves are arranged in groups of three and flutter in the slightest wind. Early Hawaiians used the bark, leaves, and purple fruit to make a blue black dye to decorate their *kapa* (bark cloth). The leaves also make a distinctive *lei* (garland).

Watch your footing while fording the stream. As always, if the water level is much above your knees, don't attempt to cross. Near the ford is a deep, inviting pool. Take a dip if you haven't already done so downstream. Tannin from the swamp vegetation colors the stream a rich brown.

On the return portion of the loop is the native shrub pū'ahanui (kanawao), a relative of hydrangea. It has large, serrated, deeply creased leaves and clusters of delicate pink flowers. Early Hawaiians used the plants for medicinal purposes.

There is an attractive option combining portions of the Alaka'i Swamp and Kawaikōī Stream hikes. Park your car at Pu'u o Kila lookout and follow the initial route description of the Alaka'i

Swamp hike. At the four-way boardwalk junction continue straight on the Pihea Trail. Cross Kawaikōī Stream and take the loop portion of that hike. Walk along Camp 10–Mōhihi Rd. and then turn right on the Alakaʻi Swamp Trail. At the familiar four-way junction turn left back onto the Pihea Trail. Total distance is 8.2 miles.

16 Waimea Canyon Vista

Length:	6.0-mile loop
Elevation Gain:	700 feet
Suitable for:	Intermediate
Location:	Kaua'i: Kōke'e State Park and Nā Pali–Kona Forest Reserve
Topo Map:	Hā'ena, Waimea Canyon, Mākaha Point

Highlights:

This winding loop follows the rim of spectacular Waimea Canyon. Along the way are scenic lookouts, a lovely waterfall, and a deep swimming hole. You may even see colorful native birds in the forest canopy.

Trailhead Directions:

Distance: (Līhu'e to Waineke trailhead) 41 miles

Driving Time: 1 1/2 hours

From Līhu'e take Kaumuali'i Hwy (Rte 50) toward Waimea.

Pass a sugar mill on the left and then Kaua'i Community College on the right.

Drive through the towns of Lāwa'i and Kalāheo.

Pass the Hanapēpē River overlook on the right.

Drive through the towns of 'Ele'ele and Hanapēpē.

Pass the Russian fort on the left and then enter Waimea town.

Look for the Waimea Baptist Church on the right. It's beige with a white steeple.

Just past the church, turn right on Waimea Canyon Rd.

Ascend gradually along the rim of Waimea Canyon.

At the stop sign turn right on Kōke'e Rd.

Pass the Kōke'e Hunter Check-in Station on the right.

Pass turnoffs to Waimea Canyon and Pu'u Hinahina lookouts on the right.

Enter Kōke'e State Park.

On the left pass the turnoff to Kōke'e Lodge and Museum. The lodge has restrooms and drinking water, and the museum has trail maps and a small pamphlet on the hike.

Shortly afterward turn right on Waineke Rd. It's marked by a sign to Camp Sloggett.

Descend gradually on the dirt road, passing a brown shed on the right.

Reach a junction (elevation 3,560 feet) (map point A). Keep left on the main road. (To the right a one-lane dirt road leads down to Camp Sloggett.)

Just past the junction, park in a small turnout on the right side of the road.

Route Description:
Continue along Waineke Rd. on foot.

Almost immediately, reach a second junction. Turn right on a one-lane dirt road leading to the Kumuwela Trail. (Waineke Rd. continues straight to join Camp 10–Mōhihi Rd.)

Just above a ditch intake and cabin, cross 'Elekeninui Stream on a stone bridge.

Reach a junction. Keep right and down on the road. (To the left the Waininiua Trail leads to Kumuwela Rd.)

Descend gradually along Kōke'e Stream, passing stands of kāhili ginger.

The road ends at a cabin with a stone chimney (map point B). Before reaching the cabin, turn left on the Kumuwela Trail.

Continue to follow the stream through dense ginger and then a grove of silk oaks.

Bear left away from the stream. Introduced blackberry, lantana, and ginger encroach upon the trail.

Climb straight up a ridge lined with native koa trees. In the valley on the left are some native 'ōhi'a trees with their delicate, red flowers.

The trail levels off and then ends at Kumuwela Rd. (map point C). Turn right. (To the left the road leads to Camp 10–Mōhihi Rd.)

Descend very gradually toward the rim of Po'omau Canyon.

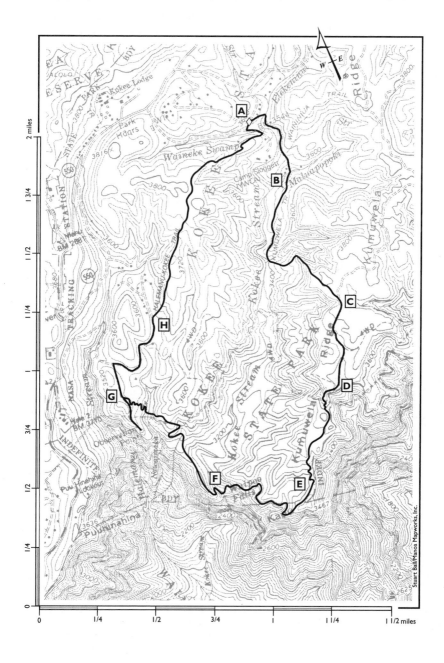

The road forks. Keep right on Kumuwela Rd. (To the left Waininiua Rd. provides access to the Ditch Trail.)

The road ends at the Kumuwela lookout, which overlooks Poʻomau Canyon (map point D). Turn right on the Canyon Trail.

Stroll through a lovely section on the canyon rim. Along the trail are koa and ʻōhiʻa trees and pūkiawe shrubs. Below are Poʻomau Canyon and Stream.

Climb briefly and then descend on five switchbacks.

Walk through an open area choked with blackberry. Watch out for thorns.

Parallel a gulch on the left in a grove of eucalyptus trees.

Descend on two switchbacks and then climb to regain the rim.

Break out into the open. The views are panoramic from two overlooks on the left (elevation 3,467 feet) (map point E). You can see ʻĀwini Falls and Kohua Ridge across Poʻomau Canyon.

Switchback twice on a deeply rutted trail. Native ʻaʻaliʻi shrubs line the trail.

Reach a third viewpoint. It has a round boulder with a comfortable flat top to sit on and look down into Waimea Canyon.

Traverse two wooded gulches.

Descend to Kōkeʻe Stream and turn left downstream.

Cross the stream near the top of lower Waipoʻo Falls. From the lip is a breathtaking view 1,500 feet straight down into the canyon.

From the falls take a makeshift trail heading up the other side of the stream.

Reach a junction (map point F). Turn right to the upper falls. (To the left the Canyon Trail continues along the rim.)

The short trail ends by a circular pool at the base of the short upper falls. The water is cool, clear, and inviting. Need I say more?

Backtrack to the junction and turn right on the Canyon Trail.

Climb an eroded slope on three poorly defined switchbacks.

Pass another lookout. The eroded rock here resembles a miniature canyon. On the left you can see a small arch in the canyon wall.

Enter a koa forest with ʻaʻaliʻi and pūkiawe shrubs.

Reach a junction. Keep left on the Canyon Trail. (To the right, the Black Pipe Trail leads to Halemanu Rd.

An irrigation ditch goes underneath the trail in a side gulch.

Climb out of the gulch on a series of short switchbacks.

Reach a junction with the Cliff Trail (map point G). Turn left for the Cliff lookout and one last view of Waimea Canyon.

Return to the junction and keep left on the Cliff Trail.

Take the unnamed dirt road at the trail end.

Reach a junction. Turn right on Halemanu Rd. (To the left the road heads back to paved Kōke'e Rd. (Rte 550).

Reach another junction. Keep left on the main road. (The dirt road on the right heads back to the Black Pipe Trail.) On the left is a plum grove.

On the right pass a palatial cabin with an expansive front lawn. A row of evergreen trees lines the road.

Just past the cabin, reach an obscure junction (map point H). Turn right on the Halemanu-Kōke'e Trail. (The road continues straight to connect with the Unnamed Trail to Faye Rd. and Kōke'e Rd.)

Climb steeply through grass and then more gradually up a ridge past some dying koa trees.

The trail levels off, ascends, and then levels off again in an 'ōhi'a forest. Look for naupaka kuahiwi shrubs with their white half-flowers in this pleasant section.

Descend gradually, switchbacking once.

Reach the end of the trail at a junction with a dirt road. Turn left on it. (To the right the road leads to Camp Sloggett.)

Reach the familiar junction with Waineke Rd. where your car is parked (map point A).

Notes:

This scenic, intricate loop is pieced together from eight different trails and dirt roads near Waimea (reddish water) Canyon. Follow the route description religiously. The junctions come fast and furiously, and several are less than obvious. Some trail sections may be partially overgrown with ginger, blackberry, or other introduced shrubs. The loop is described clockwise. You can, of course, walk the opposite way, if you are good at reading directions in reverse.

Two native trees, 'ōhi'a and koa, predominate along much of the loop. 'Ōhi'a has oval leaves and clusters of delicate red flowers. Native birds, such as the 'apapane, feed on the nectar and help in pollination. Early Hawaiians used the flowers in *lei* (garlands) and the wood in outrigger canoes. The hard, durable wood was also carved into god images for *heiau* (religious sites). Koa has sickle-shaped foliage and pale yellow flower clusters. Early Hawaiians made surfboards and outrigger canoe hulls out of the beautiful red brown wood. Today it is made into fine furniture.

The view from the lookouts on the Canyon Trail is spectacular. Po'omau (constant source) Canyon lies directly below. Across the canyon is Kohua Ridge and 'Āwini Falls. Farther along the rim you can look into Waimea Canyon, which descends all the way to the ocean. On the right are the twin cascades of Waipo'o Falls. Watch for feral goats scrambling on the cliffs and koa'e kea, the white-tailed tropicbird, soaring on the warm canyon air.

Waimea Canyon is 14 miles long and up to 2,500 feet deep. Streams carved the canyon, but a massive landslide determined its north-south orientation. Notice that all the tributary canyons, such as Po'omau, are on the left (east) side of the main canyon. Millions of years ago a slice of the island slumped, forming a north-to-south trough, known as Makaweli (fearful features) graben. Lava from Wai'ale'ale (rippling water) volcano gradually filled the graben from the east. As the volcano became extinct, streams began to erode from its summit area. The slightly higher west side of the graben blocked their normal drainage downhill. The streams diverted to the south along the graben and eventually formed Waimea Canyon.

Along the canyon rim are the native dry-land shrubs pūkiawe and 'a'ali'i. Pūkiawe has tiny, rigid leaves and small white, pink, or red berries. 'A'ali'i has narrow, shiny leaves and red seed capsules that the early Hawaiians used in *lei* making and for *kapa* (bark cloth) dye.

Spend some time at Waipo'o Falls. From the lip of the lower falls is a heart-stopping view, straight down. At the base of the upper falls is a lovely circular pool backed by cliffs and koa trees. The idyllic setting brings to mind an old Hawaiian legend about a beautiful maiden and a waterfall in Waimea Canyon.

On a dark, rainy night a baby was born, and the mother called her Ua (rain). She lived in a village along the rugged Nāpali Coast. While climbing a rope ladder above the ocean, the father accidently dropped his baby daughter. The god of waterfalls suddenly appeared out of a rainbow, caught the baby in midair, and carried her back to Waimea Canyon, where she grew up.

One day the son of a chief from Waimea village walked into the canyon to select a koa tree to build a canoe. He spotted a lovely maiden coming out of the mist in front of a waterfall. The man called to her softly, saying that he loved her. She was surprised and then pleased, but asked to be called by her real name if he was to win her love.

The chief's son returned to his village and asked all the *kāhuna* (priests) for the name of the maiden of the mist. No one could tell him. Finally, he talked to his grandmother, who had heard the story of Ua, the baby carried on a rainbow to a canyon waterfall. The man rushed back to the waterfall and called the maiden by her name. Together the couple returned to his village, were married, and lived happily for many years.

On the Halemanu-Kōke'e Trail look for the native birds 'elepaio and 'apapane. The 'elepaio is gray brown on top and has a white breast splotched with gray and black. Its dark tail is usually cocked. The 'apapane has a red breast and head, black wings and tail, and a slightly curved black bill. In flight the 'apapane makes a whirring sound as it darts from tree to tree searching for insects and nectar.

For a shorter hike to the Cliff lookout and Waipo'o Falls, park in the large turnout on the left between mile markers 14 and 15 on Kōke'e (to bend) Rd. Take the rutted dirt road on the right marked Halemanu (bird house) Valley. The road descends into the valley, swings right, and then climbs. At the first junction turn right on an unnamed dirt road. Pick up the route description in reverse at the start of the Cliff Trail. Total distance to the falls and back is about 3 miles.

17 Kukui

Length:	5.0-mile round trip
Elevation Gain:	2,200 feet
Suitable for:	Intermediate
Location:	Kaua'i: Waimea Canyon State Park and Nā Pali–Kona Forest Reserve
Topo Map:	Waimea Canyon

Highlights:

The Kukui Trail descends precipitously into spectacular Waimea Canyon. The scenery is stunning, with multicolored cliffs, eroded pinnacles, and cascading waterfalls. At the bottom, cool off in the river before the hot return uphill.

Trailhead Directions:

Distance: *(Līhu'e to Kukui trailhead) 30 miles*

Driving Time: *1 hour*

From Līhu'e take Kaumuali'i Hwy (Rte 50) toward Waimea.

Pass a sugar mill on the left and Kaua'i Community College on the right.

Drive through the towns of Lāwa'i and Kalāheo.

Pass the Hanapēpē River overlook on the right.

Drive through the towns of 'Ele'ele and Hanapēpē.

Pass the Russian fort on the left and then enter Waimea town.

Look for the Waimea Baptist Church on the right. It's beige with a white steeple.

Just past the church, turn right on Waimea Canyon Rd.

Ascend gradually along the rim of Waimea Canyon.

At the stop sign turn right on Kōke'e Rd.

Pass the Kōke'e Hunter Check-in Station on the right.

Between mile markers 8 and 9 look for the Kukui trailhead on the right by a blue emergency phone (elevation 2,900 feet) (map point A).

Park in the small turnout on the left side of the road.

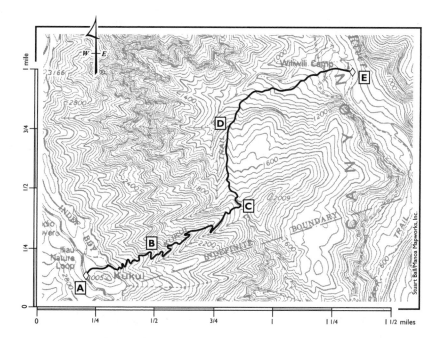

Route Description:

Climb up the embankment.

Just past a bench, reach a junction. Turn right on the Kukui Trail. (To the left a nature loop circles through a grove of native iliau shrubs.)

Pass several markers describing various native dry-land forest plants.

Reach a second junction. Again, keep right. (To the left is the nature loop.)

Pass two covered picnic tables surrounded by kī (ti) plants.

Descend steeply on six short switchbacks. Silk oaks provide some shade.

Pass another bench and lookout on the left. You can now look directly into Waimea Canyon.

The trail crisscrosses a side ridge while descending on seven long switchbacks (map point B). Don't shortcut them.

Descend straight down on a narrow eroded trail. Watch your footing. Look for kukui trees with their light green leaves in the gulch on the right.

Switchback five more times and then resume heading straight down.

Pass another bench on the right. From here is a superb view up the canyon.

The trail descends on the right side of the ridge.

Reach a signed junction in a saddle (map point C). Turn left and down on the main trail. (A side trail leads straight ahead to an overlook of the canyon.)

Descend steeply on an open, eroded slope. The trail attempts to switchback at first, but soon gives up and heads straight downhill. All around you are the sheer red and green walls of the canyon.

The trail levels off briefly by an old utility pole and then resumes the descent.

At the end of the eroded section turn sharp right into the forest toward the canyon floor (map point D).

Continue descending through introduced silk oak and guava trees on a rough, rocky trail with an occasional switchback.

Enter a grove of kukui trees. Their leaves and nuts litter the ground.

Work right, across a slope on a more gentle path.

Bear left and down along a gully. Follow the gully, first on its left and then on its right.

Contour through tall grass. The forest is now mostly koa haole with an occasional native wiliwili tree.

Bear left to begin the final descent to the canyon bottom.

Pass a line of sisal plants with their swordlike leaves.

Walk through Wiliwili Camp. It has a pit toilet and covered picnic table.

Reach a signed junction with the Waimea Canyon Trail (elevation 660 feet) (map point E). Continue straight across on a makeshift trail leading toward Waimea River. (To the left the canyon trail leads to Koai‘e Canyon and Lonomea Camp. To the right the trail heads down the canyon to Waimea town.)

Reach the Waimea River. Just upstream is a good swimming hole with a cold spring trickling into it.

Notes:

While most tourists and locals are gazing into Waimea Canyon from distant overlooks, try this adventurous hike to the canyon floor. The steep, narrow trail, however, is not for the faint of heart. The route is short, but the elevation gain is considerable, and the footing is over loose soil and rock. As you are pounding down the trail, remember that what goes down must come up.

If possible, take the hike in the early morning or late afternoon. Besides being hot, the intense midday sun washes out the vivid canyon colors: blue sky, black lava, red earth, and green vegetation. Whenever you go, drink plenty of water and use lots of sunscreen.

Before descending into Waimea (reddish water) Canyon, take the short nature loop through a grove of iliau, an unusual native shrub. It has slender, swordlike leaves clustered at the top of a woody stem. After growing for many years, the shrub flowers once during the summer and then dies. The flower stalks are tall and showy with cream-colored petals. Found only on Kaua'i, iliau is a relative of 'āhinahina, the silversword, found on Haleakalā and Mauna Kea.

The view from the picnic tables is breathtaking. Across Waimea Canyon is Wai'alae (mudhen water) Canyon with its lovely waterfall. To the left is Kaluahā'ula (reddish pit) Ridge, then Koai'e Canyon, and then Po'omau (constant source) Canyon. Farther down the trail you get a good view of the canyon floor and its red and green walls. Upstream is Po'o Kāehu, a pillar of resistant rock. Downstream is Nāwaimaka (tears) Valley with its twin falls.

Waimea Canyon is 14 miles long and up to 2,500 feet deep. Streams carved the canyon, but a massive landslide determined its north-south orientation. Notice that all the tributary canyons, such as Wai'alae, are on the far (east) side of the main canyon. Millions of years ago a slice of the island slumped, forming a north-to-south trough, known as Makaweli (fearful features) graben. Lava from Wai'ale'ale (rippling water) volcano gradually filled the graben from the east. As the volcano became extinct, streams began to erode from its summit area. The slightly higher west side of the graben blocked their normal drainage downhill. The streams diverted to the south along the graben and eventually formed Waimea Canyon.

Lining the side gulches near the canyon floor are groves of kukui trees. Their large, pale green leaves resemble those of the maple, with several distinct lobes. Early Polynesian voyagers introduced kukui into Hawai'i. They used the wood to make gunwales and seats for their outrigger canoes. The flowers and sap became medicines to treat a variety of ailments. Early Hawaiians strung the nuts together to make *lei hua* (seed or nut garlands). The oily kernels became house candles and torches for night spearfishing.

In the forested sections you may encounter a red jungle fowl (moa). It is very similar to a domestic chicken. The roosters are red brown with a black, sickle-shaped tail. The moa pokes around the underbrush, looking for seeds, fruits, and insects. The early Polynesians introduced the bird to Hawai'i. It survives only on Kaua'i because of the absence of the mongoose.

Before reaching Wiliwili Camp, look for the native tree of the same name. It has heart-shaped, leathery leaflets in groups of three. Flowers appear in the spring and are usually orange. Early Hawaiians used the soft, light wood for surfboards, canoe outriggers, and fishnet floats. The red seeds were strung together to form *lei hua*.

Around the camp you can easily recognize sisal by its swordlike leaves. At one time fibers from the leaves were made into rope, and the plant was introduced into Hawai'i in the late 1800s for that purpose. Sisal puts up a tall flower stalk every 10 years or so, on which the baby plants form.

From the camp take the short walk to Waimea River. Stretch out under a shady tree along the bank. Soak your feet or your whole body in the cool river water. Don't get too relaxed because the hard part of the hike is yet to come.

There are two good variations to the route as described. For a shorter hike, take the side trail to the canyon overlook and then return. For a longer hike take the Waimea Canyon Trail upstream, crossing the river twice. At an unmarked junction turn right on the Koai'e Canyon Trail and cross the river a third time. Follow Koai'e Stream to Lonomea Camp with its fine swimming hole. Total distance from Kukui trailhead to Lonomea and back is 12.2 miles.

Down the mountain, Mauna Loa in back. Mauna Kea hike, Hawai'i. *(Photo by Lynne Masuyama)*

Waipi'o Bay and Valley. Waipi'o Valley hike, Hawai'i. *(Photo by Deborah Uchida)*

▲ Sunrise along the Ka'ū coast. Ka'aha hike, Hawai'i. *(Photo by Deborah Uchida)*

▶ Through the native rain forest. Halema'uma'u hike, Hawai'i. *(Photo by John Hoover)*

▲ 'Ōhelo berries. Halema'uma'u hike, Hawai'i. *(Photo by Marcia Stone)*

◀ Kīlauea Iki Crater. Kīlauea Iki hike, Hawai'i. *(Photo by John Hoover)*

► 'Ōhi'a blossom. Pu'u 'Ō'ō Trail, Hawai'i. *(Photo by Marcia Stone)*

▼ *Pāhoehoe* lava. Kīlauea Crater Rim hike, Hawai'i. *(Photo by John Hoover)*

Hanakāpīʻai Falls. Hanakāpīʻai Falls hike, Kauaʻi. *(Photo by Lynne Masuyama)*

Hanakāpī'ai Beach. Hanakāpī'ai Falls hike, Kaua'i. *(Photo by Lynne Masuyama)*

◄ Nēnē, the Hawaiian goose, Nuʻalolo Valley in back. Nuʻalolo Cliff hike, Kauaʻi. *(Photo by John Hoover)*

▼ On the board-walk. Alakaʻi Swamp hike, Kauaʻi. *(Photo by John Hoover)*

▲ At Kilohana lookout.
Alaka'i Swamp hike, Kaua'i.
(Photo by John Hoover)

► 'Ōhā wai flower. Alaka'i
Swamp hike, Kaua'i. *(Photo
by John Hoover)*

KAPA'A

18 Nounou Mountain–East (Sleeping Giant)

Length:	3.8-mile round trip
Elevation Gain:	1,100 feet
Suitable for:	Novice
Location:	Kaua'i: Nounou Forest Reserve above Wailua
Topo Map:	Kapa'a

Highlights:

In profile, Nounou Mountain resembles a sleeping giant. This steady climb to the giant's head opens up spectacular views of the eastern coast and interior mountains. At the top, white-tailed tropicbirds soar gracefully overhead.

Trailhead Directions:

Distance: (Līhu'e to Nounou Mountain–East trailhead) *7 miles*

Driving Time: *1/4 hour*

From Līhu'e take Kūhiō Hwy (Rte 56) north toward Kapa'a. Cross Wailua River on a bridge.

Pass the intersection with Kuamo'o Rd. (Rte 580).

At the next traffic light by a Shell service station, turn left on Haleilio Rd.

Pass the intersection with Wailana Rd. on the right.

As the road curves left, turn right into a small paved lot and park there (elevation 120 feet) (map point A). The lot is 1.1 miles from the intersection with Route 56.

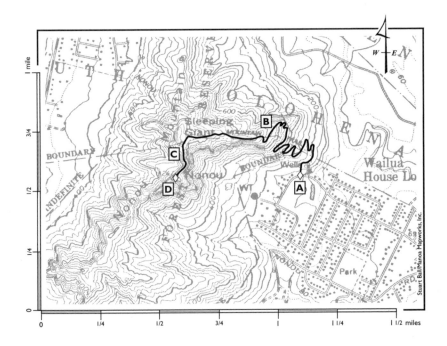

Route Description:

Climb the embankment on the right side of the parking lot to pick up the Nounou Mountain–East Side Trail.

Pass a small pumping station in a paved area below and on the right.

Ascend gradually along the slope through a mixed forest of guava and Christmas berry trees.

Switchback 10 times up the side of Nounou Mountain, also known as Sleeping Giant. The trail is rocky in spots. Look for kī (ti) plants among the scrub koa haole trees.

At the tenth switchback is a view of the giant's head. Below is the Wailua River. Beyond Līhuʻe along the coast is the massive peak of Hāʻupu, also called Hoary Head.

The trail descends briefly and then resumes climbing.

Switchback seven more times.

Gain the ridge line and turn left up it (map point B). *Mauka* (inland) are the Makaleha Mountains.

Ascend the ridge, crisscrossing it several times. Along the trail are strawberry guava and eucalyptus trees.

Pass an eroded spot with views *makai* (seaward).

Reach a signed junction in a stand of hala trees. Keep left along the ridge. (To the right the Nounou Mountain–West Side Trail descends to Kamalu Rd. [Rte 581].)

Climb through a ti grove.

Reach a flat, grassy area (giant's chest) with two covered picnic tables and an impressive view *mauka* (map point C). Look for koaʻe kea (white-tailed tropicbirds) soaring overhead.

Descend and traverse a narrow saddle in the ridge (giant's neck).

Scramble up a steep slope (giant's chin). Watch your footing on the loose dirt and rock.

Reach the summit of Nounou (giant's nose) (elevation 1,241 feet) (map point D). At the top are the remains of a triangulation station and superb views in all directions.

Notes:

The climb to the chest and head of Sleeping Giant is popular with tourists and locals alike. The route is hot and steep, but the tremendous view from the top is well worth the effort. For the most part, the trail is wide and well graded. Watch your step, however, in a few rocky, narrow spots on the switchbacks.

Along the switchbacks are kī (ti) plants. They have shiny leaves, 1–2 feet long, that are arranged spirally in a cluster at the tip of a slender stem. Early Polynesian voyagers introduced ti to Hawaiʻi. They used the leaves for house thatch, skirts, sandals, and raincoats. Food to be cooked in an *imu* (underground oven) was first wrapped in ti leaves. A popular sport with the commoners was hoʻoheʻe kī or ti-leaf sliding. The sap from ti roots stained canoes and surfboards.

Strawberry guava trees (waiawī ʻulaʻula) line the trail on the ridge. They have glossy, dark green leaves and smooth brown bark. Their dark red fruit is delicious, with a taste reminiscent of strawberries. The guavas usually ripen in August and September. Pickings may be slim, however, because of the popularity of the trail. The strawberry guava is a native of Brazil but was introduced to Hawaiʻi from England in the 1800s.

At the junction with the west-side trail is a small grove of hala trees. They have distinctive prop roots that help support the heavy clusters of leaves and fruit on the ends of the branches. Early Hawaiians braided the long, pointed leaves, called *lau hala*, into baskets, fans, floor mats, and sails.

From the overlook by the picnic tables is a marvelous view *mauka* (inland). Below is the gorge of the Wailua (two waters) River. To the west is massive, flat-topped Waiʻaleʻale (rippling water), the wettest spot on earth. Its summit, Kawaikini (the multitudinous water), is the highest point on the island at 5,243 feet. To the right (northwest) are the Makaleha (eyes looking about as in wonder and admiration) Mountains. Hanalei Valley lies beyond the low ridge joining Waiʻaleʻale and Makaleha.

While enjoying the view, consider this old story. A giant once lived in the hills behind Kapaʻa town. He was a gentle giant, always helping the Hawaiian people. They turned his footprints into fertile banana patches. The flattened hills where he rested became cultivated fields. The sleepy giant faithfully repaired houses knocked down by gusts from his yawn.

One day the giant yawned, lay down, and fell asleep—for hundreds of years. Over time the wind covered him with dirt, and shrubs and trees grew over his body. Who knows? Some day he may awaken, yawn, and sit up.

The novice hike ends at the picnic tables on the giant's chest. Continue to his head only if you feel comfortable scrambling up (and down) loose rock and dirt. At the summit is the entire panorama. In addition to the *mauka* views, you can see much of the eastern coast of Kauaʻi. Behind Līhuʻe (cold chill) and the airport is the ridge culminating in Hāʻupu (recollection) peak, also called Hoary Head.

Before heading down, look for graceful koaʻe kea or white-tailed tropicbirds, gliding overhead. They have two central tail feathers elongated into streamers. Tropicbirds feed by diving into the ocean for fish and squid. They nest in burrows or rock crevices along cliff faces.

There are two other routes to the top of Sleeping Giant. The Nounou Mountain–West-Side Trail starts from Kamalu Rd. (Rte

581) at telephone pole no. 11. The trail climbs the opposite side of the giant and joins the east-side trail just before the picnic tables. Total distance round trip is 3.3 miles.

The Kuamoʻo-Nounou Trail starts about 0.5 mile beyond the ʻŌpaekaʻa Falls turnout on Kuamoʻo Rd. (Rte 580). The route contours around the back side of the giant and joins the west-side trail. Total distance round trip is about 6 miles. If you have two cars, you can traverse the mountain by combining the east- and west-side trails. Total distance one way is 3.5 miles.

19 Kuilau Ridge

Length:	4.3-mile round trip
Elevation Gain:	700 feet
Suitable for:	Novice
Location:	Kaua'i: Līhu'e-Koloa Forest Reserve above Wailua
Topo Map:	Wai'ale'ale, Kapa'a

Highlights:

This short, pleasurable walk climbs a gentle ridge in the foothills of the Makaleha Mountains. Along the route are magnificent views of Nounou (Sleeping Giant) and massive Wai'ale'ale. The hike ends at a shady clearing ringed with ironwood trees.

Trailhead Directions:

Distance: (Līhu'e to Keāhua Arboretum) 13 miles

Driving Time: 1/2 hour

From Līhu'e take Kūhiō Hwy (Rte 56) north toward Kapa'a. Cross Wailua River on a bridge.
At the next traffic light turn left on Kuamo'o Rd. (Rte 580 west).
Pass the turnout for 'Ōpaeka'a Falls on the right.
Pass the intersection with Kamalu Rd. (Rte 581).
Reach Keāhua Arboretum at the end of the paved road.
Park in the lot on the left just before the road fords Keāhua Stream (elevation 520 feet) (map point A). Across the stream and to the left are two pit toilets.

Route Description:

Walk back along Kuamo'o Rd. for about 75 yards to reach the signed trailhead. Turn left on a dirt road that is the Kuilau Ridge Trail.
Go around a chain across the road.
Climb gradually along the left side of Kuilau Ridge through an

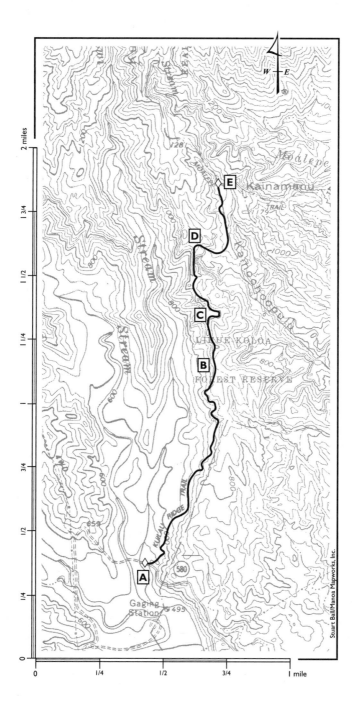

introduced forest of eucalyptus and albizia. The trail is lined with the pest plant *Melastoma*. Look for kukui trees downslope.

Gain the ridge line (map point B) and some impressive views of the surrounding mountains. *Mauka* is massive Wai'ale'ale. *Makai* is Nounou Mountain (Sleeping Giant). Farther along the ridge are the Makaleha Mountains.

Reach two covered picnic tables in a flat, grassy area (map point C). Around the clearing are some contorted native 'ōhi'a trees.

At the picnic tables turn right, following the road.

Descend briefly along a side ridge and then switchback to the left to regain the main ridge.

Switchback two more times up a steep section. From the ridge top are magnificent views in all directions.

Descend gradually along the right side of the ridge into a gulch.

Cross 'Ōpaeka'a Stream on a wooden bridge (map point D) and climb out of the gulch.

Reach the top of Kamo'oho'opulu and turn left up it.

Stroll through a level section lined with paperbark trees. Ignore an unmarked trail coming in on the right.

Reach the end of the road in a clearing ringed with ironwood trees (elevation 1,180 feet) (map point E). To the right the Moalepe Trail descends to Olohena Rd. Dead ahead is Kapehua'ala (elevation 3,200 feet), the highest peak in the Makaleha Mountains.

Notes:

Kuilau Ridge is a delightful hike—short, savory, and very scenic. Take your time on this one, or it will be over much too quickly. Stop every now and then to enjoy the view, take pictures, identify plants, whatever.

The ridge trail is actually an old road, still wide and well graded. The climb is gradual, with switchbacks on the steeper sections. The road, however, may be muddy on the level stretches along Kamo'oho'opulu (the wet ridge). Watch out for the occasional mountain biker, and a few mosquitoes at the start.

Once on the trail, look and listen for the white-rumped shama. It is black on top with a chestnut-colored breast and a long black-

and-white tail. The shama has a variety of beautiful songs and often mimics other birds. A native of Malaysia, the shama has become widespread in introduced forests such as this one.

Downslope from the road are kukui trees. Their large, pale green leaves resemble those of the maple, with several distinct lobes. Early Polynesian voyagers introduced kukui into Hawai'i. They used the wood to make gunwales and seats for their outrigger canoes. The flowers and sap became medicines to treat a variety of ailments. Early Hawaiians strung the nuts together to make *lei hua* (seed or nut garlands). The oily kernels became house candles and torches for night spearfishing.

From the road and the picnic tables are some very fine views of the surrounding peaks. *Mauka* (inland) is massive, flat-topped Wai'ale'ale (rippling water), the wettest spot on earth. Its summit, Kawaikini (the multitudinous water), is the highest point on the island at 5,243 feet. *Makai* (seaward) is Nounou with its profile of a sleeping giant. Farther along the ridge are the Makaleha (eyes looking about as in wonder and admiration) Mountains.

Around the clearing with the picnic tables are some twisted native 'ōhi'a trees. They have oval leaves and clusters of delicate red flowers. Early Hawaiians used the flowers in *lei* (garlands) and the wood in outrigger canoes. The hard, durable wood was also carved into god images for *heiau* (religious sites).

The trail ends at a pleasant spot under some ironwood trees. Relax in their shade and listen for the wind sighing through their branches. Gaze up at imposing Kapehua'ala, the highest peak in the Makaleha Mountains.

After finishing the hike, wander around the arboretum. Its lovely grounds occupy both sides of Keāhua (the mound) Stream. Along the stream are secluded picnic tables and inviting swimming holes.

As an alternative, you can take the Moalepe (chicken with comb) Trail. It starts at the end of paved Olohena Rd., off Kamalu Rd. (Rte 581) and joins the Kuilau Ridge Trail at its end. Total distance round trip is 4.5 miles. If you have two cars, go up Kuilau Ridge and down Moalepe or vice versa. Total distance one way is 4.4 miles.

20 Powerline Trail

Length:	11.3 miles one way
Elevation Gain:	1,700 feet
Suitable for:	Intermediate, Expert
Location:	Kaua'i: Līhu'e-Koloa Forest Reserve above Wailua and Halele'a Forest Reserve above Princeville
Topo Map:	Wai'ale'ale, Hanalei

Highlights:

This awesome hike traverses the divide separating Wailua Valley and Hanalei Valley. The route follows a rough dirt road built to service a transmission line. Along the way are intriguing native plants and unforgettable mountain views.

Trailhead Directions:

Because the route is point to point, this hike has two trailheads, one above Wailua and the other above Princeville.

Distance: *(Līhu'e to Keāhua Arboretum) 13 miles*

Driving Time: 1/2 hour

From Līhu'e take Kūhiō Hwy (Rte 56) north toward Kapa'a.
Cross Wailua River on a bridge.
At the next traffic light turn left on Kuamo'o Rd. (Rte 580 west).
Pass the turnout for 'Ōpaeka'a Falls on the right.
Pass the intersection with Kamalu Rd. (Rte 581).
Reach Keāhua Arboretum at the end of the paved road.
Ford Keāhua Stream.
Park in the lot on the right next to the stream (elevation 520 feet) (map point A). Across the road are two pit toilets.

Distance: *(Līhu'e to Kapaka St. end) 29 miles*

Driving Time: 1 hour

From Līhu'e take Kūhiō Hwy (Rte 56) north toward Hanalei.

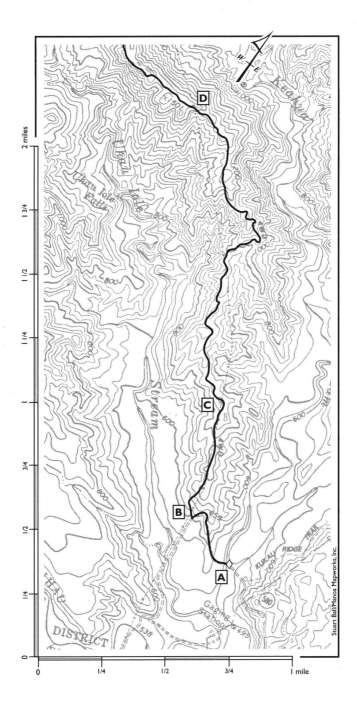

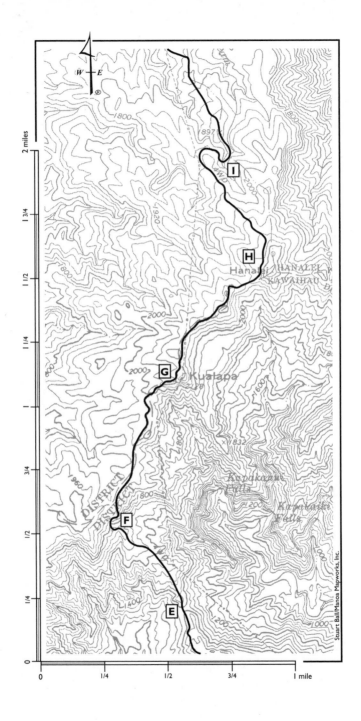

Pass the turnoff to Kīlauea Lighthouse on the right and then cross a long bridge over Kalihi Wai River.

Pass Princeville Airport on the left.

At mile marker 26 begin looking for the Princeville Ranch Stables on the left.

Turn left on Kapaka St. by the stables.

Drive 1.7 miles to the end of the pavement. Park in the dirt lot on the right (elevation 540 feet) (map point M). A water tank is visible farther up the road.

Route Description:

From the parking lot by Keāhua Stream, continue up the road, now badly deteriorated, on foot. On the side are tangled hau trees. Look and listen for the white-rumped shama in the introduced forest.

As the road swings left and down, reach a junction by a hunter checking station (map point B). Turn right and up on a dirt road that is the Powerline Trail. (To the left the main dirt road follows the powerline down to the Wailua River.)

Climb steadily under arching albizia trees.

Pass the first of many concrete pylons supporting the powerline. On the left is massive Wai'ale'ale and on the right are the Makaleha Mountains.

The road gradually ascends a ridge, switching from one side to the other. Look for native 'ōhi'a trees along the ridge top. *Makai* are views of Nounou Mountain (Sleeping Giant), and Hā'upu (Hoary Head) peak beyond the airport.

Pass close to another pylon above and on the left (map point C). Ignore service roads leading left or right to the base of each pylon.

The climb steepens. Keep your eye out for pueo, the native owl.

Pass close to a pylon above and on the right (map point D). On the right along Keāhua Stream are two lovely waterfalls, Kapaka Nui and Kapaka Iki.

After a short level section descend a saddle in the ridge (map point E).

Ascend steeply out of the saddle past a twin pylon.

The road curves right and climbs the side of a low ridge or divide.

It separates the Wailua and Hanalei drainages by connecting Wai'ale'ale and the Makaleha Mountains.

Reach the top of the divide (elevation 1,840 feet) (map point F). Turn right along it. (On the left a short road leads to an awesome overlook of much of eastern Kaua'i.)

Stroll along the relatively level ridge past a tall rusted post.

Climb gradually, passing two pylons on the right. The second one stands on Kualapa peak (elevation 2,128 feet) (map point G).

Pass a structure with attached radars. Views of Hanalei Valley begin to open up.

Ignore two service roads on the left leading down to pylons. Keep right along the main ridge.

Descend into and climb out of a small saddle.

Shortly afterward the road swings left, leaving the divide for good (map point H).

Descend gradually along a side ridge toward Hanalei. The prominent peak on the right is Namahana. On the left is fortresslike Nāmolokama Mountain.

Pass a pylon close by on the left. Look for tall native loulu palms dwarfing the scrub 'ōhi'a forest.

The road jogs right and then left. Underneath in a culvert is Ka'āpahu Stream (map point I).

Just before reaching a pylon on the left is a view of two waterfalls, cascading down the flank of Nāmolokama Mountain.

Jog left and then right to cross a small stream in a culvert (map point J).

The road hugs the pylons for a long stretch (map point K). On the right is Kalihi Wai Valley. Kīlauea Point comes into view along the coast.

The 'ōhi'a trees gradually disappear, replaced by the pest shrub *Melastoma*.

Curve left to cross another stream in a culvert (map point L).

On the right pass Kapaka, a wooded hill.

To the left is an overlook of Hanalei River and Valley. Below is a small waterfall from the stream just crossed.

Pass a hunter checking station and then a water tank on the right.

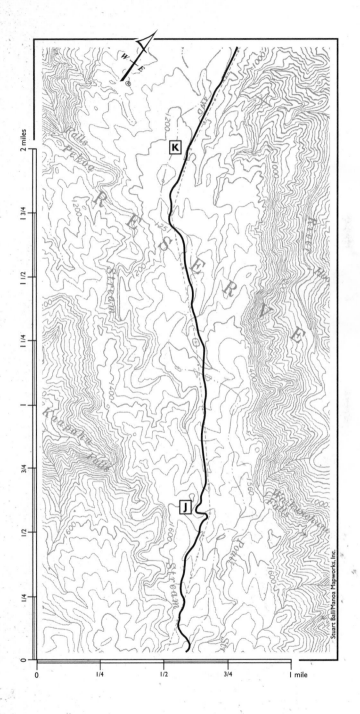

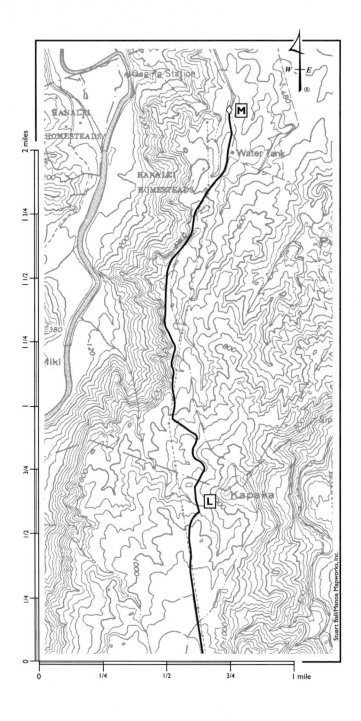

Reach the parking area at the end of paved Kapaka St. (map point M).

Notes:

The Powerline Trail is actually a dirt road that crosses the divide between Wailua and Hanalei Valleys. The road closely follows an electric transmission line and allows access to it for maintenance. If your mind can blot out the pylons and powerlines, this hike becomes one of the great wilderness walks in the Islands.

The road is a multiple-use route. You may see hunters, four-wheel-drive enthusiasts, mountain bikers, and horseback riders. To miss most of the traffic, take this hike during the week. Hunting is allowed on weekends and Mondays. Start early to complete the climbing before midday and to get the best views.

The graded route makes for a pleasant, steady hiking pace. The road, however, is muddy in the dips and in some of the level stretches. Watch your step on the steep, deeply rutted sections, which can be slippery if wet.

The views become incredible shortly after the hike starts. On the left is massive, flat-topped Waiʻaleʻale (rippling water), the wettest spot on earth. Its summit, Kawaikini (the multitudinous water), is the highest point on the island at 5,243 feet. Standing guard in front of Waiʻaleʻale is a towering rock pillar, known as Pōhakupele (lava rock). On the right are the Makaleha (eyes looking about as in wonder and admiration) Mountains. *Makai* (seaward) are Nounou with the profile of a sleeping giant and Hāʻupu peak (Hoary Head) beyond the airport.

Along the ridge line are native ʻōhiʻa trees. They have oval leaves and clusters of delicate red flowers. Early Hawaiians used the flowers in *lei* (garlands) and the wood in outrigger canoes. The hard, durable wood was also carved into god images for *heiau* (religious sites).

You may catch a glimpse of the native owl, pueo, hovering above the ridge. It is brown and white, with yellow eyes and a black bill. Unlike most owls, the pueo is active during the day, hunting birds, rodents, and insects. Early Hawaiians worshiped the owl as a god and a guardian spirit.

Along the road look for the delicate sweeping fronds of hāpu'u, the native tree fern. Its trunk consists of roots tightly woven around a small central stem. The brown fiber covering the young fronds of hāpu'u is called *pulu*.

Before reaching the divide, you can see two beautiful waterfalls along Keāhua Stream to the right. The higher one on the left is called Kapaka Nui (large raindrop), and the wider one on the right is Kapaka Iki (little raindrop). After the falls overlook, the road climbs steeply to the divide. At the top, take a well-earned break and enjoy the sights. On a clear day the view here is one of the best on the island.

The descent on the Hanalei side is long but gradual. Just put one foot in front of the other and let gravity do the rest. While cruising down the ridge, look for native loulu palms standing above the scrub 'ōhi'a forest. They have rigid, fan-shaped fronds in a cluster at the top of a ringed trunk. Early Hawaiians used the fronds for thatch. The blades of young fronds were plaited into fans and baskets.

Like the road, the views on the Hanalei side unfold gradually. On the left across the valley is fortresslike Nāmolokama (the interweaving bound fast) Mountain. Several waterfalls cascade down its flanks. On the right is Kīlauea (spewing) Point, jutting into the ocean. Eventually, you can see Hanalei River and town. Finally, the water tank near the trailhead comes into view.

As described, the route is one way from Wailua to Princeville. You can, of course, do the hike in the opposite direction. If you have only one car, start from the Keāhua Arboretum trailhead. Climb to the top of the divide and then return the way you came. Total distance round trip is 7.4 miles.

HANALEI

21 Hanakāpī'ai Falls

Length:	7.9-mile round trip
Elevation Gain:	2,000 feet
Suitable for:	Intermediate, Expert
Location:	Kaua'i: Nā Pali Coast State Park
Topo Map:	Hā'ena

Highlights:
This popular hike winds above vertical sea cliffs along the rugged Nāpali Coast. Midway is an idyllic cove with a white-sand beach. At the end is lovely Hanakāpī'ai Falls, cascading into a wide, circular pool.

Trailhead Directions:
Distance: (Līhu'e to Kē'ē Beach) 37 miles
Driving Time: 1 1/4 hours

From Līhu'e take Kūhiō Hwy (Rte 56) north toward Hanalei. Cross Wailua River on a bridge.

Drive through the town of Kapa'a.

Continue on Kūhiō Hwy along the windward coast.

Pass the turnoff to Kīlauea Lighthouse on the right and then cross a long bridge over Kalihi Wai River.

Pass Princeville Airport on the left and Princeville resort on the right. Route 56 becomes Route 560 west.

Descend into Hanalei Valley and cross the river on a one-lane bridge.

Drive through Hanalei town.

Cross a series of short one-lane bridges.

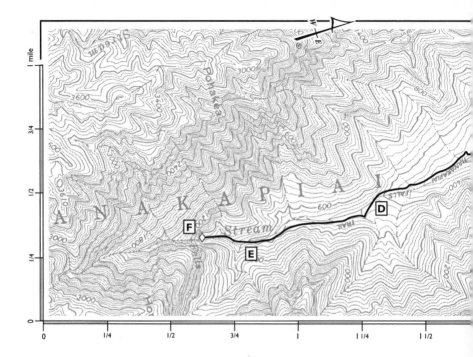

Enter Hāʻena State Park.

Reach the end of the road at Kēʻē Beach (map point A). Park on either side of the road. The state park has restrooms and drinking water.

Route Description:

Take the Nāpali Coast–Kalalau Trail that starts on the left just before the end of the paved road.

On the right pass a kiosk displaying maps and information about the trail.

Climb steadily along the Makana cliffs above Kēʻē Beach. The trail is very rocky and slippery when wet. Some sections are paved with smooth stones. Look for the native shrub naupaka kahakai, with its white half-flowers.

Work into and out of two small ravines. The first is dotted with hala trees and the second with kukui trees and kī (ti) plants.

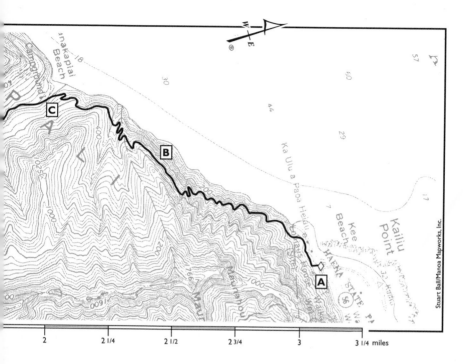

Around the corner from the second ravine is the first good view of the Nāpali Coast.

Work into and out of two more gulches. The last one has a small stream.

The trail straightens out for a while (map point B). Water seeps from the cliffs above.

Work into and out of another ravine.

Descend into a larger gulch on a series of eroded switchbacks.

Cross a double stream and climb out of the gulch.

Descend into Hanakāpī'ai Valley on two switchbacks.

Pass a brown-and-yellow tsunami marker on the right.

Cross Hanakāpī'ai Stream (map point C). If the official ford doesn't appeal to you, walk toward the beach and cross where the stream is wider and shallower.

Climb the opposite bank and reach a three-way junction. Turn sharp left upstream. (The trails straight ahead and to the right through naupaka kahakai lead to several campsites and the beach.)

Shortly afterward reach a junction near a lone ironwood tree. Turn left on the Hanakāpīʻai Falls Trail past a dilapidated shelter. (To the right the Nāpali Coast–Kalalau Trail continues along the coast. Just up the trail is an elevated compost toilet.)

Pass several campsites and a picnic table in a guava grove.

Walk across an open area used as an emergency helipad.

Climb gradually up Hanakāpīʻai Valley well above the stream.

Cross two side gullies. In between are several bamboo stands and huge mango trees. Watch for the white-rumped shama.

The trail levels off through groves of mountain apple and fragrant yellow ginger.

Walk past *loʻi*, rock-walled terraces for growing taro.

Turn right along a small channel of the main stream and then left across a side gully. Along the trail are coffee and mountain apple trees.

Ford the main channel of the stream (map point D).

Cross an island in midstream and then ford a second smaller channel.

Climb gradually along the left bank of Hanakāpīʻai Stream through terraces and coffee and mountain apple groves.

Ford two side streams and pass more terraces and bamboo.

Jog left and then right, climbing well above the stream. Through the trees is the first view of Hanakāpīʻai Falls.

Negotiate a rough, narrow section.

Descend steeply to the main stream over slippery ledges. Watch your footing.

Ford a side stream where it joins the main stream (map point E).

Pass a small waterfall from a tributary on the opposite side. Below the falls is an inviting swimming hole.

Reach a broad open basin (elevation 1,000 feet) (map point F). At the back lovely Hanakāpīʻai Falls cascades into a wide, circular pool. White-tailed tropicbirds soar above the falls along the surrounding cliffs.

Notes:

Hanakāpīʻai Falls is the classic hike in the Islands. It visits both an idyllic white-sand beach and a cascading mountain waterfall. What more could you possibly want? These twin attractions, however, make the hike popular with tourists and locals alike. If you don't like crowds, go during the week and start early.

Summer (May–October) is the best time to take this hike. Hanakāpīʻai Stream is usually lower then and thus easier to ford. The surf and the offshore current along the beach are not as strong in summer. Also, the beautiful white sand goes out to sea during winter, leaving an uninviting jumble of rock.

Several cautions are in order for this hike. The trail along the coast is slippery and eroded in spots. Do not ford the stream if the water is much above your knees. At the beach there are no life-guards. If you decide to swim, you are on your own. Finally, the trail to the falls is usually muddy and mosquitoey, sometimes narrow, and occasionally hard to follow. Look for surveyor's ribbon marking the route. If possible, wear tabis (Japanese reef walkers) with fuzzy bottoms for more secure footing.

Before starting the hike, walk to Kēʻē (avoidance) Beach. A short stroll along the beach to the right leads to a good first view of the Nāpali (the cliffs) Coast. To the left below the cliffs are the remains of a *heiau* (religious site) and a *hālau* hula platform where the ancient hula was performed.

The hike initially follows the Nāpali Coast–Kalalau Trail, an old Hawaiian route connecting the valleys along the coast. The trail was improved in the 1800s and the 1930s. The stone paving on the first section dates from that last upgrade.

Look for hala trees on the way to Hanakāpīʻai Stream. They have distinctive prop roots that help support the heavy clusters of leaves and fruit on the ends of the branches. Early Hawaiians braided the long, pointed leaves, called *lau hala*, into baskets, fans, floor mats, and sails.

About a half mile in is the first spectacular view of the Nāpali Coast. Deep valleys alternate with vertical sea cliffs. Rainfall runoff created the valleys, and wave action formed the cliffs. Where stream erosion has proceeded faster than sea erosion, the stream flows into the ocean at sea level, as at Hanakāpīʻai. The reverse situation creates a hanging valley with a waterfall cascading into the ocean, as at Hanakoa (bay of warriors), farther along the coast. From the view point you can also see the islands of Lehua and Niʻihau in the distance.

After crossing the stream, take the short side trip to the beach. It is crescent-shaped with small caves at each end. In back of the beach is the native low-lying shrub naupaka kahakai. It has bright green, fleshy leaves, and white half-flowers with purple streaks. Its round, white fruits float in the ocean, helping to spread the species to remote areas.

Hanakāpīʻai (bay sprinkling food) was the first valley along the Nāpali Coast to be settled by early Hawaiians. They lived near the beach and grew *kalo* (taro) and other crops in *loʻi* (irrigated terraces) back in the valley. You can still see the rock walls of *loʻi* on the way to the falls.

In the late 1800s Hanakāpīʻai was the site of a coffee plantation complete with a mill. The falls trail passes the wild descendants of the original trees. They have glossy, dark green leaves and white flowers. Their fruit is red, drying to black or brown. Coffee is still commercially grown on the Big Island, where it is sold as Kona coffee.

In the forest look and listen for the white-rumped shama. It is black on top with a chestnut-colored breast and a long black-and-white tail. The shama has a variety of beautiful songs and often mimics other birds. A native of Malaysia, the shama has become widespread in introduced forests such as this one.

Also along the falls trail are extensive groves of mountain apple (ʻōhiʻa ʻai). They have dark, oblong, shiny leaves. In spring their purple flowers carpet the trail. The delicious pink or red fruit usually ripens in late July or early August. If none is in reach, shake the tree and try to catch the apples as they come down. The species is native to Malaysia and was brought by early Hawaiians.

Hanakāpīʻai Falls is a welcome sight after the muddy slog up the valley. Step out on the ledges near the stream to view the falls from a distance. As the trail finally peters out, you emerge from the forest into a vast amphitheater at the back of the valley. At center stage is a dark green, circular pool. Above, the waterfall cascades from a narrow notch in the valley wall. On the sides, the towering, fluted cliffs rise over 2,000 feet to Pōhākea (white stone) peak and Hono o Nāpali (brow of the cliffs).

Take the long swim to the base of the falls. Look for koaʻe kea, the white-tailed tropicbird, soaring overhead. Or just sit and enjoy the wild, rugged beauty of this remote spot.

Instead of taking the falls trail, you can continue on the Nāpali Coast–Kalalau Trail. A good turnaround place is the highest point on the trail, marked by a huge boulder overlooking Hoʻolulu Valley. Total distance round trip for that option is 6.5 miles. The entire coastal trail is 11 miles long one way and makes a memorable backpack. See the appendix for camping information sources.

22 'Ōkolehao

Length:	3.6-mile round trip
Elevation Gain:	1,300 feet
Suitable for:	Intermediate
Location:	Hanalei National Wildlife Refuge and Halele'a Forest Reserve above Hanalei
Topo Map:	Hanalei

Highlights:
This steep climb follows a ridge route established by bootleggers during prohibition. Along the way are delicious strawberry guavas as well as the kī (ti) plants used to make the liquor *'ōkolehao*. From several overlooks you can see Hanalei River and Bay and the peaks surrounding the valley.

Trailhead Directions:
Distance: *(Līhu'e to 'Ōhiki Rd.) 29 miles*
Driving Time: *1 hour*

From Līhu'e take Kūhiō Hwy (Rte 56) north toward Hanalei.
Cross Wailua River on a bridge.
Drive through the town of Kapa'a.
Continue on Kūhiō Hwy along the windward coast.
Pass the turnoff to Kīlauea Lighthouse on the right and then cross a long bridge over Kalihi Wai River.
Pass Princeville Airport on the left and Princeville resort on the right.
Descend into Hanalei Valley and cross the river on a one-lane bridge.
Immediately after the bridge, turn left on narrow, but paved 'Ōhiki Rd.
Enter Hanalei National Wildlife Refuge.
Parallel the river, passing Haraguchi Rice Mill on the right.
Park in a dirt lot on the left (elevation 20 feet) (map point A).

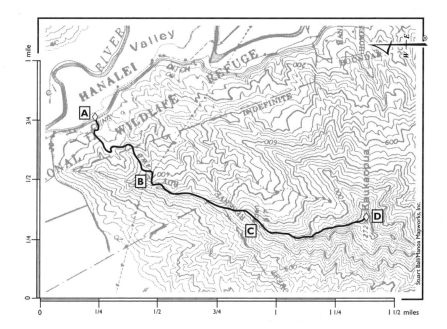

Across the road from the lot is a wooden bridge spanning an irrigation ditch. The lot is 0.6 mile from the main highway.

Route Description:

Take the wooden bridge across China Ditch.

Walk through hau and strawberry guava thickets on a path paved
with stones.

Reach a four-way junction with a dirt road. Turn right on it. (The
path continues a short distance to a *heiau* overlooking the river.)

Reach another junction by a metal gate. Turn left on a dirt road
heading uphill.

Angle steeply up the side of a ridge through koa and eucalyptus
trees.

Switchback once to the right.

Reach the ridge line near a powerline pylon in a grove of Cook
pines (map point B). Turn sharp left up the ridge.

Climb steadily along the up-and-down ridge. Strawberry guava
trees and kī (ti) plants line the trail. Above are eucalyptus and koa

trees and Cook pines. Through openings in the forest you can see Hanalei Valley and the surrounding mountains.

Leave the ridge line briefly to the left and then ascend to the right to regain it.

Climb steeply to a scenic overlook covered with ti and 'awapuhi (shampoo ginger) (map point C). The overlook was once the site of a triangulation station called Roan.

Climb steadily to a small knob in the ridge. The trail becomes rough, narrow, and overgrown in spots.

Descend the back of the knob and resume the steep ascent.

Reach a broad peak, known as Kauka'ōpua (elevation 1,272 feet), where a long side ridge comes in on the left (map point D). On the far side of the summit is a small clearing with good views *mauka*.

Notes:

While the tourist legions are marching to Hanakāpī'ai, try this nearby but less-traveled hike. The route follows a scenic ridge that separates Hanalei (crescent bay) and Wai'oli (joyful water) Valleys. The trail is not graded, though, so the climb is often steep and rough.

Before starting the hike, scan the Hanalei River for waterfowl. You may catch a glimpse of 'alae ke'oke'o, the Hawaiian coot. It is black, except for a white bill and forehead. The coot periodically dives underwater looking for vegetation, mollusks, and insects. 'Alae ke'oke'o is prominent in Hawaiian mythology.

Once on the trail, take the short side trip to the *heiau* (religious site). It overlooks *lo'i* (irrigated terraces) for growing *kalo* (taro) along the river. Namahana is the prominent peak to the right, across the valley.

Look for native koa trees on the climb to the ridge top. They have sickle-shaped foliage and pale yellow flower clusters. Early Hawaiians made surfboards and outrigger canoe hulls out of the beautiful red brown wood. Today it is made into fine furniture.

Strawberry guava trees (waiawī 'ula'ula) line the trail along the ridge. They have glossy, dark green leaves and smooth brown bark. Their dark red fruit is delicious, with a taste reminiscent of strawberries. The guavas usually ripen in late summer (July–September). The tree is a native of Brazil but was introduced to Hawai'i from England in the 1800s.

Also in abundance along the ridge trail are kī (ti) plants. They have shiny leaves, 1–2 feet long, that are arranged spirally in a cluster at the tip of a slender stem. Early Polynesian voyagers introduced ti to Hawai'i. They used the leaves for house thatch, skirts, sandals, and raincoats. Food to be cooked in an *imu* (underground oven) was first wrapped in ti leaves. A popular sport with the commoners was *ho'ohe'e kī* or ti-leaf sliding. The sap from ti roots stained canoes and surfboards.

The ti plant also had a more modern use. During prohibition in the 1920s local moonshiners distilled a liquor, '*ōkolehao*, from ti roots. '*Ōkolehao* means iron bottom, referring to the iron try-pot stills used by the bootleggers. They established this ridge route to cultivate and harvest the plants.

From overlooks along the ridge are marvelous views of Hanalei River, Bay, and town. Along the coast to the east is Kīlauea (spewing) Point and, to the west, Wainiha (unfriendly water) Pali. *Mauka* (inland) is fortresslike Nāmolokama Mountain (the interweaving bound fast). Several waterfalls cascade down its flanks.

At the Roan overlook is a stand of 'awapuhi (shampoo ginger). It is an herb with long, pointed leaves. Leaf stalks arise from a network of knobbed, underground stems. In late summer the plant sends up a flower stalk with an oblong head. Small yellow flowers emerge from the head, one at a time. Squeeze the flower head to get a sudsy, fragrant sap. Like early Hawaiians, you can use it to wash your hands or shampoo your hair.

Beyond the Roan overlook the trail becomes increasingly rough and overgrown. Watch your footing because the vegetation may conceal holes and dropoffs. On the far side of Kauka'ōpua (the horizon clouds alight) is a lookout that makes a good lunch spot and turnaround point.

MAUI

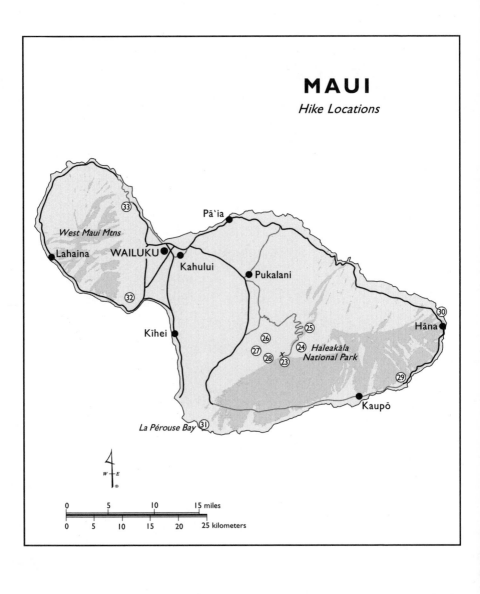

MAUI

Hike Locations

West Maui Mtns

Lahaina

WAILUKU

Kahului

Pāʻia

Pukalani

Kīhei

③③

③②

Kaupō

La Pérouse Bay ③①

⑳⑤

⑳⑥

⑳⑦

⑳⑧ ⑳③ ⑳④ *Haleakāla National Park*

③⓪

Hāna

⑳⑨

W — E

0	5	10	15 miles

0	5	10	15	20	25 kilometers

HALEAKALĀ NATIONAL PARK

23 Kaluʻuokaʻōʻō

Length:	5.0-mile round trip
Elevation Gain:	1,600 feet
Suitable for:	Intermediate
Location:	Maui: Haleakalā National Park
Topo Map:	Kilohana

Highlights:

Kaluʻuokaʻōʻō is a colorful cinder cone protruding from the slopes of Haleakalā, a dormant volcano. Heading down into its vast crater, you see the lovely ʻāhinahina, the Haleakalā silversword. The return uphill is doubly difficult because of sliding sand and the high altitude.

Trailhead Directions:

Distance: *(Kahului to Sliding Sands trailhead) 37 miles*

Driving Time: 1 1/4 hours

From Kahului take Hāna Hwy (Rte 36).

At the first major intersection turn right on Haleakalā Hwy (Rte 37).

Ascend gradually through sugarcane fields.

Pass turnoffs to Pukalani on the right and Makawao on the left.

The highway narrows to two lanes.

Turn left on Rte 377 (still Haleakalā Hwy).

Climb steadily through lush pasture land and stands of fragrant eucalyptus trees.

Pass Kula Lodge on the right.

Turn left on Haleakalā Crater Rd. (Rte 378).

Ascend steeply on a series of short switchbacks through pasture land belonging to Haleakalā Ranch.

Enter Haleakalā National Park and pay the fee at the entrance station.

Pass Park Headquarters on the right (elevation 7,030 feet). It has restrooms, drinking water, and trail information.

On the left pass the parking area for Halemau'u trailhead.

Pass Leleiwi and Kalahaku overlooks, both on the left.

Turn left into the parking area for Haleakalā Visitor Center. Park your car in the near right corner of the lot close to a horse-loading ramp (elevation 9,780 feet) (map point A). The visitor center has restrooms.

Route Description:

The Sliding Sands Trail starts by a wooden bulletin board next to the horse-loading ramp.

Briefly parallel the paved road leading to Pu'u 'Ula'ula (Red Hill), the summit of Haleakalā at 10,023 feet.

Bear left away from the road around Pākao'ao, also known as White Hill.

Reach the rim of the crater and the first of many awesome views. On the horizon to the right are the peaks of Mauna Kea and Mauna Loa on the Big Island.

Descend gradually on five long, lazy switchbacks. The trail crosses an area of gray brown and then red brown cinders known as Keonehe'ehe'e (map point B).

Pass a group of native 'āhinahina (silversword) on the right. The only other vegetation in the vicinity is the native shrubs pūkiawe and kūpaoa.

Reach a signed junction (map point C). Continue straight on a side trail to Kalu'uoka'ō'ō cone. (To the right the main trail descends to the crater floor.)

Descend, steeply at first and then more gradually. Silverswords line the trail.

Traverse a level section and then climb briefly.

Reach the rim of Kalu'uoka'ō'ō cone (elevation 8,400 feet) (map point D).

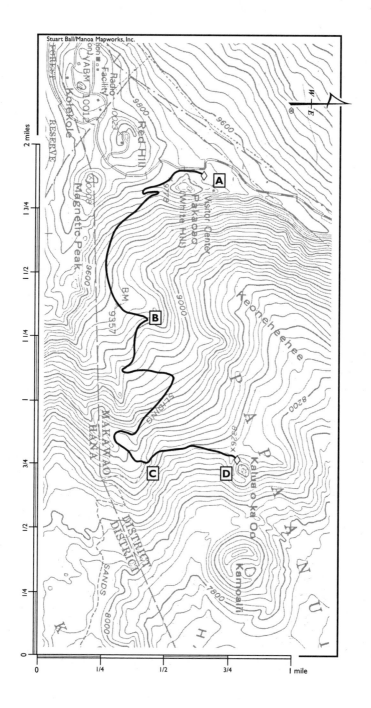

Notes:
The descent to Kalu'uoka'ō'ō (the plunge of the digging stick) cone provides a superb half-day introduction to hiking in Haleakalā (house of the sun) crater. The route is short, but the elevation gain is considerable, and the footing is over loose sand and cinders. As you are barreling down the trail, remember that what goes down must come up.

Leaving the visitor center parking lot, you quickly reach the crater rim with its panoramic view. Directly below is Kalu'uoka'ō'ō, our destination. It is the first in a line of three cinder cones leading down to the crater floor. The other two larger ones are Kama'oli'i (small native cotton bush) and Pu'u o Māui (hill of Māui).

On the left (northeast) are Kalahaku (proclaim the lord) Pali (cliff) and Leleiwi (bone altar) Pali. Beyond is Ko'olau (windward) Gap, descending to the north coast of Maui. To the east at the far end of the crater lies green Palikū (vertical cliff). To the right of Palikū and out of sight is Kaupō (landing at night) Gap, descending to the south coast of the island.

Haleakalā is a dormant volcano, but its "crater" is not really a volcanic one. The vast double amphitheater before you is more the result of wind and water erosion than volcanic activity. From opposite sides of the island two streams eroded headward and met to form a "crater." Lava from vents near the summit partially filled both deep valleys to create the wide Ko'olau and Kaupō Gaps. More recent volcanic activity produced the colorful cinder cones dotting the crater floor. The last eruption of Haleakalā was in 1790. In that eruption two small flows from the southwest rift zone outside the crater reached the ocean.

The first plant you see in the crater is 'āhinahina, the Haleakalā silversword. It has narrow, silver green leaves and a tall flower stalk. The leaves are covered with tiny hairs to conserve moisture and protect the plant from the intense sun. Other adaptations include a deep tap root to anchor the plant in high winds and a wide network of surface roots to collect water. The silversword usually grows for 15–20 years before flowering. The flower stalks usually appear in summer or early fall and have purple blossoms. After the seeds develop, the entire plant dies. Silverswords are endemic to Hawai'i, meaning they are found nowhere else. Don't approach mature plants too closely, and don't step on the baby ones.

Just after the start of the side trail to the cone, look for a huge boulder on the right. Its flat top makes a great lunch or snack spot. Spend some time there watching the interplay of sun and clouds on cones and cliffs. Let your mind drift back to ancient times, when Haleakalā was the home of Līlīnoe, a goddess of mists. She had the power to halt the eruptions from the cinder cones on the crater floor. Sometimes she clothed the summit ridge with a mantle of snow.

After reaching Kaluʻuokaʻōʻō cone, take the rough trail around its rim. The deep vent below is multicolored from the different minerals in the lava. Fiery reds and oranges predominate, but all the colors in the spectrum are there.

On the way back you rapidly learn why the trail is called Sliding Sands. The climbing is two steps forward, then one step back. Because of the high elevation, walk at a slow, but steady pace. Stop periodically to catch your breath and admire the view.

24 Sliding Sands–Halemauʻu

Length:	12.1-mile loop
Elevation Gain:	1,500 feet
Suitable for:	Expert
Location:	Maui: Haleakalā National Park
Topo Map:	Kilohana, Nāhiku

Highlights:

This magnificent loop hike winds through the vast, eroded crater of Haleakalā, a once-active volcano. Along the way are towering cliffs, colorful cinder cones, and dark lava tubes. Much in evidence are two threatened species, nēnē, the Hawaiian goose, and ʻāhinahina, the Haleakalā silversword.

Trailhead Directions:

Distance: *(Kahului to Sliding Sands trailhead) 37 miles*

Driving Time: *1 1/4 hours*

From Kahului take Hāna Hwy (Rte 36).

At the first major intersection turn right on Haleakalā Hwy (Rte 37).

Ascend gradually through sugarcane fields.

Pass turnoffs to Pukalani on the right and Makawao on the left.

The highway narrows to two lanes.

Turn left on Rte 377 (still Haleakalā Hwy).

Climb steadily through lush pasture land and stands of fragrant eucalyptus trees.

Pass Kula Lodge on the right.

Turn left on Haleakalā Crater Rd. (Rte 378).

Ascend steeply on a series of short switchbacks through pasture land belonging to Haleakalā Ranch.

Enter Haleakalā National Park and pay the fee at the entrance station.

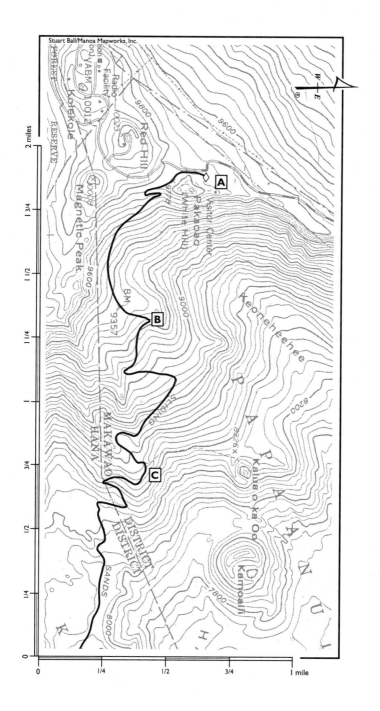

Stuart Ball/Manoa Mapworks, Inc.

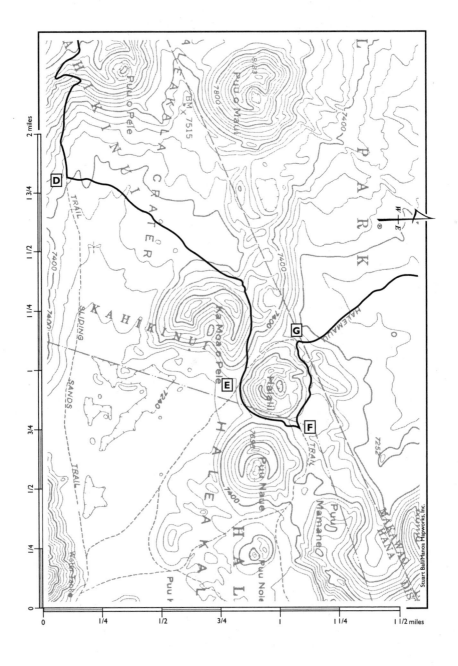

Pass Park Headquarters on the right (elevation 7,030 feet). It has restrooms, drinking water, and trail information.

On the left pass the parking area for Halemau'u trailhead (elevation 7,990 feet) (map point M). The hike ends there.

Pass Leleiwi and Kalahaku overlooks, both on the left.

Turn left into the parking area for Haleakalā Visitor Center. Park your car in the near right corner of the lot close to a horse-loading ramp (elevation 9,780 feet) (map point A). If you have two cars, drop off people and packs and shuttle one car back to Halemau'u trailhead. The visitor center has restrooms.

Route Description:
The Sliding Sands Trail starts by a wooden bulletin board next to the horse-loading ramp.

Briefly parallel the paved road leading to Pu'u 'Ula'ula (Red Hill), the summit of Haleakalā at 10,023 feet.

Bear left away from the road around Pākao'ao, also known as White Hill.

Reach the rim of the crater and the first of many awesome views. On the horizon to the right are the peaks of Mauna Kea and Mauna Loa on the Big Island.

Descend gradually on five long, lazy switchbacks (map point B). The trail crosses an area of gray brown and then red brown cinders known as Keonehe'ehe'e.

Pass a group of native 'āhinahina (silversword) on the right. The only other vegetation in the vicinity is the native shrubs pūkiawe and kūpaoa.

Reach a signed junction (map point C). Turn right, between two boulders and a lone 'ōhelo bush. The side trail straight ahead leads down to a view into Kalu'uoka'ō'ō cone.

Continue the descent on three switchbacks. The trail briefly crosses rough 'a'ā lava. Watch your footing on the loose rock.

Pass a patch of silverswords.

Cross a relatively flat area covered with red cinders. Silverswords line the trail. Kama'oli'i and Pu'u o Māui cones are on the left at a distance.

Pass Puʻu o Pele, a red cinder cone, close by on the left.

Descend to the crater floor on two switchbacks through kīlau (bracken) ferns.

Reach a signed junction by a hitching post and a māmane tree (map point D). Turn left on a side trail across the crater. (The Sliding Sands Trail continues straight, to Kapalaoa Cabin.)

Cross an old ʻaʻā flow partially buried by cinders.

Pass a small patch of silverswords. Also in this area are ʻōhelo and kūkaenēnē shrubs.

Climb steadily up the left side of Kamoa o Pele cone on red cinders. Dead ahead, at the top of the saddle, is Halāliʻi cone. In the distance along the rim is Hanakauhi peak (elevation 8,907 feet).

Descend briefly to a signed junction (map point E). Continue straight to Bottomless Pit. (The trail to the left is a shortcut to Hōlua Cabin.)

Shortly afterward reach another signed junction. This time keep left to Bottomless Pit. (To the right a side trail heads back across the crater to Kapalaoa Cabin. You can just see it near the foot of the crater wall. To the left of the cabin is vegetated Puʻu Maile cone.)

Circle Halāliʻi cone. On the right is a large red gray cone, known as Puʻu Naue.

Reach a signed junction at Bottomless Pit (map point F). Turn left on the Halemauʻu Trail toward Hōlua Cabin. (To the right the trail leads to Palikū Cabin.)

Continue to circle the base of Halāliʻi cone. At its far side are views down Koʻolau Gap and across the crater to Kalahaku and Leleiwi Palis.

Reach a signed junction (map point G). Bear right to Hōlua Cabin. (The left fork leads back to Sliding Sands Trail.)

Descend briefly and cross a basin covered with black sand, cinders, and lava rock.

Climb out of the basin on red cinders.

Reach a signed junction (map point H). Turn right on the Silversword Loop. (The main trail continues straight, to Hōlua Cabin.)

Wind through red brown cinders dotted with silverswords.

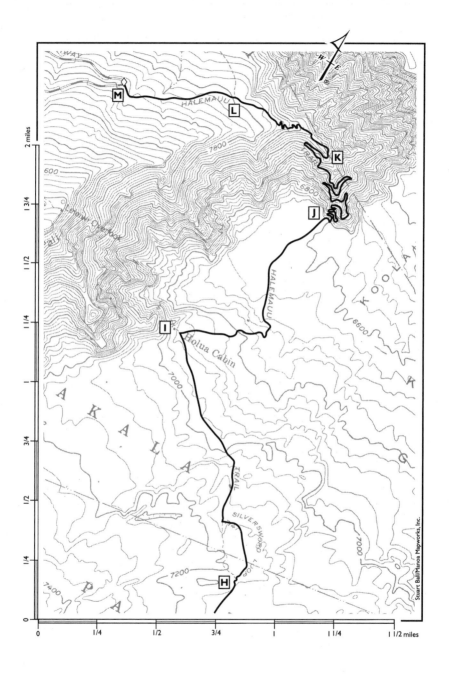

Reach a signed junction with the main trail and turn right on it.

Enter an old ʻaʻā flow partially covered with native vegetation. Look for māmane trees, and ʻaʻaliʻi, ʻōhelo, kūkaenēnē, and pūkiawe shrubs. In the distance you can see Hōlua Cabin nestled against the crater wall.

Descend briefly on a rough trail.

Reach a signed junction in front of Hōlua Cabin (map point I). Turn right on the main trail. (The trail straight ahead leads to the cabin and campground.)

Descend Koʻolau Gap, gradually at first and then more steeply through ridges of jumbled-up ʻaʻā lava.

Work left toward the crater wall as the angle of descent eases.

Cross a meadow covered with evening primrose.

Reach the base of the cliff by a wooden gate and a hitching post (map point J). Go through the gate, closing it behind you.

Begin climbing the crater wall on seven short switchbacks. The views back into the crater are spectacular. On the way up look for ʻōhelo and pūkiawe shrubs and ʻamaʻu and kīlau ferns. The young fronds of the ʻamaʻu are bright red.

Switchbacks eight through twelve are much longer and repeatedly cross a prominent side ridge in the cliff. You can now see down Koʻolau Gap as well as back into the crater.

After the twelfth switchback, follow the side ridge straight up (map point K).

Resume switchbacking as the slope steepens. The switchbacks are short and roughly parallel a fence on the right.

After the twentieth and last switchback (yes!), reach a metal gate at the crater rim. Go through the gate, closing it behind you.

Reach a junction (map point L). Keep left on the main trail. (The supply trail to the right leads down to Hosmer Grove campground.)

Ascend gradually along the slopes of Haleakalā below the crater rim. The trail is rough and eroded in spots.

Reach Halemauʻu trailhead and parking lot (elevation 7,990 feet) (map point M). If your only car is parked at Sliding Sands trailhead, hitchhike back up to it.

Notes:

The Sliding Sands–Halemau'u loop is the best day hike on Maui. The winding route provides a close-up look at the volcanic features of Haleakalā (house of the sun) crater and at the plants and birds that live there. The route also provides a challenge. It starts with a long descent on loose cinders and ends with a steep climb on narrow switchbacks. Get an early start because of the high mileage and the many points of interest.

Leaving the visitor center parking lot, you quickly reach the crater rim with its panoramic view. To the left (northeast) are Kalahaku (proclaim the lord) and Leleiwi (bone altar) Palis (cliff). Beyond is Ko'olau (windward) Gap, descending to the north coast of Maui. To the east at the far end of the crater lies green Palikū (vertical cliff). To the right of Palikū and out of sight is Kaupō (landing at night) Gap, descending to the south coast of the island.

Haleakalā is a dormant volcano, but its "crater" is not really a volcanic one. The vast double amphitheater before you is more the result of wind and water erosion than volcanic activity. From opposite sides of the island two streams eroded headward and met to form a "crater." Lava from vents near the summit partially filled both deep valleys to create the wide Ko'olau and Kaupō Gaps. More recent volcanic activity produced the colorful cinder cones dotting the crater floor. The last eruption of Haleakalā was in 1790. In that eruption two small flows from the southwest rift zone outside the crater reached the ocean.

Much of the loop hike becomes visible as you start the descent to the crater floor. Look for the Sliding Sands Trail in front and below. Try to pick out the Halemau'u (grass house) Trail as it emerges from a jumble of cones and traverses Ko'olau Gap to Hōlua (sled) Cabin. Beyond the cabin are the switchbacks climbing the crater wall.

The first plant you see in the crater is native 'āhinahina, the Haleakalā silversword. It has narrow silver green leaves and a tall flower stalk. The leaves are covered with tiny hairs to conserve moisture and protect the plant from the intense sun. Other adaptations include a deep tap root to anchor the plant in high winds and a wide network of surface roots to collect water. The silversword usually grows for 15–20 years before flowering. The flower stalks usually appear in summer or early fall and have purple blossoms. After the seeds develop, the entire plant dies. Silverswords are endemic to Hawai'i, meaning they are found nowhere else. Don't approach mature plants too closely, and don't step on the baby ones.

The middle section of the route meanders through a group of large cinder cones dotted with silverswords. According to Hawaiian legend, the cones are the handiwork of Pele, the goddess of fire. She stopped at Haleakalā on her way to the Big Island, where she currently resides in Kīlauea (spewing) Volcano. Pele created the cinder cones and the Bottomless Pit with her magic digging tool, Pā'oa.

The native dry-land vegetation at the far side of Ko'olau Gap is a welcome sight after the colorful but desolate cones. The plants have taken hold on an older 'a'ā flow that receives some moisture from the clouds advancing up the gap. Watch for māmane trees, and 'a'ali'i, pūkiawe, and 'ōhelo shrubs. Māmane has downy, oblong leaflets and clusters of bright yellow flowers. 'A'ali'i has narrow, shiny leaves and red seed capsules. Pūkiawe has tiny, rigid leaves and small white, pink, or red berries. 'Ōhelo has rounded leaves and juicy red yellow berries, about the size of blueberries. Both hikers and nēnē agree that 'ōhelo berries are delicious; try them.

The area around Hōlua Cabin makes a good rest stop before the climb out of the crater. Near the cabin are pit toilets and a water faucet. The water, however, should be boiled, filtered, or chemically treated. If you have time, explore a nearby lava tube. The directions are listed in the Notes section of the Hōlua hike.

At Hōlua Cabin you may see your first nēnē, the Hawaiian goose. The nēnē has a black face and head and a gray brown body. It lives on dry, rugged lava flows at high elevation and so has lost much of the webbing on its feet. Like its Canadian counterpart, the nēnē is a strong flyer and often honks in midflight. The nēnē is an endangered species and should be treated with respect. Don't feed them.

The Halemau'u Trail climbs out of the crater on 20 switchbacks. The path is graded, although narrow in spots. While ascending, maintain a slow but steady pace. Stop to rest occasionally and admire the view, if there is any. In the early afternoon clouds frequently ride up Koʻolau Gap and shroud the cliffs in swirling mist and cold rain.

The hike ends at Halemauʻu trailhead, which is about 6 miles from and 1,800 feet below the start of the loop. If your only car is at Sliding Sands trailhead, you could walk up the road; that is, if you have any energy left. A better alternative is to hitchhike. Rides are usually easy to catch with fellow hikers or tourists driving to the summit.

25 Hōlua

Length:	7.8-mile round trip
Elevation Gain:	1,700 feet
Suitable for:	Intermediate
Location:	Maui: Haleakalā National Park
Topo Map:	Kilohana

Highlights:

This awesome hike descends a sheer *pali* (cliff) into the crater of Haleakalā, a once-active volcano. The destination is a dark lava tube near Hōlua Cabin at the top of Koʻolau Gap. By the cabin you may encounter nēnē, the endangered Hawaiian goose.

Trailhead Directions:

Distance: (Kahului to Halemauʻu trailhead) 31 miles

Driving Time: 1 hour

From Kahului take Hāna Hwy (Rte 36).

At the first major intersection turn right on Haleakalā Hwy (Rte 37).

Ascend gradually through sugarcane fields.

Pass turnoffs to Pukalani on the right and Makawao on the left. The highway narrows to two lanes.

Turn left on Rte 377 (still Haleakalā Hwy).

Climb steadily through lush pasture land and stands of fragrant eucalyptus trees.

Pass Kula Lodge on the right.

Turn left on Haleakalā Crater Rd. (Rte 378).

Ascend steeply on a series of short switchbacks through pasture land belonging to Haleakalā Ranch.

Enter Haleakalā National Park and pay the fee at the entrance station.

Pass Park Headquarters on the right (elevation 7,030 feet). It has restrooms, drinking water, and trail information.

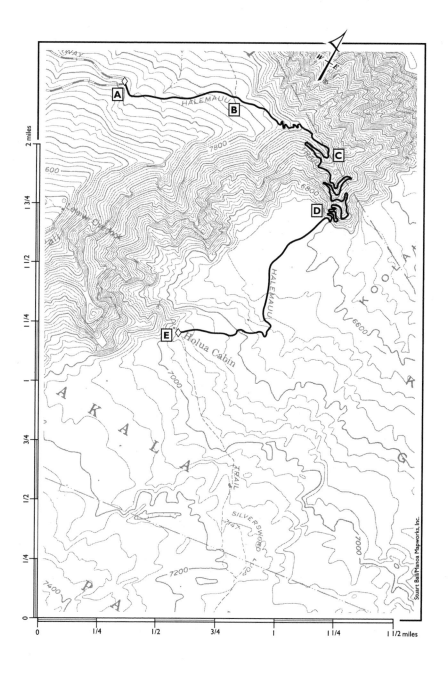

At the fourth switchback turn left to the Halemau'u trailhead.

Park in the large lot there (elevation 7,990 feet) (map point A). The lot has a portable toilet.

Route Description:

At the far end of the parking lot by a wooden bulletin board pick up the Halemau'u Trail.

Descend gradually along the slopes of Haleakalā below the crater rim. The trail is rough and eroded in spots.

Reach a junction (map point B). Keep right on the main trail. (The supply trail to the left leads down to Hosmer Grove campground.)

Go through a metal gate, closing it behind you.

Begin to switchback as the slope steepens. The trail roughly parallels a fence on the left.

Follow a prominent side ridge straight down (map point C). The views begin to open up on all sides.

Descend on five long switchbacks that repeatedly cross the side ridge. Look for 'ama'u and kīlau (bracken) ferns and 'ōhelo and pūkiawe shrubs along the trail.

Continue the steep descent on seven shorter switchbacks.

By a wooden gate and a hitching post reach the crater floor (map point D). Go through the gate, closing it behind you.

Cross a meadow covered with evening primrose.

Work left, away from the crater wall and begin to climb.

Ascend steadily through ridges of jumbled-up 'a'ā lava.

Reach a signed junction (elevation 6,900 feet) (map point E). To the right a short trail leads to Hōlua Cabin and campground. Look for nēnē hanging around the cabin.

To go to the lava tube, turn left on the Halemau'u Trail toward Palikū.

On the left pass a pit, which is actually part of a collapsed lava tube.

Just past the pit, turn right on a rough, makeshift trail. It may or may not be marked with small *ahu* (cairns).

Cross a brief stretch of *pāhoehoe* lava and then resume climbing on 'a'ā.

Reach a collapsed area that is the entrance to the lava tube.

Descend into the tube by means of a ladder.

At the bottom of the ladder walk straight ahead. (The tube also extends to the left behind you.)

Go around to the right of a boulder.

Climb steadily.

At the first fork keep left and up.

See a tiny shaft of light in the distance.

At the second fork keep left and down.

Exit through the second opening in the ceiling.

On the right pick up an obscure trail that leads back to the campground and the cabin.

Notes:

The Hōlua (sled) hike follows a short, steep, spectacular route to the floor of Haleakalā crater. Watch your footing on the narrow switchbacks; don't look and walk at the same time. Start early to ensure good views on the way down. In the early afternoon clouds frequently ride up Koʻolau (windward) Gap and shroud the cliffs in swirling mist and cold rain.

After a short traverse of the upper slopes of the volcano, the Halemauʻu (grass house) Trail reaches the crater rim and the first of many breathtaking views. To the north Koʻolau (windward) Gap descends abruptly toward the windward coast. Beyond is green Keʻanae (the mullet) Valley ending at a peninsula and village of the same name. To the east across the gap is Hanakauhi (the cover bay) Peak (elevation 8,907 feet). To the south are the sheer cliffs of Leleiwi (bone altar) Pali with the crater floor 2,000 feet below.

In addition to views, you can see various native shrubs and ferns along the switchbacks. Pūkiawe has tiny, rigid leaves and small white, pink, or red berries. ʻŌhelo has rounded leaves and delicious red yellow berries, about the size of blueberries. ʻAmaʻu ferns have short trunks, usually 1 to 2 feet high. Their fronds are bright red when young, gradually turning green with age.

The area around Hōlua Cabin makes a good rest stop before investigating the lava tube. Near the cabin are pit toilets and a water faucet. The water, however, should be boiled, filtered, or chemically treated.

At Hōlua Cabin you may see your first nēnē, the Hawaiian goose.

The nēnē has a black face and head and a gray brown body. It lives on dry, rugged lava flows at high elevation and so has lost much of the webbing on its feet. Like its Canadian counterpart, the nēnē is a strong flyer and often honks in midflight. The nēnē is an endangered species and should be treated with respect. Don't feed them.

The short walk underground through the lava tube is exciting, but a bit scary. The middle section of the tube is absolutely pitch black. Bring a powerful flashlight and extra batteries. Watch your head and hands because the lava lining the tube is often sharp and brittle. Wear a hat and gloves if possible.

Lava tubes are usually formed in *pāhoehoe* flows that are confined, such as in a gully. The top and edges of the flow cool and crust over. The lava inside continues to flow through the resulting tunnel. Eventually, the flow diminishes and stops, leaving a tube.

After the dark walk underground, sun and sky are a welcome sight. In Hawaiian, Haleakalā means house of the sun. According to legend, the sun traveled so quickly across the sky that the farmers and fishermen did not have enough time to plant crops and catch fish before night fell. The demigod Māui went to Haleakalā, where the sun's rays first struck the island. There Māui snared the sun with 16 great ropes. In return for his freedom the sun promised to travel more slowly across the sky during summer. Māui let the sun go but left some ropes tied to the sun to remind him of his promise. The people then had more time to catch fish and grow their crops. At sunset you can still see the white ropes trailing through the sky.

If you have time and energy after exploring the lava tube, continue along the Halemau'u Trail to the Silversword Loop. The loop winds through red brown cinders dotted with 'āhinahina, the Haleakalā silversword. It has narrow, silver green leaves and a tall flower stalk. The silversword is a threatened species and is found only in Hawai'i. This side trip adds about 2.5 miles to the hike.

The climb back out of Haleakalā crater is not as bad as it looks. While ascending, maintain a slow but steady pace. Stop to rest occasionally and admire the view, if there is any. Before you know it, you are on top, and the parking lot is in sight.

KULA

26 Waiakoa Loop

Length:	4.5-mile loop
Elevation Gain:	700 feet
Suitable for:	Novice
Location:	Maui: Kula Forest Reserve above Kula
Topo Map:	Kilohana

Highlights:

This short, pleasant walk loops through grassland and pine forest on the slopes of Haleakalā, a dormant volcano. Along the way are dry, rocky gulches lined with native 'ōhi'a trees. You may also see some native birds, such as 'alauahio, the Maui creeper.

Trailhead Directions:

Distance: (Kahului to Waiakoa trailhead) 24 miles

Driving Time: 1 hour

From Kahului take Hāna Hwy (Rte 36).

At the first major intersection turn right on Haleakalā Hwy (Rte 37).

Ascend gradually through sugarcane fields.

Pass turnoffs to Pukalani on the right and Makawao on the left.

After the highway narrows to two lanes, reach the first intersection with Rte 377 to Haleakalā. Continue straight on Kula Hwy (still Rte 37).

At the second intersection with Rte 377 turn left on Haleakalā Hwy. Reset your trip odometer.

Turn right on Waipoli Rd. (0.4 mile). It's the first road on the right with a stop sign.

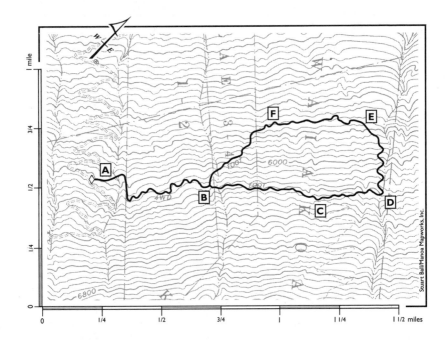

Ascend steadily through a eucalyptus forest.

After going over a cattle grate, the road becomes Polipoli Access Rd.

Switchback steadily through pasture land.

Reach a hunter check-in station on the left (5.4 miles). Park well off the road near the station (elevation 6,020 feet) (map point A).

Route Description:

Take the dirt road on the left just past the hunter check-in station.

Descend briefly and cross Kaʻonoʻulu Gulch.

The road jogs right, climbs steadily, and then jogs left.

Contour through open eucalyptus and pine forest. Ignore side tracks up and down slope. To the left you can see the West Maui Mountains.

Reach the end of the road and the start of the Waiakoa Loop Trail. Orient yourself using the colorful trail map etched in wood.

Proceed through a gate in the barbed-wire fence.

Continue to contour through pines, crossing a gully.

The trail forks, forming the loop portion of the hike (map point B). Keep right and up on the wider path.

Cross Nāʻalae Gulch and then a second smaller one.

Break out into open grassland. To the left are superb views of the West Maui Mountains.

Cross four more small gulches. The second one has an inviting slide and pool, except there is rarely any water! The gulches are all lined with native ʻōhiʻa trees.

Reach a signed junction (elevation 6,250 feet) (map point C). Continue straight on the loop trail. (To the right the Waiakoa Trail connects with the Māmane and Skyline Trails.)

Continue to contour through open grassland dotted with the native shrub pūkiawe.

Cross Keāhuaiwi Gulch (map point D), switchback once, and recross it. Look for native māmane trees in this section.

Descend steadily on five switchbacks through scattered pūkiawe and ʻōhelo shrubs.

Reenter the pine forest.

Continue to descend, first on switchbacks and then straight down.

Reach an unmarked junction (map point E). Turn left on an old dirt road.

Almost immediately, cross a gulch. On the left a short side trail leads to a lovely ʻōhiʻa and fern grotto.

Contour again, crossing several small gulches. The forest here is mostly introduced Monterey pine.

Bear left off the road (map point F) and climb steadily on six switchbacks. Look for the small, yellow green native bird called ʻalauahio (the Maui creeper).

Reach the familiar fork, completing the loop (map point B).

Backtrack to the hunter check-in station (map point A).

Notes:

The Waiakoa (water used by warriors) Loop is a gem of a hike— short, scenic, and absolutely delightful. Savor this walk; don't rush it. Look for native birds, identify some of the trees and shrubs, and enjoy the crisp mountain air.

Take this hike in the morning. Later in the day, clouds frequently roll in and blanket the slopes in mist and light rain. The loop is described counterclockwise. That way the downslope view from the grassland opens up in front of you. You can, of course, walk the route in either direction.

The loop passes through country that was once covered with a native forest of koa, ʻōhiʻa, and māmane trees. In the 1800s cattle and goat grazing and logging for firewood and fence posts destroyed much of the original forest. You can still see some remnant ʻōhiʻa lining the rocky gulches. The trees have oval, dull green leaves and clusters of delicate red flowers. Native birds, such as the ʻapapane, feed on the nectar and help with pollination.

If you're lucky, you may catch a glimpse of an ʻapapane in the forest canopy. It has a red breast and head, black wings and tail, and a slightly curved black bill. In flight the ʻapapane makes a whirring sound as it darts from tree to tree searching for insects and nectar.

In the grassland native māmane trees and pūkiawe and ʻōhelo shrubs are making a comeback. Māmane has downy, oblong leaflets and clusters of bright yellow flowers. Pūkiawe has tiny, rigid leaves and small white, pink, or red berries. ʻŌhelo has rounded leaves and delicious red yellow berries, about the size of blueberries.

The return portion of the loop goes through a forest of introduced pines planted for watershed protection. One of the species represented is a native of California, the Monterey pine. It has 4-inch needles arranged in bunches of three. The cones are lopsided at the base; the outer side has greatly swollen scales tipped with a short point.

In the pine groves you may see ʻalauahio, the native Maui creeper. It is a small, yellow green bird with a short, straight bill. Creepers move about the forest understory, taking insects from the vegetation. They frequently travel in small family groups.

27 Polipoli Loop

Length:	4.9-mile loop
Elevation Gain:	1,200 feet
Suitable for:	Novice, Intermediate
Location:	Maui: Polipoli Springs State Recreation Area and Kula Forest Reserve above Kula
Topo Map:	Lualaʻilua Hills, Mākena

Highlights:

The Polipoli Loop is a mainland-style hike with a touch of local color. The route winds through dense stands of pine, redwood, and other introduced evergreens on the slopes of Haleakalā. In the clearings you may catch a glimpse of some of the flashy native birds.

Trailhead Directions:

Distance: *(Kahului to Polipoli Springs State Recreation Area)*
            29 miles

Driving Time: *1 1/2 hours*

From Kahului take Hāna Hwy (Rte 36).

At the first major intersection turn right on Haleakalā Hwy (Rte 37).

Ascend gradually through sugarcane fields.

Pass turnoffs to Pukalani on the right and Makawao on the left.

After the highway narrows to two lanes, reach the first intersection with Rte 377 to Haleakalā. Continue straight on Kula Hwy (still Rte 37).

At the second intersection with Rte 377 turn left on Haleakalā Hwy. Reset your trip odometer.

Turn right on Waipoli Rd. (0.4 mile). It's the first road on the right with a stop sign.

Ascend steadily through a eucalyptus forest.

After going over a cattle grate, the road becomes Polipoli Access Rd.

Switchback steadily through pasture land.

Pass a hunter check-in station on the left (5.4 miles).

The pavement ends (6.3 miles).

Go over another cattle grate and pass the junction with the Boundary Trail (6.8 miles).

The dirt road forks (9.7 miles). Bear right and down. (The left fork climbs to the Skyline switchback.)

Reach the end of the road at Polipoli Springs State Recreation Area (10.3 miles). Park in the small lot there (elevation 6,160 feet) (map point A). The Polipoli area has drinking water, a toilet, covered picnic tables, and a small campground. Nearby is a lone housekeeping cabin.

Route Description:

Walk across the grassy picnic and camping area toward a colorful trail map etched in wood.

Just past the map pick up the Polipoli Trail.

Contour through Monterey pine and cypress. Look for a small yellow green native bird called 'alauahio (the Maui creeper).

Climb gradually and skirt a grassy opening in the forest.

Shortly afterward reach a signed junction with the Haleakalā Ridge Trail (map point B). Turn right on it. (To the left the ridge trail climbs to the start of the Skyline Trail at the Skyline switchback.)

Descend steadily around Polipoli Peak (elevation 6,472 feet) through eucalyptus and introduced evergreens.

As the main trail turns sharp right, reach an unmarked junction (map point C). For now take the side trail to the left.

The side trail forks. The left fork descends briefly to a cool, damp cave in a cinder cone. The right fork leads to a spectacular overlook of the leeward coast. Across 'Alenuihāhā Channel is the Big Island with its four volcanic peaks. From left to right they are Mauna Kea, Kohala, Mauna Loa, and Hualālai. Look for the native shrub pūkiawe behind the overlook.

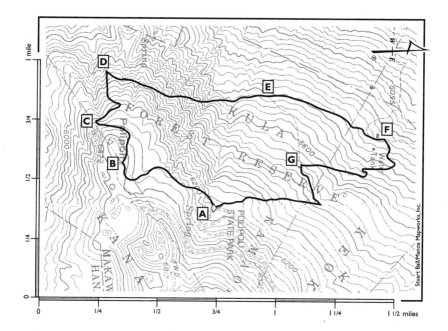

Retrace your steps to the main trail and continue down the broad ridge. Switchback twice in the steeper sections.

The trail veers right across the ridge.

Shortly afterward reach a signed junction with the Plum Trail (map point D). Turn right on it.

Descend gradually, across slopes planted with cedar and cypress.

Cross several dry gullies. Through the trees are views of the West Maui Mountains.

The trail enters a more open stand of tropical ash.

Reach a signed junction (map point E). Continue straight on the Plum Trail. (To the right the Tie Trail connects with the Redwood Trail.)

Walk through alternating groves of tropical ash and introduced evergreens.

On the left pass a dilapidated bunkhouse, built by the Civilian Conservation Corps.

Just after the bunkhouse, reach a signed junction (map point F).

Continue straight and up on the Redwood Trail. (To the left and down is the Boundary Trail that leads to the Waiohuli Trail and Polipoli Access Rd.)

Pass an abandoned ranger cabin on the right. The trail is lined with hydrangea.

Begin climbing through a grove of redwood trees.

Switchback three times to gain elevation comfortably.

By a spreading cedar reach another signed junction (map point G). Keep left, still on the Redwood Trail. (To the right the Tie Trail leads back to the Plum Trail.)

Pass a small shelter on the right.

Ascend gradually on two long switchbacks through introduced evergreens.

The Redwood Trail widens briefly and then ends at a cabin. Walk up the road from the cabin.

Reach a junction with Polipoli Access Rd. Turn right on it to return to the parking lot (map point A).

Notes:

The Polipoli Loop looks and feels just like a forest walk on the mainland. Groves of tall redwood trees remind you of northern California. Stands of pine and ash are reminiscent of the Appalachian Mountains. Only from the overlook, with the ocean below and the Big Island in the distance, is it clear that you are actually on Maui.

Morning is the best time to take this hike. Later in the day, clouds frequently roll in and envelop the slopes in mist and light rain. A late afternoon walk through the redwoods makes for a dark, eerie experience.

The drive to the trailhead is long and a bit rough. The last 4 miles are over a dusty dirt road. Although rocky in spots, the road is passable for two-wheel-drive vehicles under dry conditions. If the dirt road is muddy from a heavy rainstorm, try the Waiakoa Loop hike instead.

If not crowded, the picnic area is actually a good place to bird-watch. Look for the native 'apapane high in the forest canopy. It has a red breast and head, black wings and tail, and a slightly curved black bill. In flight the 'apapane makes a whirring sound as it darts from tree to tree searching for insects and nectar. Other birds that may frequent the area are the yellow green 'amakihi and the red-billed leiothrix.

Behind the camping area check out the route on the colorful wooden trail map. The Polipoli Loop is pieced together from four separate trails: the Polipoli, Haleakalā (house of the sun) Ridge, Plum, and Redwood. All four are well graded, and the junctions are well marked. The route is described clockwise, so you take the right fork at each major intersection.

The hike passes through country that was once covered with a native forest of koa, 'ōhi'a, and māmane trees. In the 1800s cattle and goat grazing and logging for firewood and fence posts destroyed much of the original forest. In 1912 the Polipoli area became part of the Kula Forest Reserve. To restore the watershed, the Division of Forestry began to plant trees in the 1920s. Over the next decade the Civilian Conservation Corps (CCC) continued the project, planting over 1,000 acres in introduced pines, cedar, cypress, redwoods, and tropical ash. The route goes by one of the old CCC work camps.

On the trail look for one of the introduced trees, the Monterey pine from California. It has 4-inch needles arranged in bunches of three. The cones are lopsided at the base; the outer side has greatly swollen scales tipped with a short point.

In the pine groves you may see 'alauahio, the native Maui creeper. It is a small, yellow green bird with a short, straight bill. Creepers move about the forest understory, taking insects from the vegetation. They frequently travel in small family groups.

The return portion of the loop winds through dark, damp stands of towering redwood trees. Their bark is red brown, soft, and heavily furrowed. They have narrow leaves, about 3/4 inch long. Underneath is a prominent midrib with whitish bands on either side.

Although the loop is described clockwise, you can, of course, walk it in either direction. To shorten the loop, take the Tie Trail. For a longer hike, check the wooden trail map. The Polipoli area has 10 different trails; you could easily spend several enjoyable days walking all of them.

28 Skyline Trail

Length:	15.0-mile round trip
Elevation Gain:	3,500 feet
Suitable for:	Intermediate, Expert
Location:	Maui: Kula and Kahikinui Forest Reserves above Kula, and Haleakalā National Park
Topo Map:	Lualaʻilua Hills, Kilohana

Highlights:

This arduous climb follows the southwest rift zone of Haleakalā, a dormant volcano. The goal is Puʻu ʻUlaʻula, the true summit at 10,023 feet. Along the way are native dry-land vegetation, colorful cinder cones, deep pit craters, and, quite possibly, a headache from the high altitude.

Trailhead Directions:

Distance: *(Kahului to Skyline switchback) 29 miles*

Driving Time: *1 1/2 hours*

From Kahului take Hāna Hwy (Rte 36).

At the first major intersection turn right on Haleakalā Hwy (Rte 37).

Ascend gradually through sugarcane fields.

Pass turnoffs to Pukalani on the right and Makawao on the left.

After the highway narrows to two lanes, reach the first intersection with Rte 377 to Haleakalā. Continue straight on Kula Hwy (still Rte 37).

At the second intersection with Rte 377 turn left on Haleakalā Hwy. Reset your trip odometer.

Turn right on Waipoli Rd. (0.4 mile). It's the first road on the right with a stop sign.

Ascend steadily through a eucalyptus forest.

After going over a cattle grate, the road becomes Polipoli Access Rd.

Switchback steadily through pasture land.

Pass a hunter check-in station on the left (5.4 miles).

The pavement ends (6.3 miles).

Go over another cattle grate and pass the junction with the Boundary Trail (6.8 miles).

The dirt road forks (9.7 miles). Bear left and up. (The road to the right leads down to Polipoli Springs State Recreation Area. It has drinking water, a toilet, covered picnic tables, and a small campground.)

Reach the Skyline switchback where the road crests the ridge and turns sharp left (10.4 miles). Park there well off the road (elevation 6,560 feet) (map point A). On the right is the signed junction with the Haleakalā Ridge Trail, which heads down to Polipoli Springs State Recreation Area.

Route Description:

On foot continue along the road, now called the Skyline Trail, which climbs the southwest rift zone of Haleakalā. Watch out for the occasional four-wheel-drive vehicle.

Enter a grove of eucalyptus trees.

Climb steadily on five switchbacks. The road is rocky and rutted. On the right the massive leeward slopes of Haleakalā drop steadily to the ocean. Look for Lualaʻilua Hills, a pair of eroded cinder cones downslope.

Near a flat grassy area reach a fork, known as Ballpark junction (map point B). Keep left along the ridge. (To the right is Kahua Rd., which leads to the Kahikinui Trail.)

Ascend gradually through an open forest of native māmane trees, pūkiawe and ʻōhelo shrubs, and kīlau (bracken) ferns. Superb views of West Maui start to open up on the left.

Reach a second junction. Keep right on the Skyline Trail. (To the left the Māmane Trail loops back to Polipoli Access Rd.)

Reach a third junction. Keep right on the main road. (The dirt road on the left provides access for hunters.)

Climb more steeply on two switchbacks (map point C).

Switchback twice again to ease the elevation gain.

Work left around the base of Kanahau, a large, partially vegetated cinder cone.

Reach a locked gate, blocking vehicle access (map point D).

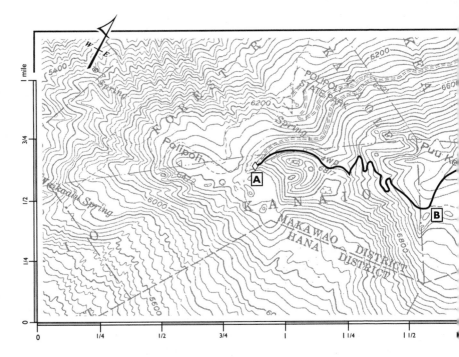

Ascend gradually on two switchbacks. The māmane disappears, and the shrubs hunker down. Look for evening primrose with its yellow flowers. You may also see some feral goats in this area.

Climb steadily on five lazy switchbacks. The pūkiawe and kīlau gradually thin and then disappear. The only remaining green among the red brown cinders is native kūpaoa.

On the left pass a low mound of red cinders known as Kalepeamoa (map point E).

Another dirt road comes in on the left. Continue straight on the Skyline Trail.

On the right pass two pit craters, the second one larger than the first.

Cross over to the right side of the ridge (map point F) and continue climbing. The view is now of the leeward slopes of Haleakalā. In the distance are the summits of Mauna Kea and Mauna Loa on the Big Island.

Go around a locked gate, blocking vehicle access.

Shortly afterward reach the end of the Skyline Trail at a junction

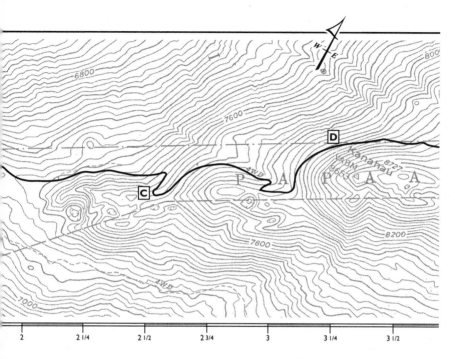

with a paved road (map point G). Turn right on it toward the summit of Haleakalā. (To the left the road leads to an FAA radar installation.)

Pass a radar complex on the left.

Reach a second junction. Keep right on the main road. (The paved road to the left leads to Science City, an astronomy center.)

Reach a third junction (map point H). This time turn left and up. (The main road continues straight to the Haleakalā Visitor Center, 0.7 mile distant.) To the right is Magnetic Peak.

Walk through a parking lot and climb some stairs to reach the top of Pu'u Ula'ula, the summit of Haleakalā (elevation 10,023 feet) (map point I). At the enclosed summit lookout is a breathtaking view into Haleakalā crater.

Notes:

Most hikers drive to the top of Haleakalā (house of the sun) and then walk down into the crater. If you want to climb the volcano, take the Skyline Trail. The trail is actually a rough dirt and cinder

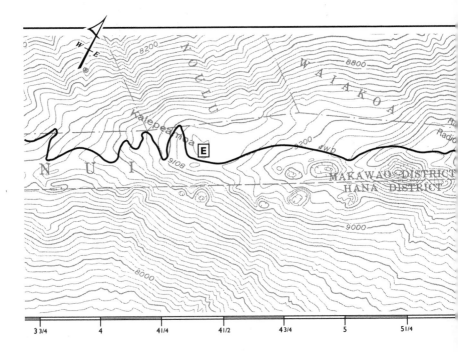

road. It ascends 6.5 miles from the Skyline switchback to a paved road leading to the summit of Haleakalā. The upper section is closed to vehicles to keep the air free of dust for the astronomy complex just below the top. The footing on the road is generally good, and the climbing is steady, but not steep. Start early because of the long mileage and large elevation gain.

Like the hike itself, the drive to the trailhead is long and a bit rough. The last 4 miles are over a dusty dirt road. Although rocky in spots, the road is passable for two-wheel-drive vehicles under dry conditions. Do not attempt to drive the dirt portion during or after a heavy rainstorm. In a four-wheel-drive vehicle you may get as far as the locked gate (map point D). From there the hike becomes a 9-mile round trip.

On the trail you climb steadily to an intersection by a flat, grassy area, locally known as Ballpark junction. In the 1930s members of the Civilian Conservation Corps played softball there during their time off. While working, they planted many of the introduced evergreens you see on the drive along the dirt road.

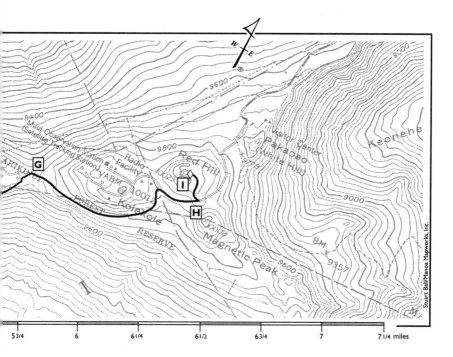

Beyond Ballpark junction, the Skyline Trail ascends through native dry-land vegetation. Look for māmane trees and pūkiawe and ʻōhelo shrubs. Māmane has downy, oblong leaflets and clusters of bright yellow flowers. Pūkiawe has tiny, rigid leaves and small white, pink, or red berries. ʻŌhelo has rounded leaves and delicious red yellow berries, about the size of blueberries.

To the west are superb views of West Maui. Downslope are upcountry Kula and the resort areas of Wailea (water of Lea) and Kīhei (cloak) along the coast. Across the isthmus you can see the West Maui Mountains and Kahului (the winning) and Wailuku (water of destruction) towns. Across ʻAlalākeiki (child's wail) Channel is the island of Kahoʻolawe (the carrying away), and across ʻAuʻau (bathe) Channel lies the island of Lānaʻi (day of conquest).

After you pass through the locked gate, the vegetation gradually disappears, revealing a moonscape of cinder cones and pit craters. The trail follows the southwest rift zone of Haleakalā. Rift zones are areas of structural weakness extending from the summit of a shield volcano. They are laced with cracks, providing passageway for rising molten rock, called magma. Two prehistoric eruption cycles, known as the Kula and the Hāna Series, produced the line of cones and craters you are slowly walking by.

The Skyline Trail reaches the 9,000-foot level at Kalepeamoa (rooster's comb), a low mound of red cinders on the left. Above 9,000 feet many people start to feel the altitude. If you have a headache, nausea, or difficulty breathing, slow your pace. Breathe deeply, rest often, and drink plenty of water. Remember you can turn around any time you feel like it.

The summit area, with its radars, observatories, and paved roads is somewhat of an anticlimax, but not for long. Climb the steps to the enclosed lookout on Puʻu ʻUlaʻula (Red Hill) and take in the awesome view of Haleakalā crater. Check out the exhibits on early Hawaiian use of the area and on the ʻuaʻu, the dark-rumped petrel, that nests near the summit.

Needless to say, the hike down is a breeze. Just put one foot in front of the other and let gravity carry you down the slopes. On the way enjoy the expansive views as the mountain unfolds in front of you.

As just described, the route is a long, round-trip climb. You can, of course, hike the trail one way, either up or down. Unfortunately, that option requires a complicated four-hour shuttle to place and retrieve cars at each end. To get to the summit trailhead, follow the directions in the Kaluʻuokaʻōʻō hike. Then drive 0.7 mile farther along the paved road to the summit parking lot. Perhaps the best alternative is for a friend to drop you off at either trailhead and pick you up at the other.

HĀNA

29 'Ohe'o Gulch

Length:	4.0-mile round trip
Elevation Gain:	900 feet
Suitable for:	Novice, Intermediate
Location:	Maui: Haleakalā National Park, Kīpahulu area near Hāna
Topo Map:	Kīpahulu

Highlights:
This hike leads into a lush, steep-walled gulch, known as 'Ohe'o. Along the route are inviting pools, early Hawaiian rock walls, and a dense bamboo grove. At the end is powerful Waimoku Falls, cascading down a fern-covered cliff.

Trailhead Directions:

Distance: *(Kahului to Kīpahulu Ranger Station) 61 miles*
Driving Time: *2 3/4 hours*

From Kahului take Hāna Hwy (Rte 36).

Reach the intersection with Haleakalā Hwy (Rte 37). Continue straight on Hāna Hwy.

Drive through Lower Pā'ia, a plantation town, and pass Ho'okipa Beach Park with its pounding surf.

Just past the last turnoff to Makawao (Kaupakulua Rd.) the road becomes Rte 360.

For the next 35 miles the narrow road winds into and out of numerous lush gulches along the windward coast of Maui. At the back of each gulch is a stream, sometimes a waterfall, and a one-lane bridge to cross them.

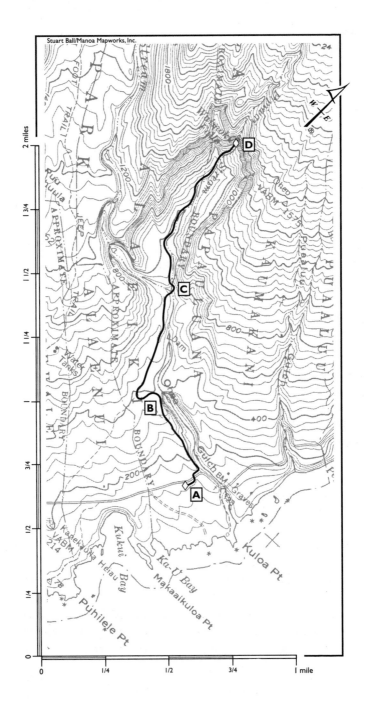

On the right pass Kaumahina State Wayside. It has restrooms and a scenic overlook of Ke'anae Peninsula.

Pass Ke'anae Arboretum on the right.

On the right pass Pua'aka'a State Wayside. It has restrooms and a short walk to a lovely pool.

On the left pass the roads leading to Hāna Airport and Wai'ānapanapa State Park.

Enter Hāna village. At the fork keep right on Rte 360.

Pass Hotel Hāna Maui and Hasegawa General Store on the left.

Just outside Hāna, Rte 360 becomes Pi'ilani Hwy (Rte 31).

The road winds into and out of several gulches.

Enter Haleakalā National Park, Kīpahulu area.

Cross 'Ohe'o Gulch on a white bridge.

Shortly afterward turn left into a gravel lot in front of Kīpahulu Ranger Station and park there (elevation 140 feet) (map point A). The station has some good exhibits, and nearby are restrooms and picnic tables. A short distance farther along the road is a campground with no drinking water.

Route Description:

From the parking lot walk back toward Hāna along the stone wall that borders the highway.

Shortly afterward reach a junction. Turn left on the Pīpīwai Trail. (To the right a path leads down 'Ohe'o Gulch past several swimming holes to Kūloa Point.)

Bear left through a break in the wall and cross the highway.

The trail jogs right, paralleling the highway and then left toward the mountains.

Ascend gradually through java plum and hala trees. Ignore the side trails on the right heading down into 'Ohe'o Gulch.

The trail forks in a pasture with scattered guava trees. Keep right.

Enter a grove of Christmas berry trees. Lau'ae ferns carpet the ground.

Reach a fenced overlook of Makahiku Falls (map point B). Take the short side trail on the right for a closer look at the falls and the large pool at its base.

Go through a gate in the fence, closing it after you.

Pass the remains of a rock wall by a spreading banyan tree. Along the trail are the tangled branches of hau trees with their yellow flowers.

Reach an obscure junction. Continue straight along the ridge. (To the right a rough trail leads down to a deep circular pool in the gulch.)

Cross 'Ohe'o Stream on a bridge (map point C). The stream splits above the crossing, forming several waterfalls. To the left is Palikea Stream, which drains the eastern side of Kīpahulu Valley. To the right is Pīpīwai Stream.

Walk through bamboo briefly and then cross Pīpīwai Stream on another bridge.

Pass several huge mango trees. Look for bird's-nest ferns nestled in the trunks and branches.

Climb gradually through a bamboo forest on a series of board-walks.

The trail forks. Keep left and up.

Descend to Pīpīwai Stream on two short switchbacks.

Ascend steadily upstream. The trail becomes rough, narrow, and wet.

Look through the trees for a glimpse of three waterfalls cascading down the cliffs ahead. The most impressive one, in the middle, is Waimoku Falls.

Ford a stream flowing from the waterfall on the left.

Reach the base of Waimoku Falls (elevation 1,000 feet) (map point D).

Notes:

'Ohe'o (gathering of pools) Gulch is a very popular tourist hike, and deservedly so. The short, well-maintained Pīpīwai (sprinkling water) Trail passes some fine swimming holes and ends at a stunning waterfall. If you want to miss the crowd, take the walk in the early morning or late afternoon. If you want to miss the mosquitoes, keep moving.

While you are hiking, keep in mind that the streams are subject to flash flooding. 'Ohe'o Gulch drains much of Kīpahulu (fetch from exhausted gardens) Valley, a huge watershed. A heavy rainstorm back in the valley can trigger a rapid increase in stream flow. If the water level rises suddenly, move to high ground immediately. The Park Service reports that 'Ohe'o Stream can rise 4 feet in 10 minutes; I don't doubt them.

The trail initially climbs alongside the gulch through a mixed forest of java plum, guava, Christmas berry, and hala trees. In the late 1800s to the early 1900s this area was planted in sugarcane and then pineapples. The sugar mill and plantation village were just down the road in Kīpahulu. Early Hawaiians also cultivated the area, as evidenced by the rock walls.

One of the trees the Hawaiians found useful was the hala. It has distinctive prop roots that help support the heavy clusters of leaves and fruit on the ends of the branches. The early Hawaiians braided the long, pointed leaves, called *lau hala*, into baskets, fans, floor mats, and sails.

Near the rock walls are some tangled hau trees. They have large, heart-shaped leaves. Their flowers are bright yellow with a dark red center and resemble those of a hibiscus. Early Hawaiians used the wood for kites and canoe outriggers, the bark for sandals, and the sap as a laxative.

'Ohe'o Stream forks at the twin bridges. The trail continues up the right fork, Pīpīwai Stream. The left fork, Palikea (white cliff) Stream, penetrates deep into Kīpahulu Valley, a biological reserve closed to the general public. The valley contains a vast koa and 'ōhi'a rain forest that provides habitat for many native birds, including the endangered nukupu'u and Maui parrotbill.

In the upper section of the streams live 'o'opu, small native fishes in the goby family. After birth the young fish swim all the way down to the ocean. To mature fully, the 'o'opu must return to the fresh water of the upper streams. The fish climbs the waterfalls by using a suction cup evolved from its lower front fins to cling to the wet rocks.

Waimoku Falls is both powerful and delicate. A wall of white water free falls from cliff to canyon bottom. Behind and to the side rivulets cascade down the banded rock. The falling water creates its own breeze laden with a fine mist. If the sun is shining, a rainbow forms across the shallow pool at the base.

After returning from the gulch hike, take the short loop walk *makai* (seaward) of the ranger station. The path descends to Kūloa Point and then returns along 'Ohe'o Stream. The stream drops to the ocean in a series of pools separated by small waterfalls. Pick a pool and take another dip.

30 Hāna-Waiʻānapanapa Coastal Trail

Length:	4.6-mile round trip
Elevation Gain:	100 feet
Suitable for:	Novice, Intermediate
Location:	Maui: Waiʻānapanapa State Park near Hāna
Topo Map:	Hāna

Highlights:

This hike follows an ancient Hawaiian path along the rugged wind-swept Hāna coast. Along the way are sea arches, tide pools, a *heiau* (religious site), and a black-sand beach. The walk ends under a shady tree at lovely Kaʻinalimu Bay.

Trailhead Directions:

Distance: *(Kahului to Waiʻānapanapa State Park) 49 miles*
Driving Time: 2 1/4 hours

From Kahului take Hāna Hwy (Rte 36).

Reach the intersection with Haleakalā Hwy (Rte 37). Continue straight on Hāna Hwy.

Drive through Lower Pāʻia, a plantation town, and pass Hoʻokipa Beach Park with its pounding surf.

Just past the last turnoff to Makawao (Kaupakulua Rd.) the road becomes Rte 360.

For the next 35 miles the narrow road winds into and out of numerous lush gulches along the windward coast of Maui. At the back of each gulch is a stream, sometimes a waterfall, and a one-lane bridge to cross them.

On the right pass Kaumahina State Wayside. It has restrooms and a scenic overlook of Keʻanae Peninsula.

Pass Keʻanae Arboretum on the right.

On the right pass Puaʻakaʻa State Wayside. It has restrooms and a short walk to a lovely pool.

On the left pass the junction with the road to Hāna Airport.

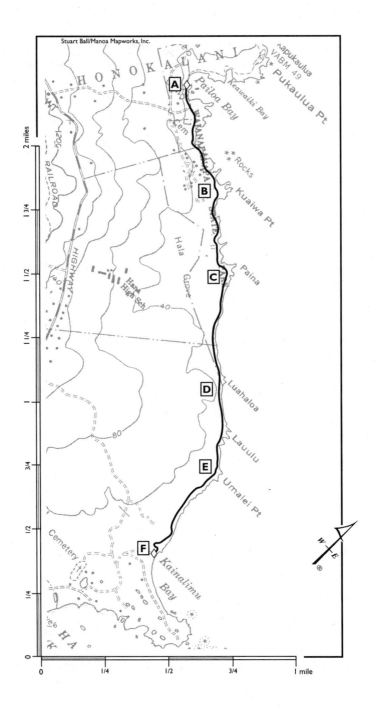

About a mile past the airport road, turn left on a paved road to Wai'ānapanapa State Park.

By the park headquarters turn left again toward the camping and picnic areas.

Park in the lot at the end of the road (elevation 40 feet) (map point A). Wai'ānapanapa State Park has drinking water, restrooms, outdoor showers, picnic tables, rental cabins, and a campground.

Route Description:

From the parking lot walk *makai* (seaward) to an overlook of Pa'iloa Bay. Below is a black-sand beach and to the right a sea arch carved out of a spit jutting into the ocean.

At the overlook turn right on a paved path along the coast. (To the left the path leads a short distance to Wai'ānapanapa Cave.)

Go through a break in a rock wall. Underfoot are the large seeds of the kamani haole (tropical almond) tree.

Reach a junction. Keep right on a dirt trail along the shoreline. (The paved path swings left and down to the black-sand beach.)

On the right pass a cemetery and the state park campground. On the left is a small craggy island with a lone palm tree on top.

The trail splits. Keep left, hugging the coast. (The wide path to the right passes another cemetery and then rejoins the coastal trail.)

Walk along the rugged shoreline made up of black, clinkery 'a'ā lava. The native shrub naupaka kahakai spills down the cliff, almost touching the water. *Mauka* (inland) is a grove of hala trees.

Pass the state park cabins on the right. Ignore the paths leading to them.

A dirt road comes in on the right (map point B). *Makai* is Kuaiwa Point with a small blowhole.

Cross a sea arch; the sea surges underneath.

Descend a short cliff face. Tide pools dot the wave-swept ledges.

Reach Ohala *heiau* (religious site). It has several platforms and massive rock walls.

At the far side of the *heiau* go through a battered fence.

The treadway becomes a line of smooth stones.

Just past a grove of ironwood trees, another dirt road comes in on the right. In the distance *mauka* lie the slopes of Haleakalā, dotted with old cinder cones of the Hāna Series of prehistoric eruptions.

Cross a flat grassy area near Pa'ina Point (map point C).

The trail turns sharp right by a rock shelter and traverses jumbled-up *'a'ā* lava covered with lichen. Smooth stones underfoot make the going easier.

Walk along a sheer cliff pounded by the surf. The footing is rough and rocky.

At Luahaloa pass a weathered shelter used by local fishermen (map point D).

Cross the base of twin Lau'ulu Point. Here the smooth wave-washed cliffs are topped by an unruly mop of *'a'ā*. At the waterline is a colorful band of pink rock.

Pass Umalei Point on the left (map point E). Small *ahu* (cairns) mark the way. You can see Ka'inalimu Bay and Nānu'alele Point farther along the coast. In back of them is Ka'uiki Head, covered with ironwoods. It is a prehistoric cinder cone and the legendary home of Māui, demigod and trickster.

Descend briefly through a shady grove of beach heliotrope. Lau'ae ferns carpet the ground.

Emerge onto the rocky beach at Ka'inalimu Bay (map point F).

Notes:

In the Hāna area most hikers take the popular trail up 'Ohe'o (gathering of pools) Gulch. While they are all jostling for space at Waimoku Falls, try this less-traveled coastal walk instead. After you pass the campground and cabins, you and a few local fishermen have this wild coast all to yourselves.

If possible, take this hike in the early morning or late afternoon. The air is cooler then, and the colors are vivid and contrasting: blue sky and sea, green vegetation, black lava, and white coral and driftwood.

Before you start the hike, a few cautions are in order. The route traverses a rocky, windswept coastline exposed to powerful currents and surf. While exploring, remember the old saying—never turn your back on the ocean. At the beaches there are no lifeguards. If you decide to swim, you are on your own.

After you pass the campground, look for the native, low-lying shrub naupaka kahakai. It has bright green, fleshy leaves, and white half-flowers with purple streaks. The unusual appearance of the flowers has given rise to several unhappy legends. According to one, a Hawaiian maiden believed her lover unfaithful. In anger she tore all the naupaka flowers in half. She then asked him to find a whole flower to prove his love. He was, of course, unsuccessful and died of a broken heart.

Near the cabins are groves of hala trees. They have distinctive prop roots that help support the heavy clusters of leaves and fruit on the ends of the branches. Early Hawaiians braided the long, pointed leaves, called *lau hala,* into baskets, fans, floor mats, and sails.

Farther along the route is Ohala *heiau,* a place of worship for early Hawaiians. The site has several platforms and massive rock walls. Beyond the *heiau,* smooth stepping-stones make the walking easier. They are the remnants of an old Hawaiian footpath, known as the King's Highway. *Ali'i* (chiefs), commoners, and tax collectors used the highway to travel between *ahupua'a* (land divisions) along the coast.

Without the stepping-stones, the trail becomes rough and obscure in spots. Watch your footing on the loose *'a'ā* lava. Look for *ahu* (cairns) marking the route. You can hardly get lost, but the walking is a lot easier if you stay on the trail.

The hike ends under a shady beach heliotrope tree partway along Ka'inalimu (seaweed procession) Bay. Find a comfortable spot and stretch out. Take in the broad sweep of the bay. Listen for the growl from the rocks as the surf rubs them together.

There are several variations on this hike. For a short 1-mile walk, go as far as the *heiau* and then turn around. For a longer hike, continue around Ka'inalimu Bay to Nānu'alele (the altar heaps) Point. You can also hike the coastal trail in the other direction for about 0.7 mile. At the overlook in the state park turn left past Wai'ānapanapa (glistening water) Cave. The route passes two small beaches and ends at Hāna Airport. Be sure to visit the cave; its haunting secret is retold on a nearby wooden sign.

KĪHEI

31 Hoapili Trail

Length:	4.2-mile round trip
Elevation Gain:	200 feet
Suitable for:	Novice
Location:	Maui: Southwest coast beyond Mākena
Topo Map:	Mākena

Highlights:
This hike follows an ancient Hawaiian footpath to the dry Kanaio coast. Along the way are historic sites, tide pools, pocket-sized beaches, and the last lava flow from Haleakalā. The walk ends at a secluded cove shaded by contorted kiawe trees.

Trailhead Directions:

Distance: *(Kahului to La Pérouse Bay) 23 miles*
Driving Time: *3/4 hour*

From Kahului take Puʻunēnē Ave. (Rte 350).

Near the sugar mill in Puʻunēnē town, bear right on Mokulele Hwy (still Rte 350) toward Kīhei.

Drive through vast fields of sugarcane. The road is lined with a windbreak of closely planted trees.

At the road end near the leeward coast, turn left on Piʻilani Hwy (Rte 31).

Pass sprawling Kīhei on the right.

Rte 31 ends abruptly. Turn right on Wailea Iki Rd. into Wailea resort area.

At the road end by Wailea Shopping Center, turn left on Mākena Alanui Rd.

The road narrows to two lanes and passes the last hotel, Maui Prince.

The road narrows some more; the pavement becomes bumpy and uneven.

Enter 'Āhihi-Kīna'u Natural Area Reserve.

The pavement ends at the La Pérouse monument. Bear right on a rough road toward the shore. Park near the beach (map point A).

Route Description:

At the beach take the dirt road along the shore of Keone'ō'io Bay, also known as La Pérouse Bay.

Pass Pa'alua *heiau* (religious site).

The road forks. Keep left heading *mauka* (inland).

Reach a junction with a well-traveled dirt road (map point B). Turn right on it. (To the left the road heads back to the La Pérouse monument.)

Walk through scattered kiawe trees on barren *'a'ā* lava from the 1790 eruption of Haleakalā. To the left and back is Pu'u o Kanaloa cone; farther upslope is Pu'u Naio. Both are prehistoric cinder cones.

Pass a small beach with tide pools in the rocks nearby.

Stroll under shady kiawe trees past old rock walls. On the right is a native wiliwili tree with its heart-shaped leaves.

The road forks, just past a vehicle turnaround (map point C). Keep left, briefly paralleling a wire fence. (The right fork hugs the shore and ends at a small cove.)

The road winds through clinkery red *'a'ā* lava.

Reach a junction near a grove of kiawe (map point D). Turn left through a vehicle barrier of cemented lava rock. (The road continues straight to a beacon at the tip of Cape Hanamanioa.)

Shortly afterward reach a signed junction. Turn right on the Hoapili Trail. (To the left a trail leads back to the main dirt road at the wire fence.)

The Hoapili Trail heads straight across the base of Cape Hanamanioa. Beautifully constructed rock causeways smooth out the dips in the lava flow. Watch your step on the loose rock, however.

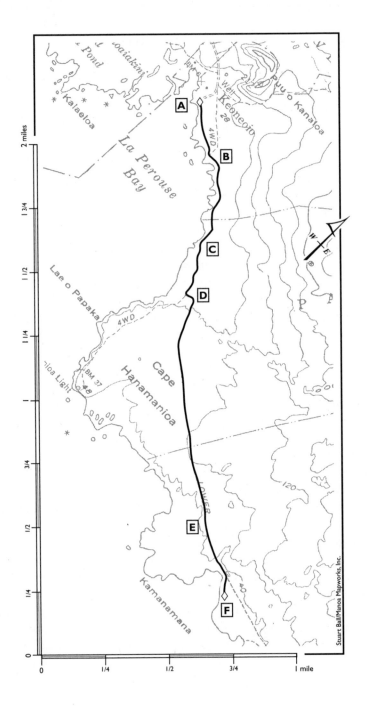

At the top of the first rise look *makai* (seaward) across 'Alalākeiki Channel to see the islands of Kahoʻolawe and Lānaʻi. In front of Lānaʻi is the islet of Molokini. Upslope is Puʻu Pīmoe, a prehistoric cone named after a demigod who lived in the sea.

Cross the base of Kamanamana Point (map point E). On the left you can look all the way up to the astronomy complex near the top of Haleakalā. In front of you extends the Kanaio coast.

Descend steeply off the lava flow to a lovely cove backed by kiawe (map point F). Look for the native shrubs naupaka kahakai and naio. Beyond is a tiny white-sand beach and rock shelves with tide pools.

Notes:

The Hoapili Trail traverses a short section of the hot, dry southwest coast. Winter (November–April) is the most comfortable time of year to take this hike. If you go in summer (May–October), start early in the morning or late in the afternoon. Besides being hot, the intense midday sun washes out the vivid coastal colors: blue sea and sky, green vegetation, black lava, and white coral and driftwood.

Leeward coasts, such as this one, generally have less-powerful surf and currents than windward coasts, especially in summer. Nevertheless, remember the old saying—never turn your back on the ocean. At the beaches there are no lifeguards. If you decide to swim, you are on your own.

The hike starts at Keoneʻōʻio (the sandy place with bonefish) Bay, also named La Pérouse after the French explorer. On 29 May 1786 he sailed along this coast in command of two frigates, *La Boussole* and *L'Astrolabe*. The expedition was met by about 150 canoes laden with trading goods. The next morning La Pérouse and a well-armed party went ashore nearby and exchanged gifts with the Hawaiian natives.

The route initially crosses a jagged *'aʻā* flow from Haleakalā (house of the sun) Volcano. In 1790 lava erupted from two vents *mauka* (inland) and poured into the ocean, creating Cape Kīnaʻu (flaw) on the western side of the bay. The date of the lava flow was estimated by comparing maps of the coastline drawn by the La Pérouse expedition of 1786 and the Vancouver expedition of 1793.

The eruption in 1790 may not have been the last for Haleakalā, which is still classified as a dormant volcano.

The *heiau* (religious site) and rock walls along the way are evidence of ancient Hawaiian use of the area. Near the walls is a native wiliwili tree. It has heart-shaped, leathery leaflets in groups of three. Early Hawaiians used the soft, light wood for surfboards, canoe outriggers, and fishnet floats. The red seeds were strung together to form *lei hua* (seed or nut garlands).

The Hoapili Trail roughly follows an old Hawaiian footpath, known as the King's Highway. *Ali‘i* (chiefs), commoners, and tax collectors used the highway to travel between *ahupua‘a* (land divisions). Hoapili, governor of Maui, had the route reconstructed in the early 1800s and gave it his name. The trail was recently restored by volunteers under the direction of Na Ala Hele, a state program involved in trail maintenance and access. The route resembles a Roman road with its straight, graded alignment.

At the end of the trail is a secluded cove and beach. Plop down underneath a shady kiawe tree and take a well-earned rest. If ambition gets the better of you, check out the tide pools or go swimming. In winter look for migratory shorebirds, such as ‘ūlili, the wandering tattler, with its yellow legs.

This stretch of coast is named Kanaio, after the naio tree. It has narrow, pointed leaves and tiny white flowers. Early Hawaiians used the hard, heavy wood for house posts and rafters and in tools for making fishnets. They also burned it as a torch for night fishing. As the wood dries, it has a fragrance similar to that of ‘iliahi (sandalwood), but the smell doesn't last as long. When the sandalwood trade with China declined in the middle 1800s, naio was offered as a substitute, but the Chinese wouldn't buy it.

You can explore farther along the Kanaio coast. A rough road leads to more coves, beaches, tide pools, and a blowhole. Other options include the side trip to the beacon at Cape Hanamanioa. On the return you can proceed straight at the signed junction, taking the trail that parallels the dirt road and ends at the wire fence.

WEST MAUI

32 Lahaina Pali

Length:	5.0-miles one way
Elevation Gain:	1,600 feet
Suitable for:	Intermediate
Location:	Maui: West Maui Mountains near Mā'alaea Harbor
Topo Map:	Mā'alaea

Highlights:
This hot, dry, but very scenic hike follows a historic horse and foot trail built in the early 1800s. Numbered signs along the route explain various points of interest. From lookouts along the cliffs you may see humpback whales in the ocean below.

Trailhead Directions:
Because the route is point to point, this hike has two trailheads, one near Mā'alaea Harbor and the other near Ukumehame Beach Park.

Distance: (Kahului to Ukumehame trailhead) 12 miles

Driving Time: 1/2 hour

From Kahului take Pu'unēnē Ave. (Rte 350) toward Pu'unēnē. Turn right on Kūihelani Hwy (Rte 380).

At the road end turn left on Honoapi'ilani Hwy (Rte 30) toward Lahaina.

Right after the turn cross a white bridge.

To get to Mā'alaea trailhead, turn right on a dirt road just after the bridge. The intersection is marked by a tall utility pole. The dirt road is well graded but very dusty.

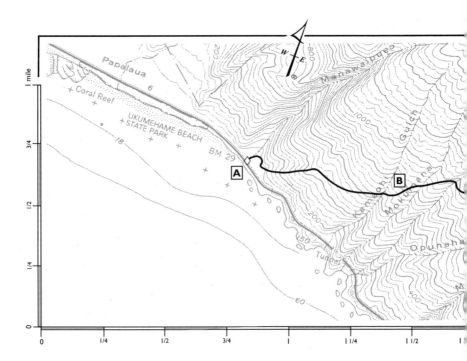

Drive through an unlocked gate, closing it behind you.

Reach a junction with another dirt road. Turn left on it. (Straight ahead is another gate leading into a pasture.)

The road parallels a ditch on the left. Watch for cattle.

Drive through a second unlocked gate, closing it behind you.

The road forks. Keep right on the more traveled route.

Pass an old gate and overgrown road on the right. Continue straight, past a raised white water pipe.

Turn right off the road into a fenced lot and park there (elevation 200 feet) (map point G).

To get to Ukumehame trailhead, continue on Route 30 after crossing the bridge.

On the left pass several turnoffs to Kīhei and Māʻalaea Harbor.

Drive by the scenic lookout at Papawai Point, also on the left.

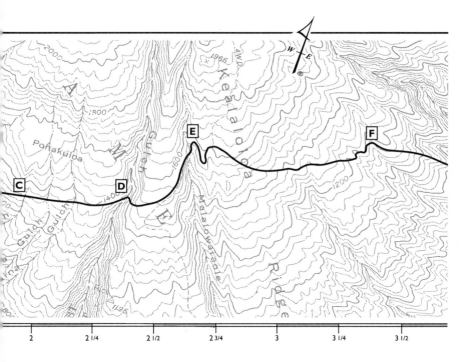

Go through a tunnel.

About 0.5 mile beyond the tunnel, turn right into a dirt area shaded by kiawe trees and park there (elevation 10 feet) (map point A). If you have two cars, drop off people and packs and shuttle one car back to Māʻalaea trailhead.

Route Description:

At the back of the parking area take the trail past some information plaques.

Climb briefly up Manawaipueo Gulch and then turn right on the old *pali* (cliff) road.

Turn left off the road onto the Lahaina Pali Trail.

Begin climbing on a series of S curves. Some sections still have the original rock pavement. Look back to see Lahaina town and the island of Lānaʻi across ʻAuʻau Channel.

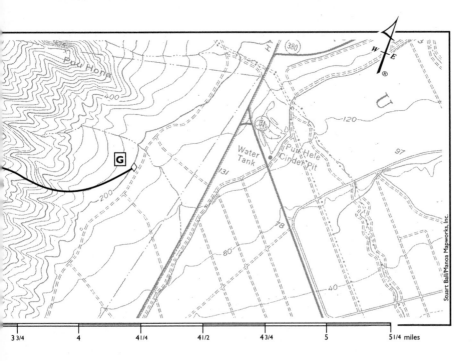

Ascend gradually, cutting across the topography. Below on the right is the portal of the Lahaina tunnel. Keep your eye out for graffiti cut in the rock by travelers long ago.

Cross Kamaohi Gulch (map point B). Several kiawe trees provide some shade.

Climb steeply alongside Mokumana Gulch and then cross it. To the right in the gulch is a grove of native wiliwili trees.

Cross Ōpūnahā Gulch (map point C).

Pass a concrete water tank for cattle on the left.

Cross shallow Makahuna and Kaʻalaina Gulches.

Descend gradually into rocky Manawainui Gulch (map point D). Rest briefly under a shady, spreading wiliwili tree.

Climb steeply out of the gulch on three switchbacks.

Contour across a broad side ridge through a field of ʻilima and lantana.

Reach the highest point along the trail (elevation 1,600 feet). To the east Haleakalā dominates the view. To its right is the islet of Molokini and the island of Kahoʻolawe across ʻAlalākeiki Channel.

After descending some stone stairs, reach a signed junction. Turn left on McGregor Point jeep road.

Cross Malalowaiaole Gulch on the road (map point E).

As the road swings sharp left up Kealaloloa Ridge, turn right and down on the Lahaina Pali Trail.

Cross a small gully and then broad Kealaloloa Ridge.

Continue to descend, traversing a series of dry gullies.

Bear right and descend steadily down a side ridge (map point F). The trail usually hugs the right side of the ridge. On steeper sections it slaloms back and forth across the ridge.

A gulch appears on the right. Look for the native shrub ʻaʻaliʻi in this stretch. Along the coast are views of Māʻalaea Harbor, Keālia fishpond, and Kīhei town. To the left of the sugarcane fields is Kahului town.

Descend more gradually through scattered kiawe trees.

Reach the fenced lot (map point G).

Notes:

This hot, dry hike is well named; in its old pronunciation Lāhainā means cruel sun and *pali*, cliff. Take this climb during the winter (November–April) when the temperature is cooler, and the sun less intense. If you must do the hike in summer, drink lots of water and use plenty of sunscreen. Whether in summer or winter, start early to avoid the heat or start very late and just go partway.

In the early 1800s the Lahaina Pali Trail was constructed across the southern slopes of the West Maui Mountains. The trail provided a more direct route between the Wailuku (water of destruction) and Lahaina districts. In 1900 prison laborers built a winding dirt road at the base of the *pali* near the coast. The trail fell into disuse because travelers preferred the ease of the dirt road and then the paved highway, constructed in 1951. The Lahaina Pali Trail was recently rebuilt by volunteers under the direction of Nā Ala Hele, a state program involved in trail maintenance and access.

The renovated route is well marked, but rough and steep in some spots. Along the way are signs explaining the points of interest. The signs are keyed to a pamphlet, Maui History and Lore from the Lahaina Pali Trail. If possible, pick one up at the Division of Forestry and Wildlife in Wailuku before starting the hike. The address is in the appendix.

After the initial climb, scan the ocean for humpback whales. They migrate from the North Pacific to Maui, arriving in October and leaving in May. While in the Maui area they occupy themselves calving, nursing, breeding, and generally horsing around.

In Manawainui (large water branch) Gulch take a well-deserved break under the shady wiliwili tree. It has heart-shaped, leathery leaflets in groups of three. Flowers appear in the spring and are usually orange. Early Hawaiians used the soft, light wood for surfboards, canoe outriggers, and fishnet floats. The red seeds were strung together to form *lei hua* (seed or nut garlands).

Just before you reach the top of Kealaloloa (the long pathway) Ridge, keep your eye out for the native shrub 'ilima. It has oblong, serrated leaves, about 1 inch long. The yellow orange flowers strung together make a regal *lei*, in both ancient and modern Hawai'i.

On the way down look for another native shrub, 'a'ali'i. It has narrow, shiny leaves and red seed capsules. Early Hawaiians used the leaves and capsules in making *lei*. When crushed, the capsules produced a red dye for decorating *kapa* (bark cloth).

As described, the route is one way from Ukumehame to Mā'alaea. You can, of course, do the hike in the opposite direction. If you have only one car, start at either trailhead, climb to the top of Kealaloloa Ridge, and return the same way. If you do not want to drive the dirt road to Mā'alaea trailhead, park on Honoapi'ilani Hwy (Rte 30) near the tall utility pole. Follow the driving instructions on foot and add about 1 mile to the one-way hike mileage.

33 Waihe'e Ridge

Length:	5.0-mile round trip
Elevation Gain:	1,500 feet
Suitable for:	Novice, Intermediate
Location:	Maui: West Maui Forest Reserve near Waihe'e
Topo Map:	Wailuku

Highlights:

This incredible hike leads deep into the wet and wild West Maui Mountains. Along the way is a rich variety of native rain forest plants. From the summit picnic table you may glimpse the deep gorges and massive ridges leading to Pu'u Kukui, one of the wettest areas on earth.

Trailhead Directions:

Distance: *(Kahului to Waihe'e Ridge trailhead) 10 miles*

Driving Time: *1/2 hour*

From Kahului take Ka'ahumanu Ave. (Rte 32) toward Wailuku. Pass Maui Community College on the right.

Enter Wailuku town. At the second traffic light turn right on Market St. (Rte 33).

Rte 33 becomes Rte 340, Kahekili Hwy.

Drive through Waihe'e village and cross Waihe'e River on a bridge.

The road narrows and curves in and out of several gulches.

Pass mile marker 6.

At 0.9 mile past the marker, turn left on a paved road to Camp Maluhia, a Boy Scout camp. The intersection is across from a house with a rock wall and a tall gate.

After driving 0.8 mile, look for a gate and a trail sign on the left. A large parking area for the camp is just beyond on the right.

Park in the grassy area near the gate (elevation 1,069 feet) (map point A). Don't block it.

Route Description:

Climb over the fence on a ladder to the left of the gate.

Ascend steeply on a one-lane paved road.

Just before the road ends at a water tank, bear left on the Waihe'e Ridge Trail.

The trail continues to climb through the overgrown pasture. Rusted metal stakes mark the right of way.

Enter a small gulch, filled with kukui and guava trees.

Go through a stile in a second fence.

Pass a grove of Cook pines on the left.

Work right, out of the gulch, through eucalyptus trees.

As the trail switchbacks to the left, reach an overlook. To the right is a waterfall along Makamaka'ole Stream. Straight ahead is Kānoa Ridge, our destination. Nearby are several small native 'ōhi'a trees with yellow flowers.

Cross over to the left side of Kānoa Ridge (map point B). The view is now of Waihe'e Valley and River. In the distance you can see Wailuku and Kahului towns and the slopes of Haleakalā.

Stroll through a lovely open stretch. Look for the native bird 'apapane flitting among the 'ōhi'a.

Go through a stile in a wire fence. The trail narrows.

Ascend steadily on a double series of short switchbacks. Watch for native hāpu'u tree ferns and kōpiko trees in this section.

At the back of a small gulch the trail levels briefly and then resumes climbing (map point C).

Bear right across a flat, marshy area (map point D). To the right is a hanging gulch leading down to Makamaka'ole Stream.

Climb Lanilili hill on a series of switchbacks. Look for hāpu'u and 'ama'u ferns and stunted 'ōhi'a with red, yellow, and salmon-colored blossoms.

Reach the flat top of Lanilili (elevation 2,563 feet) (map point E).

The trail ends at a picnic table with a superb view of the West

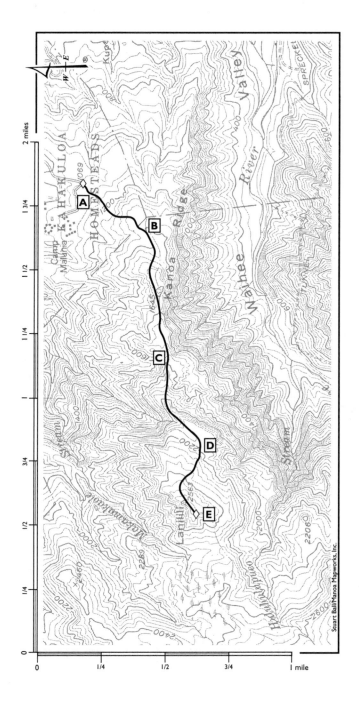

Maui Mountains. Close by is a native 'ōlapa tree with its fluttering leaves.

Notes:

Waihe'e (octopus liquid) Ridge is a misty hike through a native rain forest. Expect to get wet, and you won't be disappointed. After all, a rain forest should be experienced in the rain, right? If the weather just happens to be sunny and clear, count yourself lucky.

The ridge trail is well graded and maintained. The climbing is steady, but rarely steep. Hike as far as you want and then turn around; even going partway is worthwhile.

Along the trail are well over 50 different species of native plants that prefer a wet mountain habitat. All are identified and illustrated in a pamphlet, Waihe'e Ridge Trail Native Plant Guide, available from the State Division of Forestry and Wildlife in Wailuku. The address is in the appendix. The notes below describe a few of the more easily identified native plants.

After the overlook of Makamaka'ole (without friends) Stream, begin looking for native 'ōhi'a. When first seen along Kānoa (bowl) Ridge, they are good-sized trees. By the end of the hike, they have become small shrubs, stunted by the exposed conditions higher up. 'Ōhi'a has oval, dull green leaves and clusters of delicate red, yellow, or salmon-colored flowers. Native birds, such as the 'apapane, feed on the nectar and help with pollination.

You may catch a glimpse of an 'apapane in the forest canopy. It has a red breast and head, black wings and tail, and a slightly curved black bill. In flight the 'apapane makes a whirring sound as it darts from tree to tree searching for insects and nectar.

On the series of short switchbacks keep your eyes out for kōpiko, a native member of the coffee family. It has leathery, oblong leaves with a light green midrib. Turn the leaf over to see a row of tiny holes (*piko* [navel]) on either side of the midrib. The kōpiko produces clusters of tiny white flowers and fleshy, orange fruits.

On the upper section are two native ferns, 'ama'u and hāpu'u. You can tell them apart by the structure of their fronds. Those of 'ama'u branch once before the green segments are attached to the stem. The fronds are red when young, gradually turning green with age. Hāpu'u fronds branch several times before the green segments. Their fronds have a lacy, delicate appearance.

From the summit picnic table is a view not easily forgotten, perhaps because it is so rare. All around lies the convoluted topography of the West Maui Mountains. Massive ridges alternate with deeply dissected valleys. Below and to the west is Huluhulupueo (owl feathers) Stream that flows into Waihe'e River. Beyond the stream to the right is Keahikauō (the dragged fire), a hill rising from a swamp. The broad ridge to the southwest climbs to 'Eke Crater (elevation 4,480 feet), a flat-topped volcanic dome with a bog on top. Beyond the crater the mountains rise steadily to Pu'u Kukui (candlenut hill) (elevation 5,788 feet), one of the wettest areas on earth.

Near the picnic table is a native 'ōlapa tree. The leaves are opposite, oblong, and flutter in the slightest wind. In a special hula stance named after the tree, dancers mimic the exquisite movements of the leaves. Early Hawaiians used the bark, leaves, and purple fruit to make a blue black dye to decorate their *kapa* (bark cloth).

◀ Pūʻahanui (kanawao) flower. Alakaʻi Swamp hike, Kauaʻi. *(Photo by John Hoover)*

▼ Kawaikōī Stream. Kawaikōī Stream hike, Kauaʻi. *(Photo by Deborah Uchida)*

◄ Up the ridge. Kuilau Ridge hike, Kaua'i. *(Photo by Lynne Masuyama)*

▼ Wai'ale'ale in the clear. Powerline Trail, Kaua'i. *(Photo by Lynne Masuyama)*

▲ Along the Hāna coast. Hāna-Wai'āna-panapa Coastal Trail, Maui. (Photo by John Hoover)

◀ Along the Kanaio coast. Hoapili Trail, Maui. (Photo by Lynne Masuyama)

▲ ʻĀhinahina, the Haleakalā silversword. Sliding Sands–Halemauʻu hike, Maui. *(Photo by Deborah Uchida)*

◄ Down the switchbacks. Sliding Sands–Halemauʻu hike, Maui. *(Photo by Deborah Uchida)*

Heading into Haleakalā crater. Kaluʻuokaʻōʻō hike, Maui. *(Photo by Deborah Uchida)*

Crossing Kahana Stream. Kahana Valley hike, Oʻahu. *(Photo by Lynne Masuyama)*

Below the Ko'olau cliffs. Maunawili Trail, O'ahu. *(Photo by Deborah Uchida)*

▲ Taking a break. Maʻakua Gulch hike, Oʻahu. *(Photo by Albert Miller)*

◄ Koʻolau cliffs, Kōnāhua-nui in back. Kuliʻouʻou Ridge hike, Oʻahu. *(Photo by John Hoover)*

Cooling off at Mānoa Falls. ʻAihualama hike, Oʻahu. *(Photo by John Hoover)*

O'AHU

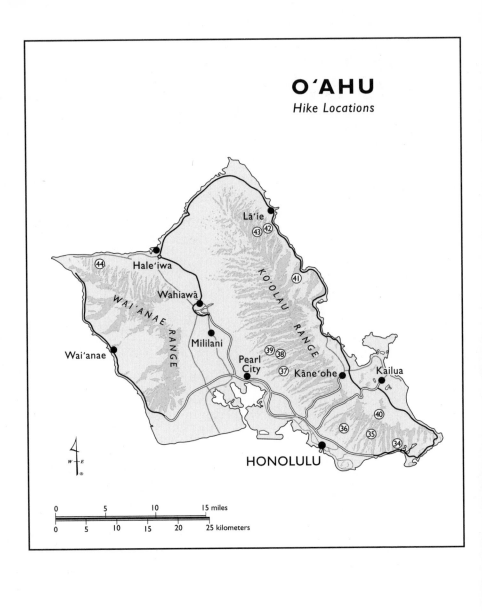

O'AHU

Hike Locations

Lā'ie

43 42

44

Hale'iwa

KO'OLAU RANGE

Wahiawā

41

WAI'ANAE RANGE

Mililani

Wai'anae

39 38

Pearl
City

37 Kāne'ohe

Kailua

40

36

35

34

HONOLULU

W — E

0	5	10	15 miles

| 0 | 5 | 10 | 15 | 20 | 25 kilometers |

EAST HONOLULU

34 Kuli'ou'ou Ridge

Length:	5.0-mile round trip
Elevation Gain:	1,800 feet
Suitable for:	Novice, Intermediate
Location:	O'ahu: Kuli'ou'ou Forest Reserve above Kuli'ou'ou
Topo Map:	Koko Head

Highlights:
This popular hike climbs a dry, shady ridge to the top of the Ko'olau Range. Along the way are some native plants and a stately forest of Cook pines. From the summit lookout are superb views of the windward coast.

Trailhead Directions:
Distance: *(Downtown Honolulu to Kuli'ou'ou trailhead) 11 miles*
Driving Time: *1/2 hour*

At Ward Ave. get on Lunalilo Fwy (H-1) Koko Head bound (east).

As the freeway ends, continue straight on Kalaniana'ole Hwy (Rte 72).

Drive by 'Āina Haina and Niu Valley Center.

Pass Holy Trinity Catholic Church on the right.

Turn left on Kuli'ou'ou Rd. and head into Kuli'ou'ou Valley.

The road jogs left and then right.

Pass Kuli'ou'ou Neighborhood Park on the right. The park has restrooms and drinking water.

At the dead end sign turn right on Kala'au Pl.

Park on the street just before it ends at a turnaround circle (elevation 260 feet) (map point A).

Bus: Route 1 to Kalaniana'ole Hwy and Kuli'ou'ou Rd. Walk 1.3 miles along Kuli'ou'ou Rd. and Kala'au Pl. to the trailhead.

Route Description:

At the back of the circle take the one-lane, paved road on the left leading down to Kuli'ou'ou Stream.

Before crossing the stream, bear right on a grassy road by a utility pole.

Enter a clearing with a lone Christmas berry tree in the middle.

The road narrows and becomes the Kuli'ou'ou Valley Trail.

Cross a small gully.

Contour above the stream through an introduced forest of Christmas berry, koa haole, and guava. Laua'e ferns and native 'ūlei shrubs cover the ground.

Reach a signed junction by some small boulders (map point B). Turn sharp right and up on the Kuli'ou'ou Ridge Trail. (The valley trail continues straight.) Just after the junction look for noni, a small tree with large, shiny green leaves and warty fruits.

Climb gradually up the side of the valley on 10 long switchbacks. After the first one are good views of Kuli'ou'ou Valley. Between the second and third switchbacks the trail splits twice. Keep right each time. After the eighth one the trail enters a grove of ironwood trees.

Ascend straight up a side ridge briefly.

Bear right off the side ridge and continue climbing via two short switchbacks.

Just before the top, work up a gully lined with ironwoods.

Reach the ridge line (map point C) and turn left up the ridge. Memorize that junction for the return trip.

Climb steadily up the ridge on its right side.

After regaining the ridge line, wind through a stand of large Cook pines.

Skirt an eroded spot.

Shortly afterward pass two covered picnic tables on the right.

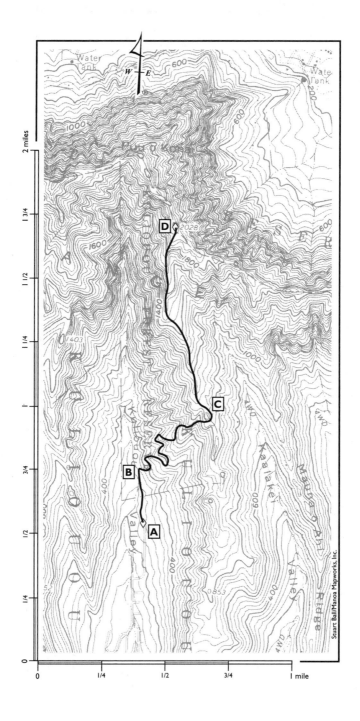

The trail climbs steeply and then levels off briefly in a lovely area lined with stately pines.

Ascend steadily along the left side of the broad ridge through Cook pines and ironwood.

Break out into the open. On the left you can see the sheer walls of Kuli'ou'ou Valley. Along the route are the native trees 'ōhi'a and lama.

The ridge narrows, and the trail becomes rough and eroded in spots. Look to the left for an unusual view of the back side of Diamond Head. To the right are Kohelepelepe (Koko Crater) and Kuamo'okāne (Koko Head) overlooking Hawai'i Kai and Maunalua Bay.

Climb steeply on plastic steps.

Reach the Ko'olau summit at an eroded hill (elevation 2,028 feet) (map point D).

Notes:

Kuli'ou'ou Ridge is a very popular route to the summit of the Ko'olau Range. The hike is reasonably short, mostly shady, and usually mud free. Novices can climb the graded switchbacks to the picnic tables. More experienced hikers can head for the summit lookout with its superb view of the windward coast.

Before you start the hike, a few cautions are in order. Look out for mountain bikers and trail runners on the switchback section. Beyond the picnic tables the trail becomes steep and eroded in spots. Watch your footing, especially on the descent. In the worst areas plastic steps have been installed to slow the erosion and stabilize the trail.

On the valley trail, look for the sprawling native shrub 'ūlei in the sunny sections. It has small, oblong leaves arranged in pairs; clusters of white, roselike flowers; and white fruit. Early Hawaiians ate the berries and used the tough wood for making digging sticks, fish spears, and 'ūkēkē (the musical bow).

Along the ridge near the picnic tables are several groves of tall Cook pines. They have overlapping, scalelike leaves about 1/4 inch long, rather than true needles. The pines were planted in the 1930s for reforestation. Discovered by Captain James Cook, they are native to New Caledonia (Isle of Pines) in the South Pacific between Fiji and Australia.

Beyond the pines the trail climbs through a more open native forest of 'ōhi'a and lama trees. 'Ōhi'a has oval leaves and clusters of delicate red flowers. Early Hawaiians used the flowers in *lei* (garlands) and the wood in outrigger canoes. The hard, durable wood was also carved into god images for *heiau* (religious sites).

Lama has oblong, pointed leaves that are dark green and leathery. Its fruits are green, then yellow, and finally bright red when fully ripe. Lama was sacred to Laka, goddess of the hula. Early Hawaiians used the hard, light-colored wood in temple construction and in hula performances.

After the steep final climb, relax on the summit and take in the magnificent view. In front of you is the broad sweep of Waimānalo (potable water) Bay. To the right the sheer summit ridge ends at Makapu'u (bulging eye) Point. Offshore is Mānana Island, a seabird sanctuary. Along the coast to the left is Kailua (two seas) Bay, stretching to Mōkapu (taboo district) Peninsula. Pu'u o Kona (hill of leeward) is the flat-topped peak on the summit ridge to the left. Wafting up on the trade winds is the earthy odor from the Waimānalo dairies and farms below.

Kuli'ou'ou means sounding knee, referring to the sound made by the *pūniu* (knee drum). Early Hawaiians made the drum out of a coconut shell. They cut off the top portion and covered it with the stretched skin of the surgeonfish, kala. The *pūniu* was tied to the right thigh of the player, just above the knee.

The Kuli'ou'ou Valley Trail is an attractive alternative for beginning hikers. Instead of turning right on the ridge trail, continue into the valley. Walk until the graded trail ends in 0.6 mile and then turn around. There are some mosquitoes by the intermittent stream in the valley.

35 Lanipō

Length:	6.7-mile round trip
Elevation Gain:	2,000 feet
Suitable for:	Intermediate
Location:	Oʻahu: Honolulu Watershed Reserve above Maunalani Heights
Topo Map:	Honolulu, Koko Head

Highlights:

This up-and-down hike follows the crest of Mauʻumae Ridge to the Koʻolau summit. Along the route you see a rich variety of native plants and a hidden volcanic crater. From the lookout on Kainawaʻaunui Peak is a splendid view of much of the windward coast.

Trailhead Directions:

Distance: *(Downtown Honolulu to Lanipō trailhead) 7 miles*

Driving Time: *1/4 hour*

At Ward Ave. get on Lunalilo Fwy (H-1) Koko Head bound (east).

Take the Koko Head Ave. exit (26A) in Kaimukī.

At the top of the off ramp, turn left on Koko Head Ave.

Cross Waiʻalae Ave.

At the first stop sign turn left, still on Koko Head Ave.

At the next stop sign turn right on Sierra Dr.

Switchback up the ridge to Maunalani Heights.

Pass Maunalani Community Park on the right and Maunalani Nursing Center on the left. The park has restrooms and drinking water.

At the end of Sierra Dr. by the last bus stop bear right and up on Maunalani Circle.

The road swings left in a broad arc.

On the right look for a chain-link fence enclosing a Board of Water Supply tank.

Park on the street next to the fence (elevation 1,040 feet) (map point A).

Bus: Route 14 to the end of Sierra Dr. Walk 0.2 mile up Maunalani Circle to the trailhead.

Route Description:

Walk back down the road to a signed junction at the corner of the fence. Turn left on the Mau'umae Trail, which follows a narrow right-of-way between two chain-link fences. The passageway is directly across from the garage of 4970 Maunalani Circle.

At the end of the fences keep left through a small grove of iron-wood trees.

Reach the crest of Mau'umae Ridge and bear right along it.

Descend moderately along the mostly open ridge. There is one rocky section. Along the trail are the Formosa koa tree and the native dry-land shrubs 'ūlei, 'a'ali'i, and 'ilima.

Pass a utility pole on the left (map point B).

Begin a long climb interspersed with two dips. On the left is Pālolo Valley and on the right, Wai'alae Nui Gulch.

After the second dip ascend steeply through native koa trees. At this point the ridge is quite massive and well forested.

After a pleasant level section through ironwood trees, climb steeply again on a badly eroded trail.

Stroll through a lovely stretch of koa and 'iliahi (sandalwood) trees.

Ascend a flat grassy knob with a 360-degree view (map point C). Look behind you for an unusual view of the back side of Diamond Head. Along the coast to the left is Maunalua Bay, Kuamo'okāne (Koko Head), and Kohelepelepe (Koko Crater).

The vegetation gradually changes from dry-land to rain forest. Native 'ōhi'a trees form a loose canopy, and uluhe ferns cover the ground.

Climb a second, shady knob topped by two Cook pines (map point D).

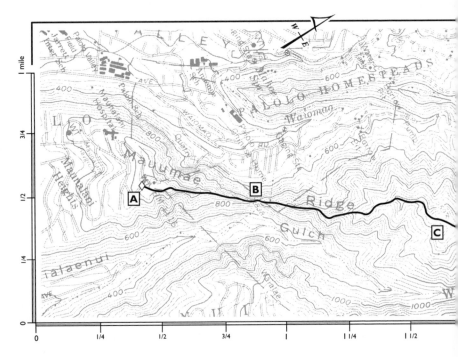

Traverse a long, relatively level section with many small ups and downs. The path leaves the ridge line for short periods.

As the trail resumes serious climbing, pass a lookout on the left above a landslide. Across Pālolo Valley is Ka'au Crater, nestled below the Ko'olau summit ridge. A waterfall cascades from the lip of the crater.

The ridge narrows, and the vegetation thins.

After a stiff climb reach a flat, open knob with a panoramic view (map point E).

Descend off the knob, passing a spindly Cook pine.

Ascend steeply on a rutted trail to a broad hump. From its top you can see the last stretch of the hike.

Descend the back side of the hump and go left around a slippery, exposed spot.

Begin the final climb to the summit along the open windswept ridge. On the right is a magnificent 'ōhi'a tree, which must be partly sheltered from the trade winds.

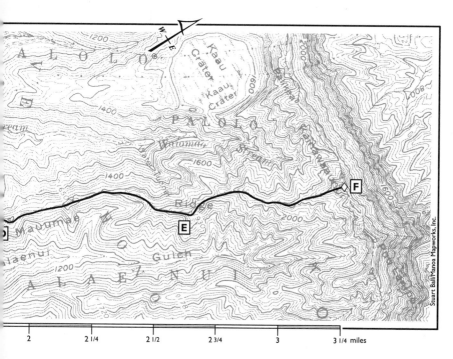

As the top nears, the trail steepens and becomes severely eroded. Reach the Koʻolau summit at a peak called Kainawaʻaunui (elevation 2,520 feet) (map point F). Look for dwarf kōpiko trees in the area.

Notes:

Lanipō is the classic Oʻahu ridge hike. It offers a challenging climb, breathtaking windward views, and a surprising variety of native plants. As a bonus, you get to see a little-known volcanic crater and a lovely waterfall.

Start early to avoid the hot sun in the open lower section of the Mauʻumae (wilted grass) Trail. Watch your footing constantly because the ungraded route is often rough, sometimes muddy, and occasionally narrow. The middle section of the trail may be overgrown with grass and scratchy uluhe ferns. The upper section is wet and cool, with vegetation stunted by the wind.

Some hikers are put off by the initial rocky descent, which, of course, must be climbed on the way back in the hot afternoon. Don't be discouraged! The native plants and the spectacular views farther in are well worth the extra effort.

On the trail look for the native dry-land shrubs 'a'ali'i and 'ilima. 'A'ali'i has narrow, shiny leaves and red seed capsules. Early Hawaiians used the leaves and capsules in making *lei* (garlands). When crushed, the capsules produced a red dye for decorating *kapa* (bark cloth). 'Ilima has oblong, serrated leaves, about 1 inch long. The yellow orange flowers strung together make a regal *lei*, in both ancient and modern Hawai'i.

In the dry lower section of the trail, koa is the most common native tree. It has sickle-shaped foliage and pale yellow flower clusters. Early Hawaiians made surfboards and outrigger canoe hulls out of the beautiful red brown wood. Today it is made into fine furniture.

Less common along the trail is 'iliahi, the native sandalwood tree. Its small leaves are dull green and appear wilted. 'Iliahi is partially parasitic, with outgrowths on its roots that steal nutrients from nearby plants. Early Hawaiians ground the fragrant heartwood into a powder to perfume their *kapa*. Beginning in the late 1700s, sandalwood was indiscriminately cut down and exported to China to make incense and furniture. The trade ended around 1840 when the forests were depleted of 'iliahi.

In the wetter middle section of the trail, native 'ōhi'a gradually replaces koa as the dominant tree. 'Ōhi'a has oval leaves and clusters of delicate red flowers. Early Hawaiians used the flowers in *lei* and the wood in outrigger canoes. The hard, durable wood was also carved into god images for *heiau* (religious sites).

From the lookout above the landslide you can see Ka'au (forty), a circular crater at the base of the Ko'olau summit ridge. The crater was probably formed by steam explosions when rising molten rock encountered ground water. Both Ka'au and Diamond Head Craters are remnants of the last volcanic activity on O'ahu, known as the Honolulu Series.

According to Hawaiian legend, the demigod and trickster Māui wanted to join all the islands together. From Ka'ena (the heat) Point on O'ahu he threw a great hook toward Kaua'i, hoping to snare the island. Initially the hook held fast, and Māui gave a mighty tug on the line. A huge boulder, known as Pōhaku o Kauaʻi, dropped at his feet. The hook sailed over his head and fell in Pālolo Valley, forming Kaʻau Crater. The crater may have been named after Kaʻauhelemoa, a supernatural chicken that lived in the valley.

Near the top keep your eye open for kōpiko, a native member of the coffee family. It has leathery, oblong leaves with a light green midrib. Turn the leaf over to see a row of tiny holes (*piko* [navel]) on either side of the midrib. The kōpiko produces clusters of tiny white flowers and fleshy, orange fruits.

From the summit lookout on Kainawaʻaunui are some impressive windward views. In front is Olomana (forked hill) with its three peaks. To the right is the broad sweep of Waimānalo (potable water) Bay. Farther along the coast are Kailua (two seas) and Kāneʻohe (bamboo husband) Bays, separated by Mōkapu (taboo district) Peninsula. You can also see the sheer Koʻolau (windward) summit ridge from flat-topped Puʻu o Kona (hill of leeward) on the right to twin-peaked Kōnāhuanui (large fat testicles) on the left. Lanipō (dense) is the broad peak close by on the right.

36 'Aihualama (via Mānoa Falls)

Length:	6.0-mile round trip
Elevation Gain:	1,400 feet
Suitable for:	Novice, Intermediate
Location:	O'ahu: Honolulu Watershed Reserve above Mānoa
Topo Map:	Honolulu

Highlights:
This hike climbs the west side of Mānoa Valley through mostly introduced forest. Along the way is lovely Mānoa Falls with its small swimming hole. At the end is a windy overlook of Nu'uanu Valley and Pali.

Trailhead Directions:

Distance: *(Downtown Honolulu to Wa'akaua St.) 5 miles*

Driving Time: *1/4 hour*

Get on S. King St. Koko Head bound (east).

Turn left on Punahou St. by the Cinerama Theater.

Pass Punahou School on the right and enter Mānoa Valley.

The road splits and narrows to two lanes. Take the left fork onto Mānoa Rd.

At the stop sign proceed straight across the intersection on a much wider Mānoa Rd.

Pass Mānoa Elementary School on the right.

Park on Mānoa Rd. just before it narrows at the intersection with Wa'akaua St. (elevation 280 feet) (map point A).

Bus: Route 5 to Mānoa Rd. and Kumuone St. Walk 0.5 mile to the start of the hike.

Route Description:
Continue along Mānoa Rd. on foot.

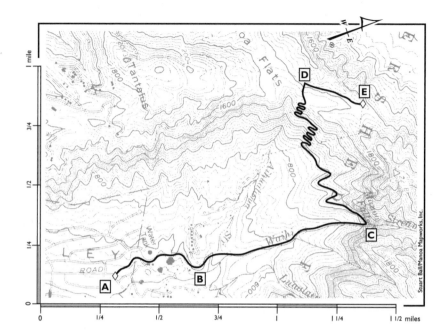

Walk underneath the pedestrian overpass at the entrance to Paradise Park.

Follow the main road as it curves left and then right around the lower parking lot of the park.

As the paved road turns left to Harold L. Lyon Arboretum, proceed straight on a gravel road (map point B).

The road narrows and becomes Mānoa Falls Trail. On the left is a hau tree tangle.

Cross a small stream on a bridge.

Swing left to parallel Mānoa Stream, which soon splits to form 'Aihualama and Waihī Streams.

Bear right and ford 'Aihualama Stream.

Cross a muddy, rooty stretch. Stay on the trail to minimize erosion.

Waihī Stream comes in on the right.

Ascend gradually alongside the stream. On the left is another hau tangle. Above are introduced albizia trees with their whitish bark and layered branches. The trail is paved with rocks in several spots.

Climb more steeply now as the valley narrows. You can see the top of Mānoa Falls through the trees.

Go through a bamboo grove.

Just before the falls, reach a signed junction with the 'Aihualama Trail in a grove of mountain apple trees. For now, continue the short distance to lovely Mānoa Falls and its small swimming hole (map point C).

Backtrack to the signed junction. Turn right and up on the 'Aihualama Trail. The path is narrow and rocky at first but soon widens.

Work in and out of three gulches cut into the side of Mānoa Valley. The third gulch has a small stream. Look for yellow ginger and red heliconia in this section.

Break out into the open near some utility lines. Below is Lyon Arboretum. Beyond, Mānoa Valley stretches to the ocean.

Climb the side of the valley on 14 switchbacks. Kī (ti) plants line the trail. After the eighth switchback are two concrete posts. Between nine and thirteen a dense stand of cinnamon trees blots out the daylight.

At the top of the ridge turn right, through a bamboo forest.

Reach a junction with the Pauoa Flats Trail (map point D). Turn right on it. (To the left the flats trail leads to the Nuʻuanu, Kalāwahine, and Mānoa Cliff Trails.) Memorize the junction for the return trip.

Walk through more bamboo and then cinnamon trees.

Reach windy Nuʻuanu Valley overlook (elevation 1,640 feet) (map point E). Nearby are some native ʻōhiʻa ʻāhihi trees, and naupaka kuahiwi shrubs with their white half-flowers.

Notes:
The 'Aihualama hike combines a pleasant walk in Mānoa (vast) Valley with a steady climb to a scenic viewpoint. The short stroll to the falls at the back of the valley is popular with tourists and locals alike, especially on weekends. Few people go beyond the falls because of the long ascent to the ridge top.

The trails making up the hike are generally well graded, although muddy and rooty in spots. The 'Aihualama Trail climbs out of the valley on long, lazy switchbacks. Because of heavy traffic, the wet and eroded sections of the Mānoa Falls Trail have been improved with gravel, plastic steps, and wooden walkways. The upgraded trail allows you to keep just ahead of the hungry mosquitoes in the valley.

Initially the falls trail passes by a tangled grove of hau trees with large, heart-shaped leaves. Their flowers are bright yellow with a dark red center and resemble those of a hibiscus. Early Hawaiians used the wood for kites and canoe outriggers, the bark for sandals, and the sap as a laxative.

Mānoa Falls makes a refreshing rest stop or a good turnaround point for novice hikers. If you can't resist, take a quick dip in the small pool there. Otherwise, wait until the return trip when you are really hot and tired. If it's late July, you may get some delicious mountain apples ('ōhi'a 'ai) from the grove in front of the falls.

The 'Aihualama area in back of Lyon Arboretum figures prominently in a grisly Hawaiian legend. The maiden Kahalaopuna was walking in Mānoa Valley with her suitor Kauhi, a chief of Kailua. Believing her unfaithful, he clubbed her to death in a fit of anger. Kauhi buried the corpse in an area known as 'Aihualama. The owl god Pueo saw the murder and the hasty burial. He flew down, retrieved the body, and brought the maiden back to life.

Unfortunately, Kahalaopuna returned to the chief, to whom she had been betrothed by her parents. Again the two walked into the valley. Again Kauhi grew angry and killed her. Pueo then retrieved the body and revived the maiden for a second time. The sequence of events then repeats itself again and again in different areas of O'ahu! Eventually the poor owl grew tired from rescuing the maiden so many times and gave up. Luckily another, less jealous suitor revived Kahalaopuna once again with the help of some spirit friends. The two married and lived happily together for a time.

Lining the middle switchbacks of the 'Aihualama Trail are kī (ti) plants. They have shiny leaves, 1–2 feet long, that are arranged spirally in a cluster at the tip of a slender stem. Early Polynesian voyagers introduced ti to Hawai'i. They used the leaves for house thatch, skirts, sandals, and raincoats. Food to be cooked in an *imu* (underground oven) was first wrapped in ti leaves. A popular sport with the commoners was *ho'ohe'e kī* or ti-leaf sliding. The sap from ti roots stained canoes and surfboards.

From the windy viewpoint you can look down into Nu'uanu (cool height) Valley with its reservoir. The massive peak across the valley is Lanihuli (turning royal chief). The saddle to the right of Lanihuli is Nu'uanu Pali (cliff). You can see the windward coast through the gap in the Ko'olau (windward) summit ridge. To the right of the Pali is mist-shrouded Kōnāhuanui (large fat testicles) (elevation 3,105 feet), the highest point in the Ko'olau Range.

Near the overlook are several native 'ōhi'a 'āhihi trees. They have narrow, pointed leaves with red stems and midribs. Their delicate red flowers grow in clusters and are similar to those of the more common 'ōhi'a. 'Ōhi'a 'āhihi is found only in the Ko'olau and Wai'anae (mullet water) Mountains on O'ahu.

The Mānoa Falls and 'Aihualama Trails are part of the Honolulu *mauka* trail system. You could easily spend a week hiking all 18 trails in the complex. One option from the same trailhead is the climb of Tantalus (Pu'u 'Ōhi'a) (elevation 2,013 feet). From the 'Aihualama Trail turn left on the Pauoa Flats Trail. At its end turn left on the Mānoa Cliff Trail. At the next junction turn sharp right on the Pu'u 'Ōhi'a Trail. Reach a one-lane paved road and follow it to the summit. Total distance round trip is 7.7 miles.

CENTRAL O'AHU

37 'Aiea Loop

Length:	4.8-mile loop
Elevation Gain:	900 feet
Suitable for:	Novice
Location:	O'ahu: Keaīwa Heiau State Recreation Area above 'Aiea
Topo Map:	Waipahu, Kāne'ohe

Highlights:
This short, pleasant hike winds through the foothills of the Ko'olau Range. Along the trail you see some native trees and the site of a plane crash. Nearby is Keaīwa *heiau*, an early Hawaiian medicine center.

Trailhead Directions:
Distance: (Downtown Honolulu to Keaīwa Heiau State Recreation Area) 11 miles

Driving Time: 1/2 hour

At Punchbowl St. get on Lunalilo Fwy (H-1) heading 'Ewa (west).

Near Middle St. keep left on Rte 78 west (exit 19B, Moanalua Rd.) to 'Aiea.

While descending Red Hill, take the exit marked Hālawa Stadium.

At the end of the long off-ramp continue straight on Ulunē St.

At the road end turn right on 'Aiea Heights Dr.

Pass 'Aiea High School on the left.

Climb gradually through 'Aiea Heights subdivision.

Reach the entrance to Keaīwa Heiau State Recreation Area.

Drive past the *heiau* and the camping area to the upper lot and park there (elevation 1,080 feet) (map point A). At the trailhead are restrooms and drinking water.

Bus: Route 11 to 'Aiea Heights Dr. and Ka'amilo St. Walk 2.0 miles along 'Aiea Heights Dr. and through the recreation area to the trailhead. Route 74 goes farther up 'Aiea Heights Dr., but it only runs on weekday mornings and afternoons.

Route Description:

At the back of the upper lot take the 'Aiea Loop Trail.

Pass a small water tank on the right.

Enter a grove of Sydney blue gum trees.

Cross an open, eroded area. On the right is a view of Diamond Head and Honolulu.

Pass a powerline tower above and to the right. Strawberry guavas line the trail.

Shortly afterward reach a junction (map point B). Continue straight on the loop trail. (The makeshift trail to the left leads down to Kalauao Stream.)

Pass a second powerline tower on the right.

Contour on the right side of the ridge just below its top.

Reach a small, grassy clearing with a bench. From there is a good view of the Wai'anae Range in the distance. The flat-topped mountain is Ka'ala, the highest point on O'ahu.

Continue contouring well below the ridge line for a stretch.

Duck under a huge tree trunk spanning the trail.

Right after the trunk the trail curves right and then left.

As it begins to curve right again, reach another junction (map point C). Continue on the wide loop trail to the right. (The narrower trail to the left is the 'Aiea Ridge Trail, which leads to the Ko'olau summit.)

Cross over to the left side of the ridge. You can see the Ko'olau Range through the native koa and 'ōhi'a trees. Look for alahe'e, a small native tree with shiny, dark green leaves.

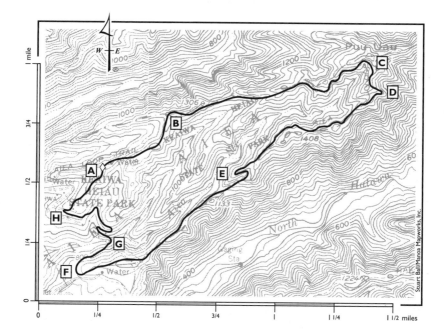

Reach the farthest point of the loop by a large 'ōhi'a tree with exposed roots (elevation 1,480 feet) (map point D). Just past the 'ōhi'a are two native 'iliahi (sandalwood) trees.

Along the first part of the return leg are views of North Hālawa Valley and the H-3 freeway on the left.

Walk under a shady mango tree and then switch to the right side of the ridge.

Descend gradually, well below the ridge line, through eucalyptus.

In a gully pass the wing section of a C-47 cargo plane on the right. A steep overgrown trail leads to other wreckage farther down the gully. The plane crashed in 1943.

Pass a powerline tower above and to the left (map point E). Pass a second one.

Stroll through a grove of Cook pines on a broad trail.

Reach a junction. Keep right on the contour trail. (The eroded trail to the left climbs to a view of Honolulu and Salt Lake.)

Go under some powerlines.

Pass another grove of Cook pines.

In a stand of albizia trees reach another junction (map point F). Bear right on the wide trail. (The left fork leads to Camp Smith.)

Switchback once and descend into a lush gulch. Look for kukui trees and yellow ginger there.

Cross intermittent 'Aiea Stream (map point G) and climb out of the gulch on a rocky, rooty trail with three switchbacks.

Switchback once again past a powerline tower on the left.

The trail levels off and enters the camping area of the park (map point H).

Turn right and climb the steps to the middle parking lot.

Turn right again and walk up the paved road to the upper parking lot (map point A).

Notes:

'Aiea Loop is a very popular hike, especially on weekends. The route is reasonably short, mostly shady, and quite scenic. It seems as though everyone who has ever hiked on O'ahu has done the loop. To avoid the crowds, go on a weekday or start early. Many people just walk partway, so the return portion is often less traveled.

The loop is a perfect hike for beginners. Built by the Civilian Conservation Corps in 1935, the path remains wide and well graded for the most part. The only rough section is the short climb out of the gulch near the end of the hike. Watch out for other trail users, such as runners, mountain bikers, horseback riders, and wayward mosquitoes.

After the first viewpoint, the trail is lined with strawberry guava trees (waiawī 'ula'ula). They have glossy, dark green leaves and smooth brown bark. Their dark red fruit is delicious, with a taste reminiscent of strawberries. The guavas usually ripen in August and September. Pickings are slim along the loop trail, however, because of its popularity. The strawberry guava is a native of Brazil but was introduced to Hawai'i from England in the 1800s.

In the forest look and listen for the white-rumped shama. It is black on top with a chestnut-colored breast and a long black-and-white tail. The shama has a variety of beautiful songs and often mimics other birds. A native of Malaysia, the shama has become widespread in introduced forests such as this one.

Near the farthest point of the loop are some native 'ōhi'a and koa trees. 'Ōhi'a has oval leaves and clusters of delicate red flowers. Early Hawaiians used the flowers in *lei* (garlands) and the wood in outrigger canoes. The hard, durable wood was also carved into god images for *heiau* (religious sites). Koa has sickle-shaped foliage and pale yellow flower clusters. Early Hawaiians made surfboards and outrigger canoe hulls out of the beautiful red brown wood. Today it is made into fine furniture.

Among the 'ōhi'a and koa is a small native tree, alahe'e. Its oblong leaves are shiny and dark green. Alahe'e has fragrant white flowers that grow in clusters at the branch tips. Early Hawaiians fashioned the hard wood into farming tools, and hooks and spears for fishing.

In the gulch on the way back is a grove of kukui trees. Their large, pale green leaves resemble those of the maple, with several distinct lobes. Early Polynesian voyagers introduced kukui into Hawai'i. They used the wood to make gunwales and seats for their outrigger canoes. The flowers and sap became medicines to treat a variety of ailments. Early Hawaiians strung the nuts together to make *lei hua* (seed or nut garlands). The oily kernels became house candles and torches for night spearfishing.

After completing the loop hike, stop at Keaīwa (mysterious) *heiau* on the way out. The ancient site is a *heiau ho'ōla* (medical center). There *kāhuna lapa'au* (healers) treated patients with herbs from the surrounding gardens. The *heiau* was probably built in the 1500s and was rededicated in 1951.

The hike is described clockwise. You can, of course, take all or part of the loop in either direction. For a much longer hike, try the 'Aiea Ridge Trail that leads to the summit of the Ko'olau Range. Turn left at the junction before the return leg of the loop. The rough 9.8-mile round trip is for experienced hikers only.

38 Waimano Ridge

Length:	14.6-mile round trip
Elevation Gain:	1,700 feet
Suitable for:	Intermediate, Expert
Location:	Oʻahu: ʻEwa Forest Reserve above Pearl City
Topo Map:	Waipahu, Kāneʻohe

Highlights:

This graded trail follows an abandoned irrigation ditch above Waimano Stream and then climbs gradually to the Koʻolau summit. Along the route are some delicious fruit and a good variety of native plants. At the top you look out to Kāneʻohe Bay on the windward side.

Trailhead Directions:

Distance: *(Downtown Honolulu to Waimano trailhead) 13 miles*

Driving Time: *1/2 hour*

At Punchbowl St. get on Lunalilo Fwy (H-1) heading ʻEwa (west).

Near Middle St. keep left on Rte 78 west (exit 19B, Moanalua Rd.) to ʻAiea.

By Aloha Stadium bear right to rejoin H-1 to Pearl City.

Leave the freeway at exit 10, marked Pearl City–Waimalu.

Turn right on Moanalua Rd. at the end of the off-ramp.

As Moanalua Rd. ends, turn right on Waimano Home Rd.

The road narrows to two lanes.

Enter the grounds of Waimano Training School and Hospital.

Look for a guard station ahead.

Park on the left in a dirt area just before the guard shack and across from the Pearl City Cultural Center (elevation 470 feet) (map point A).

Bus: Route 53 to the intersection of Waimano Home Rd. and Komo Mai Dr. Walk 1.0 mile up Waimano Home Rd. to the trailhead.

Route Description:

Continue up Waimano Home Rd. on foot.

Bear left off the road by the hunter check-in mailbox near the guard shack.

Follow the path to the left of and next to a chain-link fence.

Shortly afterward reach a signed junction (map point B). Keep right, on the Upper Waimano Trail along the fence. (To the left the Lower Waimano Trail leads down into Waimano Valley.)

Parallel the fence and the road, passing several guard rails.

Across from a low, white building turn left and down, leaving the road behind (map point C).

An abandoned irrigation ditch appears on the right.

Jump over a narrow concrete spillway.

Swing left into a side gully.

Cross over the top of an eroded side ridge. In the distance is a good view of the Wai'anae Range.

Contour along the side of Waimano Valley through strawberry guava and Christmas berry trees. Watch for an occasional native lama tree.

The ditch reappears on the right and then periodically disappears into short tunnels.

Reach a signed junction (map point D). Continue straight on the upper trail. (To the left the lower trail leads down to the floor of Waimano Valley.)

Negotiate two rock faces covered with slippery roots. Cables are provided for assistance.

Pass several large mango trees.

Descend gradually to a tributary of Waimano Stream.

Just past a dead triple-trunked tree reach a signed junction (map point E). Turn left off the wide trail and cross the stream. (The wide trail, which quickly becomes overgrown, climbs out of the valley back to Waimano Training School and Hospital.)

After crossing, turn right upstream.

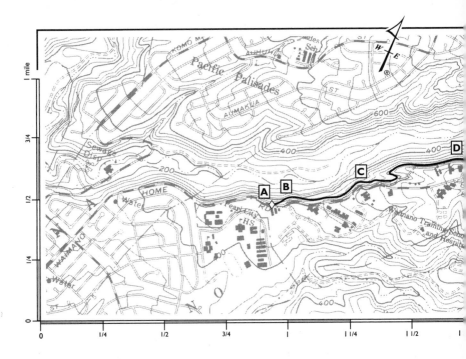

Leave the stream behind and climb a low side ridge on the left with the help of two switchbacks.

Cross over the ridge line at a grassy clearing with a covered picnic table. Nearby are some large koa and lama trees.

Contour along the left side of the ridge well above Waimano Stream. Look for mountain apple trees in this section.

Descend gradually to the stream through mountain apple groves and hau tangles. By the stream is the blocked intake for the irrigation ditch.

Almost immediately Waimano Stream forks (map point F). Cross the right fork and take the trail heading upstream along the right side of the left fork (got it?).

Climb steadily up the ridge, switchbacking four times (map point G). Tall 'ōhi'a and palm trees line the route. As the trail levels off and turns a corner, look for several 'iliahi (sandalwood) trees with their droopy leaves.

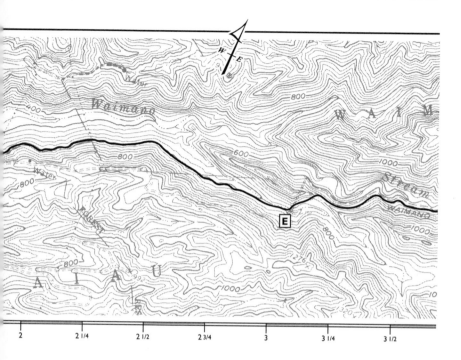

Resume contouring near the top of the ridge through native rain forest.

Reach the top of the ridge in a grove of Australian tea.

Leave the ridge line and contour on its left side. The trail is lined with native naupaka kuahiwi shrubs.

After climbing a small hump, reach an obscure junction (map point H). Continue straight on the contour trail. (To the right a trail leads down to the right fork of Waimano Stream (crossed earlier) and a dilapidated cabin built by the Civilian Conservation Corps on the far bank.)

Climb gradually, working into and out of every side gulch.

Switchback once to gain the ridge line and cross over to its right side (map point I).

Ascend steadily, weaving in and out of the side gullies just below the top of the ridge. Watch for native pūʻahanui (kanawao) shrubs and kōpiko trees along the trail.

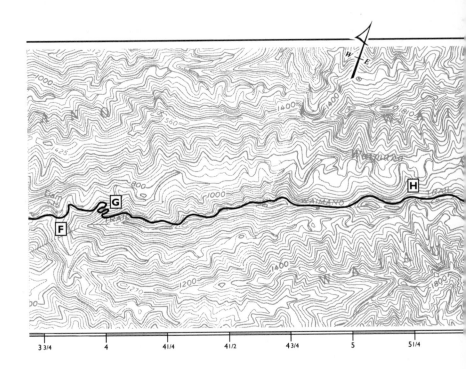

Reach the Ko'olau summit in a saddle just to the right of a large landslide (elevation 2,160 feet) (map point J).

Notes:

Don't be put off by the high mileage of this hike. The well-designed trail makes for steady, pleasant walking so the miles just seem to fly by. Soon you are in some wild country, and before you know it, you're at the summit. Leave time, though, to check out the native plants and to enjoy a delicious guava or mountain apple in season.

Built by the Civilian Conservation Corps in 1935, the Upper Waimano Trail is the best preserved of the Ko'olau ridge trails of that era. The footpath is graded, wide, and easy to follow, for the most part. Pay particular attention to the directions at the two stream crossings. Watch your step on the two rooty rock faces. From the stream to the final switchback, the trail may be somewhat overgrown with scratchy uluhe ferns and various introduced shrubs.

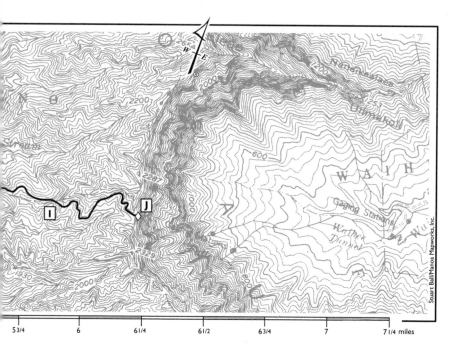

Stuart Ball/Manoa Mapworks, Inc.

| 53/4 | 6 | 61/4 | 61/2 | 63/4 | 7 | 71/4 miles |

The route initially parallels an abandoned ditch once used by the Honolulu Plantation to irrigate sugarcane. Lining the trail are strawberry guava (waiawī ʻulaʻula) trees whose tasty, dark red fruit usually ripens in August and September. Also along the path in this section are native lama trees. Their oblong, pointed leaves are dark green and leathery. The fruits are green, then yellow, and finally bright red when fully ripe. Lama was sacred to Laka, goddess of the hula. Early Hawaiians used the hard, light-colored wood in temple construction and in hula performances.

On the gradual descent to the stream and the ditch intake you pass through groves of mountain apple (ʻōhiʻa ʻai). The trees have dark, oblong, shiny leaves. In spring their purple flowers carpet the trail. The delicious pink or red fruit usually ripens in late July or early August. If none is in reach, shake the tree and try to catch the apples as they come down. The species is native to Malaysia and was brought by early Hawaiians.

After crossing Waimano (many waters) Stream, watch for the native shrub naupaka kuahiwi. It has light green, pointed leaves and half-flowers. Initially the naupaka along the trail has toothed leaves and white flowers. Closer to the summit, a slightly different variety appears with smoother leaf margins and purple streaks in the flowers.

Along the final stretch are two more native shrubs, pūʻahanui (kanawao) and kōpiko. A relative of the hydrangea, pūʻahanui has large, serrated, deeply creased leaves and clusters of delicate pink flowers. Kōpiko is a member of the coffee family and has leathery, oblong leaves with a light green midrib. Turn the leaf over to see a row of tiny holes (piko [navel]) on either side of the midrib. The kōpiko produces clusters of tiny white flowers and fleshy, orange fruits.

From the summit viewpoint you can look straight down into Waiheʻe (octopus liquid) Valley. In back is Kāneʻohe (bamboo husband) Bay stretching to Mōkapu (taboo district) Point. By the bay is Kahaluʻu (diving place) fishpond and a wooded hill, known as Māʻeliʻeli (digging). Along the summit ridge to the right is the massive unnamed peak at the head of Waimalu (sheltered water) drainage. To the left past the landslide scar is the summit of ʻEleao (plant louse). Behind the lookout is a native ʻōhiʻa tree with clusters of salmon-colored flowers.

There are two good variations to the route as described. For a short loop hike, keep left on the Lower Waimano Trail at the first junction. Descend into the valley and walk upstream. Turn right at the junction with the upper trail to complete the loop. Total distance is 2.3 miles. For a longer, more challenging route connect the Waimano Ridge and Mānana hikes. Go up Waimano, turn left along the Koʻolau summit ridge, and then go down Mānana. The 1.2-mile summit section is for experienced hikers only, because the trail there is rough, narrow, overgrown, and frequently socked in. Total distance for the open-ended loop is 14.1 miles.

39 Mānana

Length:	11.6-mile round trip
Elevation Gain:	1,700 feet
Suitable for:	Novice, Intermediate, Expert
Location:	Oʻahu: ʻEwa Forest Reserve above Pacific Palisades
Topo Map:	Waipahu, Kāneʻohe

Highlights:

This long, splendid ridge hike leads deep into the wild Koʻolau Mountain Range. Along the way is an incredible variety of native dry-land and rain forest plants. Lofty lookouts, enroute and at the summit, provide stunning views of leeward and windward Oʻahu.

Trailhead Directions:

Distance: (Downtown Honolulu to Pacific Palisades) 15 miles

Driving Time: 1/2 hour

At Punchbowl St. get on Lunalilo Fwy (H-1) heading ʻEwa (west).

Near Middle St. keep left on Rte 78 west (exit 19B, Moanalua Rd.) to ʻAiea.

By Aloha Stadium bear right to rejoin H-1 to Pearl City.

Leave the freeway at exit 10, marked Pearl City–Waimalu.

Turn right on Moanalua Rd. at the end of the off-ramp.

As Moanalua Rd. ends, turn right on Waimano Home Rd.

At the third traffic light and just before the road narrows to two lanes, turn left on Komo Mai Dr.

The road descends into Waimano Valley and then climbs the next ridge.

Drive through Pacific Palisades subdivision to the end of the road.

Park on the street just before the turnaround circle (elevation 960 feet) (map point A).

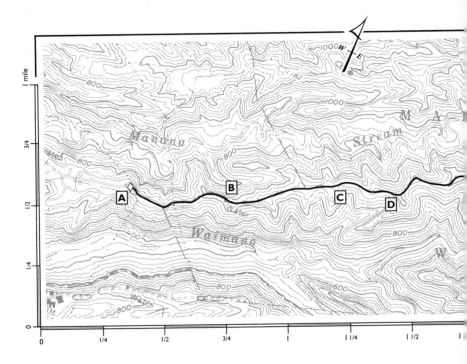

Bus: Route 53 to Komo Mai Dr. and ʻAuhuhu St. Walk 0.4 mile along Komo Mai Dr. to the trailhead.

Route Description:

At the back of the circle walk through an opening in the fence next to a gate.

Proceed up the one-lane paved road.

Reach a water tank at the road end (map point B).

Continue straight, on the Mānana Trail, through a eucalyptus forest.

Pass a utility tower on the left.

Stroll through a pleasant level section on top of the ridge.

The trail splits. Keep left, avoiding the grassy area on the right.

In a rooty clearing bear slightly left and down to continue on the main ridge.

Begin contouring to the right of a hump in the ridge (map point C).

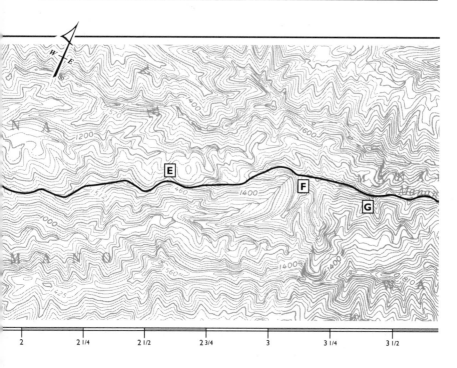

Shortly afterward the trail forks. Keep left around the hump on the main ridge. (The right fork leads down a side ridge into Waimano Valley.)

Descend briefly through an eroded section and then climb gradually through young brush box.

After another short descent the trail forks. Bear left and down (map point D).

Break out into the open. *Mauka* (inland) is a view of the entire ridge to be climbed.

Traverse a narrow, eroded stretch. Watch your footing, especially if the ground is wet.

The trail becomes a grassy avenue along the rolling ridge. Introduced pine and paperbark trees line the path. Look for the native trees koa and 'iliahi (sandalwood) and the native shrub naupaka kuahiwi.

On the left a side trail climbs to a small knob and then rejoins the main route.

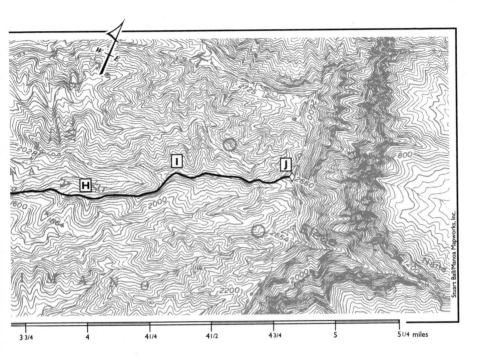

Descend a short, steep, eroded section.

Pass a covered picnic table on the right.

The introduced trees end just past the table. Look for more ʻili-ahi near the trail.

Climb steeply to the first really distinct knob in the ridge (map point E).

Descend the next dip and ascend steeply to the next hump. The native vegetation gradually changes from dry-land to rain forest. Along the route are ʻōhiʻa and kōpiko trees and hāpuʻu tree ferns.

Cross a short level section.

Climb very steeply to another knob, where a long side ridge comes in on the right (map point F).

The trail narrows and becomes rough and rooty.

Cross another level section, descend briefly, and then ascend a flat, cleared hill used occasionally as a helipad (map point G). There is a view in all directions. To leeward is Pearl Harbor and the

Wai'anae Range. On the left is a native lapalapa tree with its fluttering leaves.

Traverse a long series of small but steep knobs in the ridge.

Cross a level muddy section.

Ascend steeply to a large hill with a small clearing on top (map point H). From there is a commanding view of the ridge ahead.

Swing left and climb steadily. The vegetation becomes stunted, and the wind picks up.

Curve right, toward the Ko'olau summit as a long side ridge comes in on the left (map point I).

The main ridge narrows considerably.

Traverse a series of small humps. On the left are several native loulu palms.

The ridge broadens and levels briefly through low-lying sedge.

Cross a second series of humps on the narrow ridge.

Pass a waterfall chute down and on the right.

Climb steadily through increasing vegetation.

Reach the Ko'olau (windward) summit at a massive knob (elevation 2,660 feet) (map point J).

Notes:

Mānana is the best of the Ko'olau (windward) ridge trails. The hike offers over 2 miles of the finest open ridge walking on the island. Along the route are some intriguing native plants and a chance to glimpse some native birds. The windy finish, often in mist, is wild and wonderful. You feel as if you are on top of the world.

The Mānana Trail should appeal to all types of hikers. Novices can stroll to the picnic table. Intermediate hikers can continue to the helipad. Experts can head for the summit.

Although not graded, the trail is wide and clear to the picnic table. Watch your step, however, on the two eroded sections. Beyond the picnic table the route becomes rough, steep, narrow, and muddy, although rarely all at the same time. Between the helipad and the final climb, the trail may be overgrown with scratchy uluhe ferns and pest *Clidemia* shrubs.

On the initial trail section remember to keep left along the main ridge. Ignore the side trails leading down into Waimano (many waters) Valley on the right. Also, watch for mountain bikers, especially in the afternoon. Portions of the trail in this section are lined with strawberry guava (waiawī 'ula'ula) trees whose tasty, dark red fruit usually ripens in August and September.

After leaving the introduced forest, the route winds through a lovely open stretch still recovering from a fire in the 1970s. Making a comeback are the native trees koa and 'iliahi. Koa has sickle-shaped foliage and pale yellow flower clusters. Early Hawaiians made surfboards and outrigger canoe hulls out of the beautiful red brown wood. Today it is made into fine furniture.

Look for 'iliahi, the sandalwood tree, just past the picnic table. Its small leaves are dull green and appear wilted. 'Iliahi is partially parasitic, with outgrowths on its roots that steal nutrients from nearby plants. Early Hawaiians ground the fragrant heartwood into a powder to perfume their kapa (bark cloth). Beginning in the late 1700s, sandalwood was indiscriminately cut down and exported to China to make incense and furniture. The trade ended around 1840 when the forests were depleted of 'iliahi.

Farther along the ridge is the native rain forest, dominated by 'ōhi'a trees and hāpu'u tree ferns. 'Ōhi'a has oval leaves and clusters of delicate red flowers. Native birds, such as the 'apapane, feed on the nectar and help in pollination. Early Hawaiians used the flowers in lei (garlands) and the wood in outrigger canoes. The hard, durable wood was also carved into god images for heiau (religious sites). Beneath the 'ōhi'a are hāpu'u tree ferns with delicate sweeping fronds. Their trunks consist of roots tightly woven around a small central stem. The brown fiber covering the young fronds of hāpu'u is called pulu.

At the helipad is a magnificent lapalapa tree. Its roundish leaves are arranged in groups of three and flutter in the slightest wind. Early Hawaiians used the bark, leaves, and purple fruit to make a blue black dye to decorate their kapa. The leaves also make a distinctive lei.

Beyond the helipad watch for the 'elepaio, a small native bird. It is brown on top with a black breast and a dark tail, usually cocked. 'Elepaio are very curious, which is why you can sometimes see them. If you are very lucky, you may catch a glimpse of an 'apapane in the forest canopy. It has a red breast and head, black wings and tail, and a slightly curved black bill. In flight the 'apapane makes a whirring sound as it darts from tree to tree searching for insects and nectar.

On the final climb look for the native loulu palm emerging out of the mist. It has rigid, fan-shaped fronds in a cluster at the top of a ringed trunk. Early Hawaiians used the fronds for thatch and plaited the blades of young fronds into fans and baskets.

As you near the top, listen for the Japanese bush warbler, a bird often heard, but rarely seen. Its distinctive cry starts with a long whistle and then winds down in a series of notes. There seems to be at least one bush warbler at the top of every Ko'olau ridge trail.

The view from the summit lookout is exceptional, weather permitting. Ka'alaea (yellow earth) Valley lies 2,000 feet below. The windward coast stretches from Kualoa (long back) to Makapu'u (bulging eye) Points. In Kāne'ohe (bamboo husband) Bay you can see three enclosed fishponds, Mōli'i (small section), Kahalu'u (diving place), and He'eia, from left to right. On the left are four windward valleys: Waiāhole (mature āhole fish water), Waikāne (water of Kāne), Hakipu'u (hill broken), and Ka'a'awa (the wrasse fish). Dominating those valleys is the massive peak Pu'u 'Ōhulehule (joining of waves hill). In the distance to the right is triple-peaked Olomana (forked hill).

There are two good variations to the route as described. For a short valley hike, keep right at the junction by the hump. The side trail descends steeply into Waimano Valley and ends at a small waterfall and swimming hole. Total distance round trip is 3.2 miles. For a longer, more challenging route connect the Mānana and Waimano Ridge hikes. Go up Mānana, turn right along the Ko'olau summit ridge, and then go down Waimano. The 1.2-mile summit section is for experienced hikers only, because the trail there is rough, narrow, overgrown, and frequently socked in. Total distance for the open-ended loop is 14.1 miles.

WINDWARD SIDE

40 Maunawili Falls

Length:	2.6-mile round trip
Elevation Gain:	400 feet
Suitable for:	Novice
Location:	Oʻahu: Waimānalo Forest Reserve above Maunawili
Topo Map:	Koko Head, Honolulu

Highlights:

This short hike winds along Maunawili Stream past remnant coffee groves and taro terraces. From a ridge lookout you can see the Koʻolau Range and Kāneʻohe Bay. At the end is lovely Maunawili Falls, cascading into a deep swimming hole.

Trailhead Directions:

Distance: *(Downtown Honolulu to Maunawili subdivision) 12 miles*

Driving Time: *1/4 hour*

At Punchbowl St. get on Pali Hwy (Rte 61 north) heading up Nuʻuanu Valley.

Go under the Pali through the twin tunnels.

At the first traffic light (Castle junction) continue straight on Kalanianaʻole Hwy (still Rte 61).

At the third traffic light turn right on ʻAuloa Rd.

Almost immediately the road forks. Keep left on Maunawili Rd.

Drive through Maunawili subdivision.

The road narrows and winds through a forested area.

At the end of Maunawili Rd. turn right on Kelewina St.

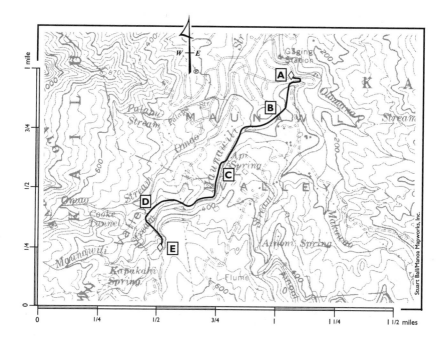

Park on the street near that intersection (elevation 160 feet) (map point A).

Bus: Route 70 to Maunawili Rd. and Aloha 'Oe Dr. Walk 0.3 mile along Maunawili Rd. to the trailhead.

Route Description:

Walk back to the intersection and turn right on a one-lane private road.

Just before the road swings right, reach a signed junction. Turn right on the access trail to Maunawili Falls.

Climb some steps through a hau tangle.

Parallel the private road above Olomana Stream.

Climb gradually and cross over a side ridge under some power-lines.

Descend to Maunawili Stream and ford it (map point B). Watch your footing on the slippery rocks.

Go through a break in a stone wall and turn left upstream through a coffee grove.

Follow the stream under a canopy of mango and monkeypod trees. Red ginger lines the trail.

Cross Maunawili Stream again and turn right upstream paralleling another stone wall.

Walk through a level section on a rocky trail. Overhead are mango, coffee, and kukui trees; underfoot are kukui nuts.

Jump over a small stream channel coming from 'Api spring on the left.

Ford Maunawili Stream for the third time. At the crossing are 'ape plants with huge, heart-shaped leaves.

Shortly afterward reach the boundary of the Waimānalo Forest Reserve and the start of the official Maunawili Falls Trail (map point C).

Climb steadily above the stream. Look for purple Philippine ground orchids.

Gain the top of a side ridge (elevation 460 feet) and turn left uphill. *Mauka* are imposing views of the Ko'olau Range.

Ascend gradually along the ridge.

Just before an ironwood grove, reach a signed junction (map point D). Turn left off the ridge. (Straight ahead the Maunawili Falls Trail climbs to a junction with the Maunawili Trail.)

Descend steeply on plastic steps. Kī (ti) plants anchor the eroding slope.

Reach Maunawili Stream where it forks under a spreading mango tree. Cross the right fork.

Proceed up the right side of the left fork. Walk in the stream at first and then pick up a rocky, slippery trail.

Reach Maunawili Falls and swimming hole (map point E).

Notes:
Volunteers under the direction of the Sierra Club Hawai'i Chapter completed this new access to Maunawili (twisted mountain) Falls in October 1996. Since then, the hike has proven very popular, especially on sunny weekend afternoons. The route is short, pleas-

ant, and leads to a superb swimming hole. To avoid the crowds, go on a weekday or start early.

Before you begin hiking, several cautions are in order. The route initially follows a public right-of-way through private property; stay on the trail. The path is well built but may be muddy and deteriorated in spots from the heavy traffic. Watch your footing while crossing the stream. If possible, wear tabis (Japanese reef walkers), which can grip wet, slippery rocks. As always, do not ford the stream if the water is much above your knees. Finally, don't feed the mosquitoes.

On the trail, look and listen for the white-rumped shama. It is black on top with a chestnut-colored breast and a long black-and-white tail. The shama has a variety of beautiful songs and often mimics other birds. A native of Malaysia, the shama has become widespread in introduced forests such as this one.

After the first stream crossing are groves of Arabian coffee trees. They have glossy, dark green leaves and white flowers. Their fruit is red, drying to black or brown. Coffee was introduced to Hawai'i in the early 1800s and was widely cultivated in valleys along streams. Coffee is still commercially grown on the Big Island, where it is sold as Kona coffee.

Before reaching 'Api spring, the trail is covered with fallen nuts from kukui trees. Their large, pale green leaves resemble those of the maple, with several distinct lobes. Early Polynesian voyagers introduced kukui into Hawai'i. They used the wood to make gunwales and seats for their outrigger canoes. The flowers and sap became medicines to treat a variety of ailments. Early Hawaiians strung the nuts together to make *lei hua* (seed or nut garlands). The oily kernels became house candles and torches for night spearfishing.

Near the spring look for the 'ape plant with its huge, heart-shaped leaves. It is a close relative of *kalo* (taro), the staple food of early Hawaiians. Like taro, the tubers of 'ape are inedible unless specially prepared. Early Hawaiians created patterns on gourd bowls using a dye made from crushed 'ape leaves.

From the short ridge section are impressive views. *Mauka*

(inland) are the sheer, fluted cliffs of the Koʻolau (windward) Range. Kōnāhuanui (large fat testicles) (elevation 3,150 feet) is the massive peak above Nuʻuanu (cool height) Pali. Along the summit ridge to the left is Mount Olympus. *Makai* (seaward) is triple-peaked Olomana (forked hill) and Kāneʻohe (bamboo husband) Bay, ending at Mōkapu (taboo district) Point.

After a steep descent back to the stream, you soon reach Maunawili Falls. At its base is the large, lower pool encircled by fern-covered cliffs. Up a slippery slope is a second, smaller pool where the waterfall splits in two. Enjoy a refreshing swim in the cool mountain water. If you plan to jump into the lower pool from the cliffs, be sure to check its depth first!

For a longer hike, continue up the ridge on the falls trail to the junction with the Maunawili Trail. Turn left or right and go as far as you want. The 10-mile Maunawili Trail contours along the base of the Koʻolau cliffs from the Pali lookout to Waimānalo.

41 Kahana Valley

Length:	6.4-mile double loop
Elevation Gain:	400 feet
Suitable for:	Novice, Intermediate
Location:	Oʻahu: Kahana Valley State Park
Topo Map:	Kahana, Hauʻula

Highlights:

This double-loop hike meanders around a vast, undeveloped windward valley. The intricate route has numerous junctions and stream crossings. Along the stream are deep, inviting pools and groves of mountain apple.

Trailhead Directions:

Distance: *(Downtown Honolulu to Kahana Valley State Park)*
        25 miles

Driving Time: *3/4 hour*

At Punchbowl St. get on Lunalilo Fwy (H-1) heading ʻEwa (west).

Take Likelike Hwy (exit 20A, Rte 63 north) up Kalihi Valley through the Wilson Tunnel.

The highway forks. Keep right for Kahekili Hwy (Rte 83 west).

Kahekili becomes Kamehameha Hwy (still Rte 83), which continues up the windward coast.

Drive through the villages of Kahaluʻu and Waiāhole to Kaʻaʻawa.

Pass Crouching Lion Inn on the left.

The road curves left to go around Kahana Bay.

Cross Kahana Stream on two bridges.

By a large palm grove turn left into Kahana Valley State Park.

Pass the green Orientation Center on the right. It has restrooms and drinking water. A shelf by the front door contains park brochures and trail maps.

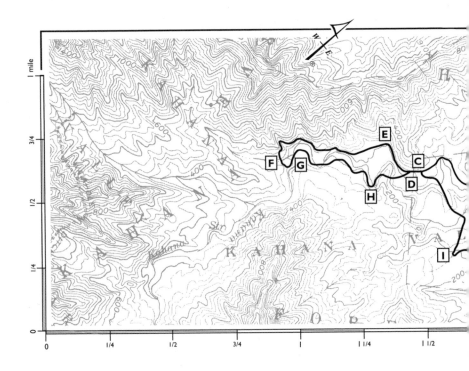

Drive another 0.5 mile into the valley on the paved road.

Park in a cleared area on the right just before a locked gate (elevation 20 feet) (map point A).

Bus: Route 55 to the entrance of Kahana Valley State Park. Walk 0.6 mile along the park access road to the trailhead.

Route Description:

Continue along the paved access road on foot.

Pass houses on both sides of the road.

Go around a second locked gate. The road narrows to one lane.

Climb steadily through introduced forest. Pu'u Piei is the sharp peak on the ridge to the right.

Reach a junction marked by a hunting area sign (map point B). Turn left and down on a dirt road. (The paved road curves right and up through a locked gate.)

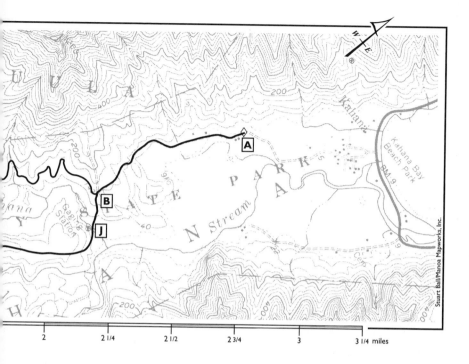

Almost immediately reach a signed junction. Turn right on to the Nakoa Trail. (The dirt road descends to Kahana Stream and is the return portion of the hike.)

Contour along the side of the valley through hala groves and hau tangles. Look for an occasional hāpuʻu tree fern and some mountain apple trees in this long section. In the openings you can see Puʻu Manamana and Puʻu ʻOhulehule on the ridge to the left.

In a stand of kukui trees jog left and down into a gully to avoid a landslide.

Turn right and climb up the gully.

Bear left out of the gully and resume contouring in a grove of hala.

Work into and out of a side gulch with an intermittent stream.

Descend briefly and ford a small stream in a second gulch.

Descend into a third gulch on one switchback and cross another stream.

Pass a rusted triangular base on the right.

Shortly afterward reach a four-way junction in a clearing surrounded by hala trees (map point C). Continue straight across. (To the left the Nakoa Trail descends to Kahana Stream and is the return portion of the hike. To the right a trail leads to a water tank and the paved access road.)

Pass several observation bunkers hidden in the trees on the left.

Shortly afterward reach a fork (map point D). Take the right fork. (The left fork leads down to Kahana Stream and is the return portion of the hike.)

Contour above Kahana Stream under magnificent albizia trees.

Cross a side stream on a slippery rock surface. Just before the crossing is a grove of mountain apples.

Cross a second side stream by two mango trees.

Reach an obscure junction in a flat area with scattered ginger (map point E). Continue straight on the trail into the valley. (To the left a trail provides a shortcut to Kahana Stream.)

Cross several side streams in groves of mountain apple. The trail is narrow and rough in spots.

Reach another obscure junction by a large side stream (elevation 360 feet) (map point F). Swing left and parallel the side stream. (To the right is the upper trail, which crosses the side stream and continues to the back of the valley.)

Cross the side stream and leave it behind.

Reach Kahana Stream and turn left downstream.

Ford the main stream just after it bends to the left, forming a lovely pool (map point G). The side stream that you crossed earlier comes in on the left.

Continue downstream, hugging the right bank.

The stream splits. One of the channels may be dry.

Ford the stream to the left bank.

Cross the stream to the right bank by two large albizia trees with white-flecked trunks.

Pass a large mango tree with exposed roots on the left bank of the stream.

Ford the stream to the left bank just before it turns sharp left (map point H). Nearby is a large mango tree and another deep inviting pool.

Continue downstream briefly and reach an obscure junction. Turn right and cross Kahana Stream to the right bank. (To the left a short trail leads back to map point E on the contour trail.)

The stream splits briefly. Traverse the island in between and then return to the right side.

Reach a large mango tree and a lovely pool.

Ford the stream there to the left bank and enter a bamboo grove.

Ascend through the grove, leaving the stream behind.

Work left and then straight up the slope on a narrow, rutted trail.

Reach the familiar junction with the contour trail (map point D). Keep right.

Reach the four-way junction again (map point C). This time turn right downhill on the continuation of the Nakoa Trail.

Descend steadily along a terrace through hala.

Enter a hau grove.

Shortly afterward ford Kahana Stream and turn right upstream.

Ascend steadily on a terrace just below the ridge line.

Reach a signed junction at the ridge line (map point I). Turn sharp left down the ridge. (To the right a faint trail continues up the ridge.)

Descend gradually down the flat ridge through hala.

Break out into the open briefly. The peak on the ridge to the left is Pu'u Piei.

Veer right, off the ridge line on to a terrace.

The trail curves left to reach Kahana Stream by a gaging station (map point J).

Ford the stream for the last time on a small dam. Watch your footing because the concrete is very slippery. At the dam is a large swimming hole popular with valley residents.

Climb gradually on an eroded dirt road.

Cross a small 'auwai (ditch) for irrigating lo'i.

Reach the familiar junction by the hunting area sign (map point B). This time turn right on the paved access road to reach your car.

Notes:

This hike is an intriguing double loop in a largely undeveloped valley on the windward side. The initial stretch leaves something to be desired, but the stream loop is perhaps the most beautiful valley walk on the island. The water rushing by is cool and clear, and the pools are deep and inviting. There are few things better in life than spending a sunny afternoon by Kahana Stream.

Kahana (cutting) Valley is a unique state park, established to foster and spread native Hawaiian culture. About 30 families live in the lower section of the valley. They are helping to restore some of the ancient sites, such as Huilua (twice joined) fishpond and lo'i (irrigated terraces for growing kalo [taro]). Years ago, the ahupua'a (land division) of Kahana supported a thriving community based on ocean fishing, taro farming, and fish raising.

The trails in this wet valley are invariably muddy, sometimes overgrown, and occasionally obscure. Watch your footing while crossing the stream. If possible, change to tabis (Japanese reef walkers) for better traction on the slippery rocks. As always, do not ford the stream if the water is much above your knees.

Unfortunately, this magnificent valley harbors a large mosquito population. Local mosquitoes are usually laid back, but not so in Kahana. Bring insect repellent or cover up or keep moving. For lunch, pick a sunny pool with a breeze, and you won't be constantly bothered.

On the first section of the Nakoa Trail are groves of tangled hau trees with large, heart-shaped leaves. Their flowers are bright yellow with a dark red center and resemble those of a hibiscus. Early Hawaiians used the wood for kites and canoe outriggers, the bark for sandals, and the sap as a laxative.

Also common in the valley is the hala tree. It has distinctive prop roots that help support the heavy clusters of leaves and fruit on the ends of the branches. Early Hawaiians braided the long, pointed leaves, called lau hala, into baskets, fans, floor mats, and sails.

The wet side gulches are lined with kukui trees. Their large, pale green leaves resemble those of the maple, with several distinct lobes. Early Polynesian voyagers introduced kukui into Hawai'i.

They used the wood to make gunwales and seats for their outrigger canoes. The flowers and sap became medicines to treat a variety of ailments. Early Hawaiians strung the nuts together to make *lei hua* (seed or nut garlands). The oily kernels became house candles and torches for night spearfishing.

On the second loop look for mountain apple trees ('ōhi'a 'ai) along the contour trail. They have dark, oblong, shiny leaves. In spring their purple flowers carpet the trail. The delicious pink or red fruit usually ripens in late July or early August. If none is in reach, shake the tree and try to catch the apples as they come down. The species is native to Malaysia and was brought by early Hawaiians.

The walk along the stream is very pleasant, but the trail there may be obscure in spots. Follow the directions closely. Surveyor's ribbon of various colors may mark the correct route, but don't count on it. If you do lose the trail, continue walking downstream until you pick it up again. Watch for the bamboo grove on the left bank where the trail leaves the stream for good.

There are several variations to the route as described. You can, of course, do one or both loops in the opposite direction. However, the hike is complicated enough without having to read the narrative in reverse. For a short novice outing, walk only the first loop, on the Nakoa Trail. Be sure to visit the lovely pool near the bamboo by keeping left and down at the junction with the contour trail (map point D). Total distance for the first loop is 4.8 miles. To shorten the second loop, turn left off the contour trail at map point E to reach the deep pool by the mango tree near map point H.

42 Hau'ula-Papali

Length:	7.4-mile double loop
Elevation Gain:	700 feet (Hau'ula), 800 feet (Papali)
Suitable for:	Novice, Intermediate
Location:	O'ahu: Hau'ula Forest Reserve above Hau'ula
Topo Map:	Hau'ula

Highlights:

This intricate double loop traverses the foothills of the windward Ko'olau Range. From secluded viewpoints you look down into deep, narrow gulches. Along the way are groves of stately Cook pines and some remnant native vegetation.

Trailhead Directions:

Distance: **(Downtown Honolulu to Hau'ula Beach Park) 30 miles**

Driving Time: **1 hour**

At Punchbowl St. get on Lunalilo Fwy (H-1) heading 'Ewa (west).

Take Likelike Hwy (exit 20A, Rte 63 north) up Kalihi Valley through the Wilson Tunnel.

The highway forks. Keep right for Kahekili Hwy (Rte 83 west).

Kahekili becomes Kamehameha Hwy (still Rte 83), which continues up the windward coast.

Drive through the villages of Ka'a'awa and Punalu'u to Hau'ula. Pass a fire station on the left and cross a bridge.

Look for Hau'ula Beach Park on the right. At the park are restrooms and drinking water.

Park on Kamehameha Hwy at the far end of the beach park near Hau'ula Congregational Church (map point A).

Bus: Route 55 to Kamehameha Hwy and Hau'ula Homestead Rd.

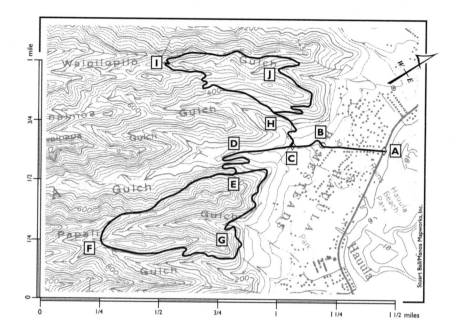

Route Description:

Continue along Kamehameha Hwy on foot.

At the first intersection turn left on Hau'ula Homestead Rd.

As the road curves left, proceed straight on Ma'akua Rd.

As the pavement ends, pass a private driveway on the left.

The road forks by a utility pole (map point B). Take the left fork and go around a chain across the road.

The road crosses a stream bed and swings right.

Shortly afterward reach a signed junction (map point C). Keep left on the dirt road. (To the right is the Hau'ula Loop Trail, which is described later on.)

The road straightens out briefly by a concrete retaining wall.

Just before the road curves right, reach a second signed junction (map point D). Bear left and down off the road onto the Papali-Ma'akua Ridge Trail. (Straight ahead the road leads to the Ma'akua Gulch Trail.)

Almost immediately cross Ma'akua Stream and climb the embankment on the far side.

Work right and then left through a hau grove.

Climb gradually up the side of Maʻakua Gulch on eight switch-backs. At the sixth one is a good view of Hauʻula town and the ocean.

At the eighth switchback the trail splits, becoming a loop (map point E). Turn sharp right and start the loop in a counterclockwise direction.

Ascend steadily up the side of the gulch heading *mauka* (inland) through a mixed introduced forest. You can look deep into Maʻakua Gulch through breaks in the trees. Keep your eyes peeled for tasty banana lilikoʻi.

Reach the ridge line and stroll along it under shady Formosa koa trees.

Bear left off the ridge and descend gradually into Papali Gulch. Look for the native shrub naupaka kuahiwi and purple Philippine ground orchids in this section.

Cross the stream (map point F) by a stand of kukui trees and turn left downstream.

Climb gradually out of the gulch.

Gain the ridge line briefly near some Cook pines.

Switch to the right side of the ridge and descend partway into Punaiki Gulch on a series of switchbacks.

Contour around the front of the ridge. There are good views of Hauʻula town and the ocean.

Descend once again into Papali Gulch and cross the rocky stream bed (map point G).

Climb out of the gulch on switchbacks.

Contour along the front of the next ridge.

A cliff overhangs the trail on the left.

Reach the end of the loop (map point E). Bear right and down.

Retrace your steps to the dirt road and its junction with the Hauʻula Loop Trail (map point C).

Turn left off the road onto the trail.

Follow Hānaimoa Stream briefly and then cross it.

Ascend through ironwoods on two long switchbacks. At the first switchback look for noni with its large, shiny leaves.

The trail splits, becoming a loop (map point H). This time keep left and start the loop in a clockwise direction.

Climb *mauka* up the side of Hānaimoa Gulch on several switch-backs.

Reach the ridge line and cross over it.

Descend gradually into Waipilopilo Gulch.

Cross the stream there (map point I) and climb out of the gulch.

Reach the ridge line and turn right heading *makai* (seaward). Below on the left are the sheer walls of Kaipapa'u Gulch. Look for a few native 'ōhi'a trees and pūkiawe shrubs along the trail.

Descend steadily along the top of the ridge. Steps are provided at a steep, eroded section.

Bear right off the ridge line through a grove of Cook pines. The ground is covered with lau'ae ferns.

Descend into Waipilopilo Gulch once again (map point J) and then climb out of it.

Contour around the front of the ridge through Cook pines and ironwoods. Through a break in the trees you can see down the windward coast to Māhie Point on the far side of Kahana Bay.

Reach the end of the loop (map point H) and turn left.

Retrace your steps back to the dirt road (map point C).

Turn left on it to return to the highway (map point A).

Notes:

The Hau'ula-Papali hike is perfect for beginners. The two loops are short, mostly shady, and surprisingly scenic. Along the trail are some easily identified native and introduced plants. Although in the same general area, each loop is different, so try them both.

The route narrative describes the Papali (small cliff) loop first in a counterclockwise direction and then the Hau'ula (red hau tree) loop in a clockwise direction. You can, of course, do just one or both loops in either order or direction. The Hau'ula loop is some-what easier and more popular than Papali. Neither loop is crowded, however, probably because of their distance from Honolulu.

The trails making up the loops are wide, well graded, and easy to follow, for the most part. Watch your step, however, while crossing the rocky streambeds in the gulches. The Papali loop may be over-grown in spots with introduced shrubs.

On the trail, look and listen for the white-rumped shama. It is black on top with a chestnut-colored breast and a long black-and-white tail. The shama has a variety of beautiful songs and often mimics other birds. A native of Malaysia, the shama has become widespread in introduced forests such as this one.

On the descent to Papali Gulch is the native shrub naupaka kuahiwi. It has light green, toothed leaves and white half-flowers. The unusual appearance of the flowers has given rise to several unhappy legends. According to one, a Hawaiian maiden believed her lover unfaithful. In anger she tore all the naupaka flowers in half. She then asked him to find a whole flower to prove his love. He was, of course, unsuccessful and died of a broken heart.

In Papali Gulch look for a stand of kukui trees. Their large, pale green leaves resemble those of the maple, with several distinct lobes. Early Polynesian voyagers introduced kukui into Hawai'i. They used the wood to make gunwales and seats for their outrigger canoes. The flowers and sap became medicines to treat a variety of ailments. Early Hawaiians strung the nuts together to make *lei hua* (seed or nut garlands). The oily kernels became house candles and torches for night spearfishing.

Above Kaipapa'u (shallow sea) Gulch on the Hau'ula loop are a few 'ōhi'a, the dominant tree in the native rain forest. They have oval leaves and clusters of delicate red flowers. Early Hawaiians used the flowers in *lei* (garlands) and the wood in outrigger canoes. The hard, durable wood was also carved into god images for *heiau* (religious sites).

On the return leg of the Hau'ula loop you pass through a forest of tall Cook pines. They have overlapping, scalelike leaves about 1/4 inch long, rather than true needles. The pines were planted in the 1930s for reforestation. Discovered by Captain James Cook, they are native to New Caledonia (Isle of Pines) in the South Pacific between Fiji and Australia.

For a totally different experience, try the Ma'akua Gulch hike. It starts at the same trailhead, but involves rock hopping up a stream in a narrow canyon.

43 Ma'akua Gulch

Length:	6.0-mile round trip
Elevation Gain:	900 feet
Suitable for:	Intermediate
Location:	O'ahu: Hau'ula Forest Reserve above Hau'ula
Topo Map:	Hau'ula

Highlights:

This hike explores a deep and narrow windward gulch. Along the winding route are multiple stream crossings and groves of mountain apple. At the end is a delightful waterfall and swimming hole surrounded by towering cliffs.

Trailhead Directions:

Distance: (Downtown Honolulu to Hau'ula Beach Park) *30 miles*

Driving Time: *1 hour*

At Punchbowl St. get on Lunalilo Fwy (H-1) heading 'Ewa (west).

Take Likelike Hwy (exit 20A, Rte 63 north) up Kalihi Valley through the Wilson Tunnel.

The highway forks. Keep right for Kahekili Hwy (Rte 83 west).

Kahekili becomes Kamehameha Hwy (still Rte 83), which continues up the windward coast.

Drive through the villages of Ka'a'awa and Punalu'u to Hau'ula. Pass a fire station on the left and cross a bridge.

Look for Hau'ula Beach Park on the right. At the park are restrooms and drinking water.

Park on Kamehameha Hwy at the far end of the beach park near Hau'ula Congregational Church (map point A).

Bus: Route 55 to Kamehameha Hwy and Hau'ula Homestead Rd.

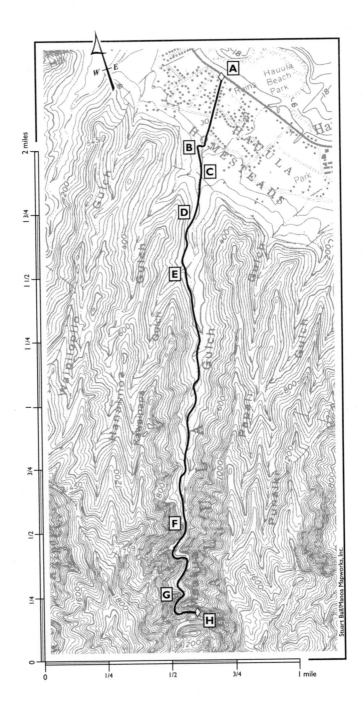

Route Description:

Continue along Kamehameha Hwy on foot.

At the first intersection turn left on Hau'ula Homestead Rd.

As the road curves left, proceed straight on Ma'akua Rd.

As the pavement ends, pass a private driveway on the left.

The road forks by a utility pole (map point B). Take the left fork and go around a chain across the road.

The road crosses a stream bed and swings right.

Shortly afterward reach a signed junction (map point C). Keep left on the dirt road. (To the right is the Hau'ula Loop Trail.)

The road straightens out briefly by a concrete retaining wall.

Just before the road curves right, reach a second signed junction (map point D). Continue straight on the road. (To the left is the Papali-Ma'akua Ridge Trail.)

Climb gradually above Ma'akua Stream on the road.

Pass a water pumping station on the right.

As the road, now paved, switchbacks to the right, continue straight, through a gap between a stone wall and a concrete retaining wall.

Pick up the Ma'akua Gulch Trail.

Descend briefly through tangled hau trees.

In a grove of ironwoods cross Kawaipapa Stream, which comes in from the right (map point E).

Descend gradually to Ma'akua Stream through mixed forest. Look for noni with its large, shiny leaves.

Ford Ma'akua Stream in a stand of hala trees.

Shortly afterward cross the stream a second time through a hau tangle.

After the third ford, parallel the stream briefly under kukui trees.

Beyond the fourth crossing the trail becomes rocky, rooty, and usually muddy. Walk through groves of mountain apple for the next 10 crossings. Above the mountain apple are kukui and an occasional mango tree.

At the sixth ford the stream bed splits in two. After crossing, jog left and then right upstream.

The trail briefly follows a rocky gully after the eighth crossing.

At the eleventh ford, the valley walls begin to close in. Walk in the stream bed for a short distance before crossing to the opposite bank.

Walk in the stream bed for a longer stretch at the fourteenth crossing.

At the fifteenth ford, a small side stream comes in on the right (map point F). If you have tabis (Japanese reef walkers), put them on here.

Beyond the fifteenth crossing the stream becomes the trail more often than not. Look for short trail sections on the inside bends of the stream.

Wind past a waterfall chute, carved out of the near vertical cliffs on the right (map point G).

Pass a lone loulu palm near a large boulder in the stream.

Pass a second, larger waterfall chute on the left.

Shortly afterward reach a point where the gulch narrows to 5 feet across (map point H).

Wade or swim through the narrows to reach a circular pool with a small waterfall. There the slippery cliffs block farther progress upstream.

Notes:

This spectacular hike is a walk on the narrow side. Ma'akua Gulch is not wide to begin with, and it just keeps getting narrower. Toward the back the stream bends around towering rock dikes. Near-vertical waterfall chutes scour the cliffs. At the end you can touch the wall on either side with your outstretched arms.

July and early August are the best months to take this hike. The mountain apples are in season then. Also, the midday sun is high enough to reach the pool at the end of the hike. Without the sun, the back of the gulch becomes a cold, damp hollow.

Before you start the hike, a few cautions are in order. Watch your footing on the slippery rocks in the streambed. Don't hesitate to get your boots wet if the rock hopping becomes dicey. Around the fifteenth crossing switch to tabis (Japanese reef walkers), if possible. Their fuzzy bottoms provide secure footing for the final stretch in the stream. You can, of course, wear tabis for the whole hike if the bottom of your feet can take the pounding.

Ma'akua Stream is subject to flash flooding during very heavy rains. If the water suddenly rises much above your knees, head for the nearest high ground and wait there for the stream to go down. It is far better to be stranded for half a day than to get swept away.

The trail is usually rocky and rooty, sometimes muddy, and occasionally obscure. Each bank at a stream crossing may be marked with surveyor's ribbon of various colors, but don't count on it. If you lose the trail, keep walking upstream until you find the route again. The lower portion of the gulch is the home of some very persistent mosquitoes.

At the first few stream crossings are groves of tangled hau trees. They have large, heart-shaped leaves. Their flowers are bright yellow with a dark red center and resemble those of a hibiscus. Early Hawaiians used the wood for kites and canoe outriggers, the bark for sandals, and the sap as a laxative.

After the third ford, kukui trees form much of the forest canopy. Their large, pale green leaves resemble those of the maple, with several distinct lobes. Early Polynesian voyagers introduced kukui into Hawai'i. They used the wood to make gunwales and seats for their outrigger canoes. The flowers and sap became medicines to treat a variety of ailments. Early Hawaiians strung the nuts together to make *lei hua* (seed or nut garlands). The oily kernels became house candles and torches for night spearfishing.

Underneath the kukui are dense stands of mountain apple trees ('ōhi'a 'ai). They have dark, oblong, shiny leaves. In spring their purple flowers carpet the trail. The delicious pink or red fruit usually ripens in late July or early August. If none is in reach, shake the tree and try to catch the apples as they come down. The species is native to Malaysia and was brought by early Hawaiians.

After the fifteenth ford, the stream trail winds around steep, narrow side ridges jutting into the gulch. Look at the exposed rock where the ridge meets the stream. The rock is part of a dike complex in the northwest rift zone of the old Ko'olau volcano. Rift zones are areas of structural weakness extending from the summit of a shield volcano. Rising molten rock or magma worked its way into cracks in the rift zone and solidified. The resulting dikes are sheet-like, vertical intrusions of hard, dense rock. Over the years the stream has eroded the softer surrounding material, leaving the dikes exposed.

The hike ends at a lovely waterfall with a deep, dark pool. To get to it, you must wade or swim through a short narrows. Before taking the plunge, look up and around at the close confines. Above, a blue ribbon of sky is all that separates the sheer, fern-covered canyon walls. The only egress is the sparkling ribbon of water soon lost from sight around a bend.

If you don't like rock hopping and cold swimming, try the Hau'ula-Papali hike that starts from the same trailhead. From the Papali loop you can look down into Ma'akua Gulch.

NORTH SHORE

44 Keālia

Length:	6.6-mile round trip
Elevation Gain:	2,000 feet
Suitable for:	Intermediate
Location:	Oʻahu: Kuaokalā and Mokuleʻia Forest Reserves above Mokuleʻia
Topo Map:	Kaʻena

Highlights:
This hot, dry hike ascends a steep *pali* (cliff) enroute to the summit of the Waiʻanae Range. While climbing, you may see fixed-wing gliders soaring above the north shore of Oʻahu. At the end is a scenic overlook of an undeveloped leeward valley.

Trailhead Directions:

Distance: (Downtown Honolulu to Dillingham Airfield) 35 miles
Driving Time: 1 hour

At Punchbowl St. get on Lunalilo Fwy (H-1) heading ʻEwa (west).

Near Middle St. keep left on Rte 78 west (exit 19B, Moanalua Rd.) to ʻAiea.

By Aloha Stadium bear right to rejoin H-1 to Pearl City.

Take H-2 freeway (exit 8A) to Wahiawā.

As the freeway ends, continue on Rte 99 north (Wilikina Dr.), bypassing Wahiawā.

Pass Schofield Barracks on the left.

The road narrows to two lanes, dips, and then forks. Take the left fork toward Waialua (still Wilikina Dr., but now Rte 803).

Wilikina Dr. becomes Kaukonahua Rd. (still Rte 803).

At Thomson Corner (flashing yellow light) continue straight on Farrington Hwy (Rte 930).

At the small traffic circle bear left under the overpass to Mokulēʻia.

Pass Waialua High School on the left.

Drive through Mokulēʻia.

On the left pass Dillingham Airfield and Glider Port, surrounded by a green fence.

At the far end of the runway turn left through an access gate in the fence by a low-flying aircraft warning sign. The gate is open from 7 a.m. to 6 p.m. daily.

Go around the end of the runway and head back along the other side.

Pass a low concrete building on the left.

Turn left into the paved lot in front of the airfield control tower and park there (elevation 20 feet) (map point A).

Bus: None within reasonable walking distance of the trailhead.

Route Description:

From the lot walk back across the access road and proceed along a wide, badly paved road heading *mauka* (inland).

By a trail sign go around a chain across the road.

Almost immediately the road forks. Take the left fork, keeping a large concrete building on your right.

The road narrows to a gravel track through koa haole trees.

Another road comes in on the left. Keep right.

Reach a low green fence with an unlocked gate (map point B).

Go through the gate and immediately bear left on the Keālia Trail.

Work toward the base of the cliffs through grass and koa haole.

Pass a utility pole on the right.

Ascend the *pali* gradually on 19 switchbacks. Watch your footing on the loose rock. After the second switchback look for kukui and wiliwili trees. At the third is a lone noni shrub. After the fourth, views of the north shore begin to open up. On the upper switchbacks are large native wiliwili and alaheʻe trees.

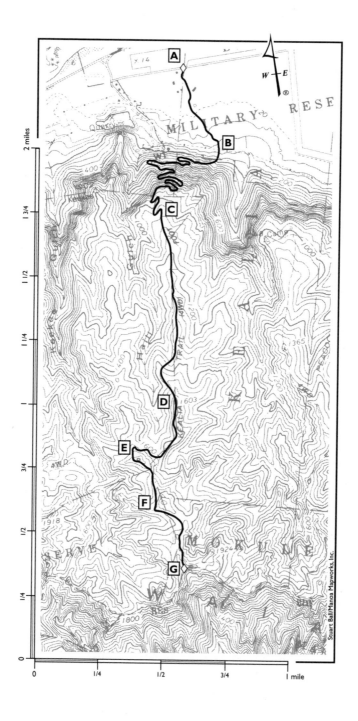

Reach the top of the cliff at an ironwood grove (map point C).

Pick up a dirt road at the far end of the grove.

Ascend gradually up the wide ridge through a forest of silk oaks and Christmas berry. Look for the native shrub 'a'ali'i along the roadside.

Reach a junction by an old fence line. Turn right, still on the main road. (To the left a less-traveled road heads downhill.)

Continue climbing through introduced forest. Young pines line the road in the open sections.

Pass a rusted water tank on the left.

Enter Kuaokalā Public Hunting Area (map point D).

The road levels, dips briefly, and then resumes climbing around a hump in the ridge.

As the road curves left in a eucalyptus grove, reach a junction (map point E). Continue left on the main road. (To the right a less-traveled dirt road heads downhill.)

Ascend steeply up the side of the hump and then descend just as steeply to a saddle on the ridge.

Climb steadily until the road ends at a signed T junction (map point F). Turn left on Kuaokalā Access Rd. toward Mākua Valley. (To the right the access road leads to Ka'ena Point Satellite Tracking Station.)

On the right pass a wildlife restoration project with a small water tank and trough.

Reach a signed four-way junction. Bear slightly right and up on the Kuaokalā Trail, a less-traveled dirt road. (Kuaokalā Access Rd. veers left.)

Reach the road end at an overlook of Mākua Valley (elevation 1,960 feet) (map point G).

Notes:

Keālia means salt encrustation. The name probably refers to sea salt along the coast, but it is also an apt description of your shirt after you finish the hike. Keālia is a hot, dry, unrelenting climb to the summit ridge of the Wai'anae Range. Switchbacks on the *pali* (cliff) and a dirt road to the top ease the gradient somewhat. Magnificent views and interesting plants and birds make the effort worthwhile.

The best time to take this hike is from February to April. The weather is cooler then, and you miss the pig and bird hunting seasons. Whenever you go, drink plenty of water and use lots of sunscreen.

The initial switchback section is clear and well graded. You are hiking up a cliff, though, so watch your footing constantly. Don't sightsee and walk at the same time. On the road look out for the occasional four-wheel-drive vehicle. At the lookout don't even think of descending into Mākua Valley. It is a military range used for live-fire exercises.

On the switchbacks, look for native wiliwili trees. They have heart-shaped, leathery leaflets in groups of three. Flowers appear in the spring and are usually orange. Early Hawaiians used the soft, light wood for surfboards, canoe outriggers, and fishnet floats. The red seeds were strung together to form *lei hua* (seed or nut garlands).

Above the fourth switchback are superb views of the beautiful north shore of Oʻahu. Along the coast are the towns of Waialua and Haleʻiwa (house of the frigate bird). Beyond are Waimea (reddish water) Bay and Sunset Beach. In the distance is the Koʻolau (windward) Range. Directly below lies Dillingham Airfield. The large pond nearby is actually a quarry once used to mine rock for the airstrip and other construction projects. Look for fixed-wing gliders soaring above cliff and ocean. You may also see sky divers with their colorful parachutes.

Along the upper switchbacks is the native tree alaheʻe. Its oblong leaves are shiny and dark green. Alaheʻe has fragrant white flowers that grow in clusters at the branch tips. Early Hawaiians fashioned the hard wood into farming tools, and hooks and spears for fishing.

Along the switchbacks and the road is a variety of introduced birds. Much in evidence is the white-rumped shama, a Malaysian songbird with a chestnut-colored breast. Watch for the red northern cardinal from the mainland and the red-crested cardinal from South America. Listen for the cackling cry of the Erckel's francolin, a brown game bird introduced from Africa. Look and listen for the iridescent peacock with its wailing call.

On the first road section look for native ʻaʻaliʻi shrubs. They have narrow, shiny leaves and red seed capsules. Early Hawaiians used the leaves and capsules in making *lei* (garlands). When crushed, the capsules produced a red dye for decorating *kapa* (bark cloth).

After the uphill road walk, the summit lookout is a welcome sight. A thousand feet below lies the green expanse of Mākua (parents) Valley leading to the ocean. In back are the dark, sheer walls of ʻŌhikilolo (scooped-out brains) Ridge. To the left the Waiʻanae (mullet water) summit ridge gradually rises to flat-topped Kaʻala (the fragrance), the highest peak on the island.

For a longer hike continue along the Kuaokalā (back of the sun) Trail to the right until turnaround time. The trail hugs the rim of Mākua Valley and then follows the coastal cliffs to Kaʻena (the heat) Point Satellite Tracking Station. For access through the tracking station to the Kuaokalā Trail, get a hiking permit and map from the Division of Forestry and Wildlife in Honolulu. See the appendix for the address.

APPENDIX:
TRAIL AND CAMPING
INFORMATION SOURCES

Hawai'i (the Big Island)

Hawai'i Volcanoes National Park
Superintendent
Hawai'i Volcanoes National Park, HI 96718
Phone: 808-985-6000

For: park brochure, trail map, backcountry camping, car camping
at Nāmakani Paio

Volcano House
P.O. Box 53
Volcano, HI 96718
Phone: 808-967-7321
For: rental cabins

State Parks
Division of State Parks
P.O. Box 936
(75 Aupuni St., Rm 204)
Hilo, HI 96721
Phone: 808-974-6200

For: state parks brochure, car camping, rental cabins at Kalōpā
Native Forest State Park, Mauna Kea State Recreation Area,
Kīlauea State Recreation Area, and Hāpuna State Recreation Area

State Forest Reserves
Division of Forestry and Wildlife
19 E. Kawili St.
Hilo, HI 96720
Phone: 808-974-4221

For: island recreation (trail) map, backcountry camping

Kaua'i

State Parks

Division of State Parks
3060 'Eīwa St., Rm 306
Līhu'e, HI 96766
Phone: 808-274-3444

For: state parks brochure, car camping, and backcountry camping in Nā Pali Coast State Park

Kōke'e Lodge
P.O. Box 819
Waimea, HI 96796
Phone: 808-335-6061

For: rental cabins in Kōke'e State Park

Kōke'e Museum
Kōke'e State Park

For: trail maps and pamphlets for the Kōke'e area

State Forest Reserves

Division of Forestry and Wildlife
3060 'Eīwa St., Rm 306
Līhu'e, HI 96766
Phone: 808-274-3433

For: island recreation (trail) map, plant trail guides, and backcountry camping

Maui

Haleakalā National Park

Superintendent
Haleakalā National Park
P.O. Box 369
Makawao, HI 96768
Phone: 808-572-4400

For: park brochure, trail map, backcountry camping, cabin rental, car camping at Hosmer Grove and 'Ohe'o

State Parks

Division of State Parks
54 S. High St., Rm 101
Wailuku, HI 96793
Phone: 808-984-8109

For: state parks brochure, car camping, cabin rental at Wai'āna-panapa State Park and Polipoli Springs State Recreation Area

State Forest Reserves

Division of Forestry and Wildlife
54 S. High St., Rm 101
Wailuku, HI 96793
Phone: 808-984-8100

For: island recreation (trail) map, plant and historical trail guides, and backcountry camping

O'ahu

State Parks

Division of State Parks
P.O Box 621
(1151 Punchbowl St., Rm 131)
Honolulu, HI 96809
Phone: 808-587-0300

For: state parks brochure, car camping

Friends of Mālaekahana
56-335 Kamehameha Hwy
Kahuku, HI 96731
Phone: 808-293-1736

For: cabin rental at Mālaekahana State Park

State Forest Reserves
Division of Forestry and Wildlife
1151 Punchbowl St., Rm 131
Honolulu, HI 96813
Phone: 808-587-0166

For: island recreation (trail) map, individual trail maps, and back-country camping

SUGGESTED REFERENCES

Ball, Stuart M., Jr. *The Backpackers Guide to Hawai'i*. Honolulu: University of Hawai'i Press, 1996.

———. *The Hikers Guide to O'ahu*. Honolulu: University of Hawai'i Press, 1993.

Berger, Andrew J. *Hawaiian Birdlife*, 2d ed. Honolulu: University of Hawai'i Press, 1988.

Bier, James A. Map of Hawai'i, 5th ed. Honolulu: University of Hawai'i Press, 1988.

———. Map of Kaua'i, 4th ed. Honolulu: University of Hawai'i Press, 1991.

———. Map of Maui, 5th ed. Honolulu: University of Hawai'i Press, 1988.

———. Map of O'ahu, 5th ed. Honolulu: University of Hawai'i Press, 1992.

———. O'ahu Reference Maps, 3d ed. Champaign, Illinois.

Bryan's Sectional Maps of O'ahu, 1999 ed. Honolulu: EMIC Graphics, 1998.

Carlquist, Sherman. *Hawaii, a Natural History*, 2nd ed. Lāwa'i, Hawai'i: Pacific Tropical Botanical Garden, 1980.

Chisholm, Craig. *Hawaiian Hiking Trails*. Lake Oswego, Oregon: The Fernglen Press, 1989.

Curtis, Carlton C., and S. C. Bausor. *The Complete Guide to North American Trees*. New York: Collier Books, 1967.

Daws, Gavan. *Shoal of Time: A History of the Hawaiian Islands*. Honolulu: University of Hawai'i Press, 1974.

Department of Geography, University of Hawai'i. *Atlas of Hawaii*, 2d ed. Honolulu: University of Hawai'i Press, 1983.

Department of Health. What is Leptospirosis? (pamphlet). Honolulu, 1992.

Department of Land and Natural Resources. 'Awa'awapuhi Botanical Trail Guide (pamphlet). 1988.

————. A Guide to the Forest Trails on Maui (pamphlet). 1977.

————. Hawai'i State Parks (pamphlet). 1997.

————. Pihea Trail Plant Guide (pamphlet). 1991.

————. Recreation Map of Eastern and Western Kauai. Honolulu.

————. Recreation Map, Island of Maui. Honolulu, 1990.

————. Waihe'e Ridge Trail Native Plant Guide (pamphlet). 1993.

Emerson, Nathaniel B. *Pele and Hi'iaka*. Honolulu: 'Ai Pōhaku Press, 1997.

Hawaii Audubon Society. *Hawaii's Birds*. Honolulu, 1989.

Hargreaves, Dorothy, and Bob Hargreaves. *Tropical Trees of Hawaii*. Kailua: Hargreaves Company, 1965.

Hazlett, Richard W., and Donald W. Hyndman. *Roadside Geology of Hawai'i*. Missoula: Mountain Press Publishing Company, 1996.

James, Van. *Ancient Sites of O'ahu*. Honolulu: Bishop Museum Press, 1991.

Kalākaua, David. *The Legends and Myths of Hawai'i*. Honolulu: Mutual Publishing, 1990.

Kane, Herb Kawainui. *Pele: Goddess of Hawaii's Volcanoes*. Captain Cook: The Kawainui Press, 1987.

Kirch, Patrick V. *Legacy of the Landscape*. Honolulu: University of Hawai'i Press, 1996.

Kōke'e Natural History Museum. Hiking Kaua'i's Highlands on Koke'e Trails (pamphlet).

Krauss, Beatrice H. *Plants in Hawaiian Culture*. Honolulu: University of Hawai'i Press, 1993.

Lamoureux, Charles H. *Trailside Plants of Hawaii's National Parks*. Hawai'i Natural History Association and Hawai'i Volcanoes National Park, 1976.

Macdonald, Gordon A., Agatin T. Abbott, and Frank L. Peterson. *Volcanoes in the Sea: The Geology of Hawaii*, 2d ed. Honolulu: University of Hawai'i Press, 1990.

McMahon, Richard. *Camping Hawai'i: A Complete Guide*. Honolulu: University of Hawai'i Press, 1994.

Merlin, Mark. *Hawaiian Forest Plants*. Honolulu: Pacific Guide Books, 1995.

Miller, Carey D., Katherine Bazore, and Mary Bartow. *Fruits of Hawaii*. Honolulu: University of Hawai'i Press, 1991.

Nā Ala Hele, Hawai'i Trail and Access System. Maui History and Lore from the Lahaina Pali Trail (pamphlet).

National Park Service. Haleakalā National Park (pamphlet).

———. Hawaii Volcanoes National Park (pamphlet).

———. 'Ohe'o (pamphlet).

Petersen, Lisa. *Mauna Loa Trail Guide*, 2d ed. Hawai'i Natural History Association, 1992.

Pukui, Mary Kawena, and Caroline Curtis. *Hawai'i Island Legends*. Honolulu: Kamehameha Schools Press, 1996.

Pukui, Mary Kawena, and Samuel H. Elbert. *Hawaiian Dictionary*, revised and enlarged ed. Honolulu: University of Hawai'i Press, 1986.

Pukui, Mary Kawena, Samuel H. Elbert, and Esther T. Mookini. *Place Names of Hawaii*, revised and enlarged ed. Honolulu: University of Hawai'i Press, 1981.

Sohmer, S. H., and R. Gustafson. *Plants and Flowers of Hawai'i*. Honolulu: University of Hawai'i Press, 1987.

Sterling, Elspeth P., and Catherine C. Summers. *Sites of Oahu*. Honolulu: Bishop Museum Press, 1978.

U.S. Geological Survey. Hawaii Volcanoes National Park and Vicinity (map). 1986.

Valier, Kathy. *On the Nā Pali Coast: A Guide for Hikers and Boaters*. Honolulu: University of Hawai'i Press, 1988.

Wagner, Warren L., Derral R. Herbst, and S. H. Sohmer. *Manual of the Flowering Plants of Hawai'i*. 2 vols. Honolulu: University of Hawai'i Press and Bishop Museum Press, 1990.

Westervelt, William D. *Myths and Legends of Hawaii*. Honolulu: Mutual Publishing Company, 1987.

Wichman, Frederick B. *Kauai Tales*. Honolulu: Bamboo Ridge Press, 1989.

INDEX

References to maps are in **boldface.**